Church
LEADERSHIP

Books Authored or Co-authored by Lawrence O. Richards

Children's Ministry: Nurturing Faith Within the Family of God
(formerly *A Theology of Children's Ministry*)

Christian Education: Seeking to Become Like Jesus Christ
(formerly *A Theology of Christian Education*)

Church Leadership: Following the Example of Jesus Christ
(formerly *A Theology of Church Leadership*)

Lay Ministry: Empowering the People of God
(formerly *A Theology of Personal Ministry*)

Expository Dictionary of Bible Words

A Practical Theology of Spirituality

Youth Ministry: Its Renewal in the Local Church

Church
LEADERSHIP

Following the Example
of Jesus Christ

LAWRENCE O.
RICHARDS &
CLYDE
HOELDTKE

Ministry
Resources
Library

Zondervan Publishing House • Grand Rapids, MI

CHURCH LEADERSHIP
Copyright © 1980 by The Zondervan Corporation

MINISTRY RESOURCES LIBRARY is an imprint of Zondervan Publishing House,
1415 Lake Drive S.E., Grand Rapids, Michigan 49506.

Library of Congress Cataloging in Publication Data

Richards, Larry, 1931–
    Church leadership.

    Rev. ed. of: A theology of church leadership.
    Includes index.
    1. Christian leadership. I. Hoeldtke, Clyde. II. Richards, Larry, 1931–
    . A theology of church leadership. III. Title.
BV652.1.R52   1988   262'.1   88-9079
ISBN 0-310-52091-6

Edited by Leslie Keylock and Gerard Terpstra
Designed by Paul M. Hillman

Printed in the United States of America

88 89 90 91 92 93 94 / CH / 12 11 10 9 8 7 6

CONTENTS

ILLUSTRATIONS

*Exercises

PREFACE

In approaching any complex issue, it is important to have a perspective. How will we approach the subject? What data will we accept as authoritative? What basis is there for commitment to our conclusion?

Perspective is somewhat easier for the Christian to achieve than for others. At least it is easier for those Christians who believe that God has spoken and that His revelation provides insight into reality available from no other source. We can, of course, listen respectfully to ideas that come to us from the behavioral sciences or human history. But although we listen with respect, we always evaluate in the light provided by revelation. Ultimately commitment to any course of action must be rooted in the conviction that our choices are in harmony with revealed truth.

Today many are troubled or uncertain about the nature of revealed truth. Has God through revelation chosen to communicate Himself? Or does He communicate true information? Or both? Or perhaps neither? And how are we to approach Scripture, which is generally accepted as the primary avenue of Christian revelation?

In this book I take a simple approach. I affirm that God through His written Word both meets us in person and reveals true information not available through other sources. What "no eye has seen, no ear has heard, no mind has conceived" about God's plans and purposes "God has revealed . . . to us by his Spirit" (1 Cor. 2:9-10). To say that such information is "true" is to affirm a belief about reality. God has cut through mankind's conflicting and confusing notions to give us a picture of reality on which we can stake our very lives. From Scripture we learn the nature of God, man, and the universe. We also learn about the structure of healthy relationships between God and man, among human beings, and between man and his social and physical environment. Thus study of Scripture is in essence an effort to see all things from God's point of view, in the conviction that He who created, redeemed, and unshakably establishes His purposes has the only trustworthy perspective on reality available to us.

None of this denies that God speaks to His people by His Spirit in additional ways. He whispers within us, calls out through fellow believers, guides by circumstances. Yet these and other avenues through which God's voice comes are not open to objective verification. They are not a portrait of reality.

They themselves demand some external revelation against which they can be tested for trustworthiness. And so we are always driven back to Scripture.

And so too we are forced into Scripture for an understanding of leadership in Christ's church. Here in the written Word we find a unique description of the church and a clear explanation of how leaders function in it. Our goal must be to see the biblical perspective. Our commitment must be to let that perspective shape us and our ministries.

And so in this book we are struggling toward a *theology* of church leadership. We come to Scripture to discover critical issues related to church leadership and then we follow the logic of God to discover who we are and how we are to function.

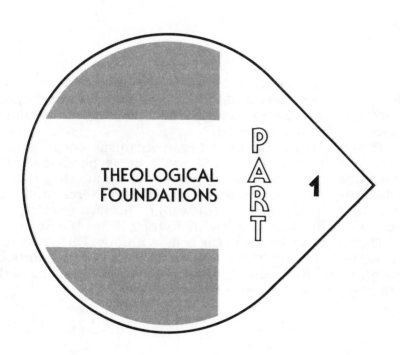

THEOLOGICAL
FOUNDATIONS

PART

1

In part 1 we ask the following basic theological questions: How are we to understand the church (discussed in chapters 1-5)? And how are we to understand leadership in the church (discussed in chapters 6-10)?

The church of Jesus Christ is an organism, not an institution. As a living organism, it has a living head—the Lord Jesus Christ. Its members are not static nor are they isolated individuals who come together for certain exercises of worship. As part of a vibrant fellowship, they are growing and maturing, and there is a vitality to their life in the Spirit.

The role of the leader in the body is unique. Patterned after the example of Christ, the leaders fill the role of servants. In teaching and in modeling, their goal is the edification—the building up—of the body of Christ in love.

PART 1

THEOLOGICAL FOUNDATION

The Church

Christ Is Head: The Basic Reality
A Living Organism: Key to Self-Understanding
Toward Maturity: The Body Grows
Incarnation: The Church in Mission
Theological Implications of the Incarnation

Leadership

The Task of Leadership: A Healthy Body
The Identity of the Leaders: Servants
The Leader's Method: Modeling
The Leader's Method: Teaching
The Leader's Goal: Edification

The basic reality that Scripture presents is that the church is a living organism with Jesus Christ Himself functioning as head. In seeing Jesus as head, we must take seriously the notion that He is not head "emeritus." He is not some titular "chairman of the board" who is given nodding acknowledg-

CHRIST IS HEAD: THE BASIC REALITY

ment while others run His organization. He is not the retired founder of the firm. No, God has appointed Jesus "to be head *over everything for the church, which is his body" (Eph. 1:22-23; emphasis added).*

Angels seated on a great stone jolted from its track announced the new era. Gesturing toward the empty tomb, they proclaimed, "He is not here; he has risen" (Matt. 28:6). The Jesus men put to death could not be held by the grave. The power of God exploded in the battered corpse and Jesus Christ was raised to new life.

The great exposition on the church in Ephesians includes a prayer in which Paul pleads that we be given eyes to see the reality of God's new-life power. He asks that we might grasp the hope set before us. In the resurrected Jesus, you and I have the promise of God's incomparably great power unleashed *now*, for us. The power that infuses the church is "like the working of his mighty strength, which he exerted in Christ when he raised him from the dead and seated him at his right hand in the heavenly realms" (Eph. 1:19-20). That power flows from Jesus into us.

In his prayer Paul also affirms the extent of Jesus' power. We must see Jesus set by God "far above all rule and authority, power and dominion, and every title that can be given, not only in the present age but also in the one to come" (Eph. 1:21). The living Jesus holds ultimate power over the universe and all its personalities. No one can claim an authority or title equal to His. He is "far above all."

C H A P T E R **1**

Then Paul reveals the appointment of Jesus to the position in which His power is to be exercised. "God placed all things under his feet," Paul writes, "and appointed him to be head over everything for the church, which is his body, the fullness of him who fills everything in every way" (Eph. 1:22-23).

The thrust of Paul's argument is clear:

1. Jesus lives.
2. Jesus possesses ultimate power.
3. Jesus is God's gift to us, appointed to be head over everything for us.

Our struggle to understand leadership must begin with the recognition that in the church we are dealing with a *living* Christ; that this Jesus acts in "the present age" as well as "the one to come"; and that it is God's express intention that Jesus is to function as "head over everything for the church, which is his body." Whatever role human leadership may play in the church, it must not intrude into the realm of Jesus' headship or claim His prerogatives. Jesus, and Jesus alone, is head of the body.

15

HEAD

Old Testament usage

To grasp the role Jesus plays in the church and to avoid overstepping our function as human leaders in Christ's body, it is important to understand what it means for anyone to be "head."

In the Old Testament we see many different usages of "head" *(r'osh)*. Individuals could be "heads of their families" (Exod. 6:14) and stand either as progenitors or elders (cf. Num. 7:2). Headship also speaks in the Old Testament of authority and leadership. Moses made some "to have authority over you—as commanders" (Deut. 1:15). Jephthah accepted military control over the forces of Israel and agreed to be head over them (Judg. 11:11). The heads of tribes were chiefs (2 Chron. 5:2), even as the "head" cities in a region were chief cities.

Brown, Driver, and Briggs in their *Hebrew and English Lexicon of the Old Testament* suggest these dominant usages of *r'osh:*

1. literally, of the physical head of a person or animal;
2. of the top of a mountain or hill: ears on a stalk of grain;
3. chief city, nation, priest, or head of a family, apparently combined with the idea of first in a series;
4. front, as in the forefront of battle [the leader's place], or, of time, the beginning or first [as "of months"];
5. chief, or choicest [the best].

There is no question that in the Old Testament the term *head (r'osh)* was applied to human leaders. Their headship involved an authority that was judicial and/or authoritative. It is also clear that leaders were organized into hierarchies. Institutions were set up by procedures like that of Moses, who followed the advice of Jethro to "select capable men from all the people—men who fear God, trustworthy men who hate dishonest gain—and appoint them as officials over thousands, hundreds, fifties and tens" (Exod. 18:21). In this leadership system, Moses, the responsible leader, delegated authority on a graduated scale; only difficult cases worked their way up through the system to come to his attention. As for the rest, the leaders were taught "the decrees and laws," and Moses as trainer showed "them the way to live and the duties they [were] to perform" (v. 20). "Heads" of institutions were this kind of leader.

New Testament usage

The New Testament usage of the Greek word translated "head," *(kephalē)* is not the same. There are only about

16

seventy-five occurrences of *kephalē*. Examining these occurrences, we make a number of striking observations.

In the Gospels, thirty-one of the thirty-three usages speak of a person's physical head. The other two refer to the "head of the corner" (i.e., cornerstone). In Acts, one of the five occurrences also refers to the cornerstone; the other four refer to someone's physical head. There are twelve occurrences in the Epistles, most referring to Jesus as head over the church, or obliquely to a similar relationship between husbands and wives. *Neither in any of these nor in Revelation's eighteen uses of "head" is there any indication that "headship" refers to leaders in the body of Christ!*

The hierarchical "headship" pattern of leadership, demonstrated so clearly in the institutions of Old Testament Israel, does not find expression in the New Testament.

Head of the body

One reason for this difference between the Testaments is seen in the assertion (repeated in Eph. 1:22; 4:15-16; Col. 1:18) that Jesus is head of the body. Jesus' church is not an institution. It is an organism. A living organism can have only one head, and the function of the head can never be "delegated" to other parts of the body. An institution, on the other hand, having no organic relationship between its individual members and its head, *must* delegate authority and responsibility

This distinction must be taken seriously. In an organism, each individual part is in intimate connection with the head, and the head sends impulses and commands directly to it. In a sense, the head of an organism is in immediate and personal touch with each member, and each member is in immediate and personal touch with the head. If we are a body and Jesus is our head, then organizational structures and leadership functions should vary significantly from forms and functions appropriate to any other kind of organization—even those institutions ordained by God for His Old Testament people. To grasp the reality on which our understanding of leadership in the church must be based, we must accept the necessity of drawing principles and practices normatively from the New Testament. In the New Testament the people of God are organically related to Jesus as a body is to its head. Principles from the Old Testament, in which the people of God were associated with one another in a national institution or in tribal institutions, hold no normative parallels for our understanding!

HEADSHIP

Too often the image we have of "headship" in the church reflects the Old Testament hierarchical leadership structure. This distortion combines with the connotations of "headship" in contemporary institutions to cloud our understanding of headship in the church. What we must do is examine headship as it is expressed in several New Testament passages concerning Jesus' relationship to the church.

1 Corinthians 11

The women in Corinth were overjoyed by the realization that in Christ there is neither "Jew nor Greek, slave nor free, male nor female, for you are all one in Christ Jesus" (Gal. 3:28). Lifted by Paul's teaching to full personhood, the Corinthian women seem to have affirmed their new freedom in inappropriate ways. They began to resent the traditional symbols of their femaleness (such as veils worn at worship) and insisted that they be treated as if they were men.

Paul's response in the Corinthian correspondence is to point out that there *are* differences between men and women. To affirm her full personhood, a woman does not need to become a man! In the body men and women are interdependent (v. 11), as they are in society. Each is equally important; neither men nor women need to deny their nature to find full acceptance and value.

To make this point Paul uses several different arguments to show that God intentionally made men and women different. His first argument involves the idea of "headship" by noting that the head of Christ is God, the head of every man is Christ, and the head of womankind is man. It is important in understanding Paul's argument to see that "head" here has nothing to do with authority (as in the Old Testament sense of a "chief" or "ruler"). Rather, as F. F. Bruce suggests, "head" refers to "source" or "origin." The Father is the source of Jesus' life. Jesus is the source of man's life (cf. John 1:4; Col. 1:16). As the Genesis account records, man is the source of woman; God used Adam's rib to demonstrate forever the identity of man and woman as copossessors of full humanity.

Following the same line of reasoning, Paul points out that the man, formed in the image of God, is the "glory" of God, for the man reflects in his personhood what God is. In the same way woman is the "glory" of man, for she reflects in her personhood what man is.

In this passage, then, "headship" speaks not of power or a

right to rule but of the origin or source of all that constitutes identity between those who are linked in a common sharing of life.

Ephesians 1:22

In Ephesians, Jesus, made "head over all things" for the benefit of the church, which is His body, is shown as exalted "far above all rule and authority and power and dominion." The point of this passage is not to affirm Jesus' "right to rule" in virtue of His headship. Jesus' right to rule and to demand our obedience stems from the fact that He is Lord. The point the passage makes is that He who is our head is the supreme power in all the universe! It is His supreme power that is at work in those who believe (1:17-23).

Ephesians 4:15

Here believers are pictured in their organic relationship with Jesus in the process of growth. "We will in all things grow up into him who is the Head, that is, Christ." The passage goes on to affirm that Jesus' role as head is one of supplying and guiding growth. It is "from him [that] the whole body . . . grows and builds itself up in love" (4:16).

Ephesians 5:21–30

In this passage marriage and the relationship between husband and wife are related to Jesus' headship. Paul teaches that the husband is the head of the wife "as Christ is the head of the church, his body, of which he is the Savior" (5:23).

The reference in verse 22 exhorting wives to "submit" to their husbands has been taken to teach a superior/subordinate relationship, with control/obedience implied. But, as Bauer points out, the Greek word translated "submission" here *(hypotassō)* speaks of "submission in the sense of voluntary yielding in love."[1] The focus of the word is not on a relationship of control/obedience, but on a deeply personal relationship of initiating love and responsiveness.

The notion that this passage teaches some kind of superior/subordinate relationship is further demonstrated to be inadequate by Paul's exhortation in verse 21 to "submit to one another out of reverence for Christ." The same Greek word is used, and what is taught is not some revolving hierarchy in

---

[1]Walter Bauer, *Greek-English Lexicon of the New Testament and Other Early Christian Literature.* Ed. and tr. W. F. Arndt and F. W. Gingrich (Chicago: University of Chicago Press; Grand Rapids: Zondervan; 1956), p. 855.

which first one person, and then another, is superior, but rather a deeply personal and loving life style for all believers, in which each of us accepts the twin responsibilities of loving others and responding to their love for us.

In interpreting this passage, particularly in applying it to marital relationships, it is important to see *how* Jesus is portrayed to function as head. Again, as in the other headship passages, control and obedience are not implied! Instead, men are exhorted in marriage to *be* head "as Christ is the head," and this is said to involve His being its Savior. Christ as head, the passage continues, "loved the church and gave himself up for her to make her holy, cleansing her by washing with water through the word, and to present her to himself as a radiant church, without stain or wrinkle or any other blemish, but holy and blameless" (vv. 25-27). It is "even so" that husbands should love their wives.

In this picture, then, headship (that of Jesus and that of a husband) involves:
1. accepting a delivering (savior) role in the relationship,
2. loving,
3. self-giving and self-sacrifice,
4. always seeking the benefit and transformation of the one it serves.

Colossians 1:18

In this great passage on the superiority of Jesus, His primacy over everything is affirmed. It is in the context of being "before all things" (v. 17), and "the beginning and the firstborn" (v. 18), that Jesus is also said to be "head of the body" (v. 18). *The New International Dictionary of New Testament Theology* points out that "in Greek anthropology the head takes precedence over all other members."[2] In this New Testament context, the emphasis seems to be on the priority or primacy of Jesus.

Colossians 2:10

In this verse Paul, in answering the heresy of those who saw Jesus as an inferior creation, insists that "in Christ all the fullness of the Deity lives in bodily form." Because of our relationship to Jesus as the body of which He is the head, we in fact "have been given this fullness." In Him we are exalted high "over every [competing] power and authority."

---

[2]Colin Brown, ed. (Grand Rapids: Zondervan, 1976), 2:157. This work will hereinafter be abbreviated NIDNTT.

Colossians 2:19

In this passage believers are warned to maintain their connection to the head, seeking the meaning of their life in relationship to Jesus, for it is from Him alone that "the whole body, supported and held together by its ligaments and sinews, grows as God causes it to grow."

In Summary

Our review of the New Testament references to headship has been revealing. First, there is no hint in Scripture of the concept expressed in the *Random House Dictionary of the English Language* definition of *headship* as "the position of head or chief; chief authority; leadership; supremacy" (p. 653). Headship in the New Testament does not imply *position* but rather *relationship.* Authority, with its right to control and demand obedience, is not suggested. The fact that the living head of the church, Jesus, is a person with supreme authority is presented to comfort and assure it of His ability to meet its needs. Again, the appropriateness of our response to Jesus with joyful obedience is rooted in the fact that He is our Lord, not that He is our head.

Second, the functions of Jesus as head are clearly delineated in the New Testament passages. As head He is the source and origin of our life. As head He is the one who sustains the whole body and supplies all we need for growth. As head He is the one who has committed Himself to serve us and is able to bring saving transformation to our personalities. He stoops to lift us up and present us without stain or wrinkle or any blemish, holy and blameless.

Third, the New Testament concept of headship is completely different from that of the Old Testament. The difference hinges on the fact that in the New Testament we are dealing with a living organism, with all its parts in organic relationship to a living head. Old Testament headship is hierarchical and implies lines of authority and responsibility. New Testament headship is organic. Even in the relationship between Jesus and His followers, authority is not implied when headship is discussed. We cannot, therefore, build our concept of leadership in the church on what the Old Testament idea of headship may imply or even express. The fact that the church is a living organism means that we must start afresh and work only from the organic perspective if we are to understand the New Testament view of leadership.

Fourth, much of our thinking about the marriage relationship has been distorted by importing into the New Testament teaching about headship concepts that it does not contain. Paul's argument in Ephesians 5 is not that a husband has a superior position in relationship to his wife and therefore the right to make decisions. Instead, Paul's argument is that in the marriage relationship the husband is to function just as Jesus functions with the church *in respect to saviorhood.* The husband is to focus on his wife and her needs, to serve her and lift her up, and to be committed to the fulfillment of her potential as a person.

Fifth, with the exception of Paul's reference to the husband's function in the marriage relationship as being like Jesus' "savior" or "servant" function on behalf of the church, there is no indication that church leaders are to be viewed as "heads" within the body. Even in Ephesians 5 Paul's argument focuses on an analogy to *one aspect* of Christ's headship, rather than on the identity of the husband as head over his wife with Christ as head over the church.

If we are ever tempted to extend this analogy to suggest authoritarian roles for church leaders, we will be driven by the biblical data to the position that leadership involves our giving ourselves up for those we serve (v. 25) and committing ourselves as holy and blameless expressions of Jesus to the fulfillment of the Christian community and the Christian individual. We surely find no basis here for claiming a position of authority over the church or for claiming a right to make decisions and command obedience. If there is any basis for human leaders to claim such a control or command a position in the church, that basis must be found somewhere other than in the New Testament presentation of headship.

THE IMPORTANCE
OF UNDERSTANDING HEADSHIP

One of our greatest problems in understanding God's perspective on reality is caused by the impressions people have of the meaning of the words used in Scripture. Typically we each import into our reading of the Bible preformed meanings and connotations. What we hear is not the unclouded voice of God, but echoes of the voices of our culture and society.

This is certainly true with the concept of "head" and "headship," as is demonstrated by the many books and articles on marriage that build their teaching on the idea that the man must always be the "head of the home." If diagramed, the relationship proclaimed on the basis of the headship doctrine is typically shown in the form of a "chain of command," with God → husband → wife → children lined up one under the other in a descending order of authority and power. When Christians are shown diagrams of the "ideal family" (like the three shown on this page), many select the "chain of command" formulation because they believe it is "biblical."

FIGURE 1
FAMILY RELATIONSHIPS

Chain of Command	Partnership	Equality

G = God
H = Husband
W = Wife
C = Children

Drawing such models is helpful because they make visible and concrete some of the underlying notions we associate with headship. A great variety of implications can be conveyed by such models. For instance, the *size* of the circles is significant. Is there a difference in the importance of the persons in the system? Is there a difference in power? The *distance* between the circles is significant. How close is the relationship between the persons? Is the relationship one of role and status, or is it one of interpersonal intimacy? The *ordering* of circles is another factor that conveys significant insights. Is one "over" the others? Are they side by side, or overlapping? Such models are helpful because they bring into the open meanings and connotations about "headship" that might otherwise never have been expressed or examined. They not only help us clarify our impressions but also urge us on to question the true shape of the reality that Scripture reveals.

It is helpful to aid us in understanding more of what Jesus' headship over the church implies for His body and its leadership if we isolate three ways of representing headship that may or may not be in harmony with revelation but that are more or less familiar in our culture.

The command model

The first is the "over/under" concept of headship that reflects both the Old Testament usage of the term *head,* and contemporary institutional structures. In this model the emphasis is on authority, decision making, and control. Here obedience is seen as the appropriate expectation of and response to leadership.

The sharing model

The second is the "side by side" concept, in which the emphasis is on sharing and sustenance. Individuals are perceived as sharing various functions as well as their lives, and the stress is on relationship rather than role.

The servant model

The third model places the "head" in a position *under* the other person, closely linked, yet seeking to support and lift. This model reflects the "gave himself for" emphasis of Ephesians 5, in which the husband, like Jesus, subordinates himself to the needs and development of the wife in the relationship.

These three models can be diagramed as follows:

FIGURE 2
MODELS OF HEADSHIP

Command	Sharing	Servant

H = Head

24

What is significant is that each of these three models *suggests a range of predictable behaviors.* That is, we can expect a person who has one of these three images of what headship involves to tend to behave in predictable ways in a relationship in which he or she is perceived as "head." For instance, the chart on page 26 suggests a number of behavioral predictions about the way a husband would likely act or feel toward his wife in each of the three models given above. Look at the chart, check any predictions with which you agree, and jot down a few predictions of your own in the space provided.

Harmony With Scripture

With some of the notions of what headship implies more clearly defined, we can compare them with the Scriptures and see how closely each corresponds with what is revealed there.

Reviewing what we have discovered by looking at the function of Christ as head, we can immediately reject the "chain of command" model as inappropriate for Christian relationships. In the New Testament, headship does not refer to authority but to relationship. It does not imply a command/obedience hierarchy, but rather sustenance and support.

The "sharing" model does seem to catch many of the sustenance and support aspects of headship. In it, the relationship rather than authority seems important, and closeness is highly valued. Yet it falls short of representing Jesus' function in the church and, to the extent that they are analogous, the husband's function in the family.

If we take seriously the "gave himself" language of Scripture, what we have called the "servant" model best captures the implications of headship. The "head" voluntarily chooses to spend himself on behalf of the other and makes it his goal to nurture, support, and build up the one with whom he is in relationship. Yet, strikingly, when we speak of leadership in the church or family, *this model of headship seems strange to the people of God.* Rather than letting our perceptions be shaped by Scripture, we have let our perceptions distort the vision of reality given in the Word of God!

Yet it is vital for us to understand the truth about headship. If we are to serve as leaders in the body of Christ, whatever that leadership may involve, it cannot be biblical if it is constructed on a distorted idea of what headship means. We dare not misunderstand what it means for Jesus to be head of the body and what it means for human beings to shape their own ministry with others on the pattern established by our Lord.

FIGURE 3
HUSBAND'S ROLE IN HEADSHIP MODELS

Command Model	Sharing Model	Servant Model
A husband who sees his headship in terms of this model will be likely to	A husband who sees headship in terms of this model will be likely to	A husband who sees headship in terms of this model will be likely to
• make most significant decisions himself	• make decision making a 50/50 matter	• engage in consensus rather than authoritarian or compromise decision making
• share few if any feelings	• share himself and his feelings more fully	• actively seek and try to understand his wife's thoughts, feelings, and needs
• perceive headship in terms of authority and the right to require obedience	• adopt compromise as the best way to resolve differences	• encourage his wife to develop her full potential and use all her abilities
• stereotype male and female roles in family and society	• value intimacy over performance of "wife" role tasks	• be more interested in personal growth and development than tasks and roles
	• consider his wife's feelings and ideas	• place high priority on time with his wife and family
• make strict divisions between "women's work" and "men's work" around the home	• be unthreatened by the possibility of his wife working outside the home	
	•	•
• not want his wife to work outside the home		•
	•	•
• be strongly against ERA		•
	•	•
•		•
•	•	•

Christ Is Head: The Basic Reality

PROBE

▶ case histories
▶ discussion questions
▶ thought provokers
▶ resources

1. What form(s) of headship have you personally experienced? For instance, what concept of headship was expressed in the relationships in your family?

   On a sheet of paper draw a model of the relationships in the family in which you grew up. Use circles, remembering that you can vary the size of the circles, the distances between them, and their ordering on the page. Use an 8½ x 11 sheet of paper.

   When this picture has been drawn, explain to another person what the significant elements represent. Then from your drawing see if you can suggest the influence your family had in shaping your own perception of headship.

2. On the following page is a chart to be filled out by you or by a group. It reproduces the three models of headship diagramed in this chapter. In the spaces on the chart, fill in *ideas* as to how a pastor or other leader in a local church might act or feel if he viewed "headship" in terms of each of the three models. Use the "husband" models diagramed above as a guide.

3. Ted Engstrom summarizes his purpose in the following paragraph. From this paragraph, would you conclude that Engstrom favors any one of the three models of headship shown on the above chart? Why, or why not?

   This book has been written to help the Christian leader to get a clearer picture of what he wants to do and be in a church or an organization, and how to get there. When we use the term leader in this book, we see him as one who guides and develops the activities of others and seeks to provide continual training and direction. This includes the president, administrator, executive, pastor, director, superintendent, supervisor, department head, and so on. It is a broader term than the popular term manager, which traditionally is associated more with industry or commerce.[3]

4. Do you believe "pastor" should be included with "president," "executive," and "superintendent" in the list of leaders given by Engstrom above? Why, or why not?

---

[3]Ted. W. Engstrom, *The Making of a Christian Leader* (Grand Rapids: Zondervan, 1976), Introduction.

FIGURE 4
CHURCH LEADER'S ROLE IN HEADSHIP MODELS

Command Model	Sharing Model	Servant Model
A pastor who sees headship in terms of this model will be likely to	A pastor who sees headship in terms of this model will be likely to	A pastor who sees headship in terms of this model will be likely to
• • • • • • •	• • • • • • •	• • • • • • •

PART 1

THEOLOGICAL FOUNDATION

The Church

Christ Is Head: The Basic Reality
A Living Organism: Key to Self-Understanding
Toward Maturity: The Body Grows
Incarnation: The Church in Mission
Theological Implications of the Incarnation

Leadership

The Task of Leadership: A Healthy Body
The Identity of the Leaders: Servants
The Leader's Method: Modeling
The Leader's Method: Teaching
The Leader's Goal: Edification

If we are to understand who we are as the church, we must begin by affirming our identity as Christ's body. No approach to organization and administration can reach sound conclusions apart from the recognition that, in essence, we Christians are members of a living organism. Every principle

A LIVING ORGANISM: KEY TO SELF-UNDERSTANDING

of organization must flow from this understanding; every practice must be in full harmony with it. We can never be effective leaders in the church until we realize, with Paul, that we "are the body of Christ, and each one of [us] is a part of it" (1 Cor. 12:27).

There is a tremendous difference between "are like" and "are." If Scripture were to suggest that the community of Christians is like a body, we might look for points of resemblance and even appreciate them. But we might look for other analogies as well and feel no obligation to take any of them seriously. After all, *resemblance* is not identity. And resemblance is always limited: the church might resemble a body in some respects and not in others. We would then be able to choose which set of characteristics we wanted to build our understanding of church leadership on.

But the Bible does not say that the church *resembles* a body. It insists that the church of Christ *is* a body. In this chapter, then, we are clearly dealing with a reality; we are confronting a concept that is at the heart of the nature of the church. Since we are dealing with identity rather than resemblance, we are not free to note parallels and then ignore their practical implications. We must take with complete seriousness the nature of the church as a living organism, particularly those specific points of identity the Bible stresses. Our understanding of the tasks of human leaders and their ministries must grow out of our understanding of the church as a living organism in which leaders play a significant part.

BODY

The Greek word for body, *sōma,* has no real equivalent in Old Testament usage. When *sōma* is used by the translators of the Septuagint, it seems to reflect the general understanding of "body in the sense of the whole person."[1] Thus, "body" is used virtually in the sense of "person."

There is a wide range of usages of *body* in the New Testament, most of which reflect general Greek usages. In one special usage, Paul selects *body* not only to stress the fact that Jesus' death was real (and to counter developing Gnosticism) but also to show that Calvary represents our Lord's total self-giving. Here too *sōma* is more than the physical body; it is the person himself. NIDNTT thus concludes that typically *sōma* denotes man as a whole, man as a person.[2]

We see this meaning particularly in the interplay between *sōma* ("body") and *sarx* ("flesh") in Romans 7. Here *sōma* clearly represents man as a person in contrast to *sarx,* which, used here as a moral term, stresses the existence of the powers of sin within the person.

---

[1]NIDNTT, 1:233.
[2]Ibid., p. 234.

When the Bible speaks of the church as the "body of Christ," we must assume it is not only affirming the unity of the Christian community but also the fact that "the body of Christ" cannot be separated from Christ Himself. As our head, Jesus has called us into a relationship in which we identify with Him and in which He identifies Himself with us.

In passages where the "body of Christ" is developed, more than union and identity with Christ are affirmed. Several major passages show that the church *is* an organism and is designed to function as an organism. Growth is possible only when members are intimately linked with one another, free, like cells in a body, to share sustenance and strength with one another. Ministry is related to the differences that exist in the members of Christ's body, even as hand and foot and eye are able to make their contribution to the whole because of their differences in form. In spite of those differences, however, all are part of the one body and share its life. In it, all diverse and contrasting parts are harmonized by God's design into one coordinated, living being.

Scripture suggests that because the church *is* a living organism, the very body of Jesus, it also *functions* as a living organism.

Wofford and Kilinski write:

> The church of today is failing to fulfill its purpose largely because it has ceased to be an organism. A church in which one person preaches, a few teach, and a few others work in an administrative ministry, but the vast majority simply listen, learn, and follow without becoming functioning members of the body, is not an integrated organism. . . . In the face of the demands of today's society, the survival of the church is dependent upon its being "fitted and held together by that which every joint supplies, according to the proper working of each individual part" to fulfill its purposes in Christ.[3]

We can agree with Wofford and Kilinski's major premise. Since the church *is* an organism, it must be structured and led as an organism if it is to be effective. Leadership in the church of Christ demands that we rediscover and reaffirm the nature of the church as body and that we learn how to help the church *be* and *become* what it ought to be.

INSTITUTION OR ORGANISM?

We just noted Wofford and Kilinski's evaluation that the church today is failing to fulfill its purpose "because it has ceased to be an organism." Yet even those most sensitive to

---

[3]Jerry Wofford and Kenneth Kilinski, *Organization and Leadership in the Local Church* (Grand Rapids: Zondervan, 1973), p. 134.

the nature of the church as an organism find difficulty in giving that perception a controlling role in the organization of the local congregation. There seems to be great difficulty in translating biblical concepts into lifestyle without drawing on cultural patterns that are not in harmony with Scripture.

In her book, *Focus on People in the Church*,[4] Lois LeBar seeks to encourage warm relationships and mutual ministering. Yet when it comes to structuring a church to achieve these ends, the principles of organization expressed in her charts are typical of military, business, and other nonorganic institutions (see organizational charts, p. 34 and 35).

What is wrong with this type of organization? Essentially it is *institutional*, not *organic*. It implies and requires a different set of leadership principles and styles to make it function from that required by a living organism.

For example, the structure shown on the charts implies an over/under (superior/subordinate) relationship between leaders and those led. The structure diagramed is essentially a *control* structure, designed to give those in the "over" roles control over the individuals in roles underneath. This form of organization also leads to the definition of persons by their institutional role or function rather than by relationship or personhood. ("I am a Sunday school teacher" or "I am the superintendent of our Sunday school" are descriptions of a person by his function in the institution.) In an institutional organization, there are many pressures for decision making to take place at the top. Difficult decisions are usually pushed up the chart for superiors in the chain of command to make. Also in this structure certain types of communication (generally ideas related to task, and cognitive data) are perceived by the members as being appropriate, but other kinds of data (feelings and personal experiences) are not seen as appropriate for sharing.

Each of the above is characteristic of institutional forms of organizing groups of people. Yet none of these things are characteristic of an organism! In an organism, control is not distributed (delegated) but retained by the head. In an organism the members are not in a superior/inferior relationship to each other. Every member is essential to the wholeness of the being. Members in a body can function only when they are in an intimate relationship with the members next to them. Yet institutional organization creates "layers" that lead to interpersonal distance. In an organism each member is always viewed in integral relationship with the whole, and its

[4]Old Tappan, N.J.: Fleming H. Revell, 1968.

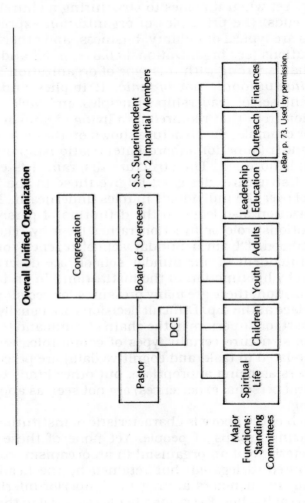

FIGURE 5
ORGANIZATIONAL CHARTS

Overall Unified Organization

Congregation

Board of Overseers

S.S. Superintendent
1 or 2 Impartial Members

Pastor

DCE

Major
Functions:
Standing
Committees

Spiritual
Life

Children

Youth

Adults

Leadership
Education

Outreach

Finances

LeBar, p. 73. Used by permission.

Board of Christian Education

```
                        Pastor
                          |
                  Board of Christian Ed.
                          |
          DCE
           |
```

| Director of Leadership Education | Director of Children's Division | Director of Youth Division | Director of Adult Division | Sunday School Supt. | Director of Children's Churches | Director of Weekday Clubs |

Departments

| Cradle Roll | Nursery | Beginner | Primary | Junior |

Agencies

| Sunday School | Junior Church | Weekday Club | Camp | VBS |

The Sunday School

Classes

```
Superintendent
Asst. Supt.
        |
   S.S. Council
        |
  Secretary
  Treasurer
```

Departments

| Cradle Roll | Nursery | Beginner | Primary | Junior | Junior High | Senior | College & Career | Young Adults | Middle Adults | Senior Adults | Home Dept. |

LeBar, p. 74. Used by permission.

function, though honored, is not a basis for its identity with the body. In an organism, cells have permeable membranes, and all of life is shared by one cell with all the others to which it is most intimately linked.

It is not necessarily wrong to adopt and use forms from our culture or society for the expression of our faith life. But where there is a basic antagonism between the biblical reality of our faith life and the essence of certain cultural forms, the cultural forms must be decisively rejected, and forms suited to express the theological reality must be developed to replace them.

THE REALITY OF THE BODY

Among the passages in the New Testament that give insight into our understanding of the church, two are especially clear. Ephesians 4:12-16 speaks of the growth of the organism and its members within the framework of organic relationships. The joining and linking of each member of the body in an intimate relationship and the contributing of each part to the others as it functions within that relationship are essential. Each member has a ministering work

> so that the body of Christ may be built up until we all reach unity in the faith and in the knowledge of the Son of God and become mature, attaining the full measure of the fullness of Christ.
>
> Then we will no longer be infants, tossed back and forth by the waves, and blown here and there by every wind of teaching and by the cunning and craftiness of men in their deceitful scheming. Instead, speaking the truth in love, we will in all things grow up into him who is the Head, that is, Christ. From him the whole body, joined and held together by every supporting ligament, grows and builds itself up in love, as each part does its work.

The second passage is 1 Corinthians 12:12-31. It says that we form *one* body. Differences within the body do not make some parts better than (superior to) others; there is an interdependence. The *wholeness* of the body must always be affirmed and expressed, even though differences in gifts lead to different functions for individual members. What is more, arranging the parts in the body is God's own prerogative and work (v. 18). Whatever organizational approaches we may take, the wholeness, integration, and freedom of members to be responsive to God's arrangement of their lives must be preserved within and by the structure.

About the body, Paul says in 1 Corinthians 12:12-20, 27:

> The body is a unit, though it is made up of many parts; and though all its parts are many, they form one body. So it is with Christ. For we were all baptized by one Spirit into one body—whether Jews or Greeks, slave or free—and we were all given one Spirit to drink.

Now the body is not made up of one part but of many. If the foot should say, "Because I am not a hand, I do not belong to the body," it would not for that reason cease to be part of the body. And if the ear should say, "Because I am not an eye, I do not belong to the body," it would not for that reason cease to be part of the body. If the whole body were an eye, where would the sense of hearing be? If the whole body were an ear, where would the sense of smell be? But in fact God has arranged the parts in the body, every one of them, just as he wanted them to be. If they were all one part, where would the body be? As it is, there are many parts, but one body. . . .

Now you are the body of Christ, and each one of you is a part of it.

Scripture teaches that in its essential nature the church is a living organism. We are members of a body, not an institution. Any expression the church takes must be an expression in harmony with its nature, not a stumbling copy of man's notions for organizing institutions.

LEADERSHIP ROLES

We are still far from reaching a definition of leadership for the church and examining leadership roles and resources. Yet we can see already that church leadership must be "body leadership." It cannot simply be institutional leadership.

This point is made much more strongly by the apostle Paul, who reports in Ephesians 4 that leaders are Christ's gift to His church. Personnel gifts have a special purpose. Leaders are given to equip members of the body to make their own contribution to the organism. Paul says it was Jesus "who gave some to be apostles, some to be prophets, some to be evangelists, and some to be pastors and teachers, *to prepare God's people for works of service, so that the body of Christ may be built up until we all reach unity in the faith*" (Eph. 4:11-13; italics added).

- Leaders have a special function in the body.
- Leaders are to prepare other members for ministry.
- Leaders who function in this way will find the local body growing up until it reaches unity in the faith.

Yet this is just the problem with imposing an institutional form of organization on the church. That kind of structure places leaders in *controlling* rather than *equipping* roles.

In chapter 1 we saw that the Old Testament idea of headship did involve individuals as leaders over hierarchical structures. It is possible to analyze from Scripture the roles of Old Testament leaders. Strikingly, they are the same roles given leaders within the structures of modern institutions. The organizational form of business, the military, and Old Testament institutions is essentially the same:

1. It centralizes control in an individual or small group.
2. It distributes that centralized power by giving leaders responsibility for the behavior of others below them.
3. It incorporates a "judge" role in leadership, where the behavior and disputes of others are evaluated and decisions are made.
4. It focuses attention on deviant behavior and problem solving.
5. It organizes relationships by their place in the structure, and structures contact between persons so that leaders tend to relate to the supervisors above them, to their peers, or to their subordinates. This tends to focus communication on task accomplishment rather than on personal experience and needs.

Institutional forms of organization, then, *tend to create or impose a leadership role* that involves (1) control; (2) authority over and responsibility for the behavior of others; (3) judging, evaluating, and decision making; (4) concentration on problem resolution and reduction of deviant behavior; and (5) interpersonal contact primarily with others for whom the leader performs tasks or with those who perform tasks for him.

These elements are implicit in the organizational structure of all institutions. We can see them in Old Testament institutions, too:

The next day Moses took his seat to serve as judge for the people, and they stood around him from morning till evening. When his father-in-law saw all that Moses was doing for the people, he said, "What is this you are doing for the people? Why do you alone sit as judge, while all these people stand around you from morning till evening?"

Moses answered him, "Because the people come to me to seek God's will. Whenever they have a dispute, it is brought to me, and I decide between the parties and inform them of God's decrees and laws."

Moses' father-in-law replied, "What you are doing is not good. You and these people who come to you will only wear yourselves out. The work is too heavy for you; you cannot handle it alone. Listen now to me and I will give you some advice, and may God be with you. You must be the people's representative before God and bring their disputes to him. Teach them the decrees and laws, and show them the way to live and the duties they are to perform. But select capable men from all the people—men who fear God, trustworthy men who hate dishonest gain—and appoint them as officials over thousands, hundreds, fifties, and tens. Have them serve as judges for the people at all times, but have them bring every difficult case to you; the simple cases they can decide themselves. That will make your load lighter, because they will share it with you. If you do this and God so commands, you will be able to stand the strain, and all these people will go home satisfied."

> Moses listened to his father-in-law and did everything he said. He chose capable men from all Israel and made them leaders of the people, officials over thousands, hundreds, fifties, and tens. They served as judges for the people at all times. The difficult cases they brought to Moses, but the simple ones they decided themselves.
>
> Then Moses sent his father-in-law on his way, and he returned to his own country (Exod. 18:13-27).

Now that we have looked at the leadership responsibilities imposed by the institutional form of organization, it is striking to see how many of these roles are carried out by the head of an organism.

FIGURE 6
INSTITUTIONAL HEADSHIP IN AN ORGANISM

The responsibility	How carried out in an organism
Control	The head makes decisions, communicating them directly to members of the body, which respond to carry out those decisions.
Behavior	The head is responsible for controlling, correcting, and directing the organization's members.
Judging, evaluating	The head makes choices based on data drawn from all members and systems within the body.
Problem resolution	The head organizes the resources of the body to heal, correct, and take appropriate action.

It seems clear from this analysis that when we do organize a Christian community as though it were an institution, we place human leaders in roles that are not *equipping* roles. In fact we also infringe on the prerogatives of the true head of the body, Jesus Himself.

What seems necessary, then, if we are to develop a New Testament understanding of church leadership, is decisively to reject approaches to organizing the life of a congregation that are institutional, and seek instead organizational forms that are organic. Organic organization must be patterned on the nature of the living body of Christ; it must preserve the prerogatives given in any organism to its head; and it must define the functions of leadership in terms that *facilitate the functioning of the body under Christ's headship, as described in Ephesians.*

THEOLOGICAL FOUNDATION

PROBE
▶ case *histories*
▶ *discussion questions*
▶ *thought provokers*
▶ *resources*

1. Research done by Rensis Likert in the sixties in the Institute of Social Research led to descriptions of effective and ineffective organizations. Here are a number of characteristics of each type. Look over the two lists, and (1) determine which is most descriptive of the structure and functioning of your own local church and (2) which is *most compatible* with an organism (body) in contrast to an institution.

FIGURE 7
CHARACTERISTICS OF
INEFFECTIVE VS. EFFECTIVE ORGANIZATIONS

Ineffective	Effective
General meetings are large, formal	The small group is the basic action unit
There is little personal interaction of the leaders with the membership	Communication flow is sustained by having committees and departments linked by common members
There is little board participation in departmental meetings	Each unit has a person on the board as a member
Leaders are more active than in effective organizations	There is free flow of communication from the leader of the organization to individual members
Many members are not personally familiar with others, reducing warmth and openness	Organization sustains a minimum number of organizational "layers"
Board members are viewed as visitors to departmental meetings rather than as members	Members feel leaders have an attitude of acceptance and support
Members feel leaders have little interest in their ideas	Members feel they have more influence and receive more encouragement to be involved from other members than from official leaders
Members feel they have little influence on the organization	

NOTE: "Effective" and "ineffective" refer to high or low membership involvement and interest and high or low performance results.

2. Compare the organizational chart of your local church with the charts on pages 34–35. Are you structured more like an institution or an organism?

3. If your church's organizational structure is institutional, can you see any of the resultant leadership behavior patterns the author suggests are created or imposed by such a structure?

A Living Organism: Key to Self-Understanding

One way to find out is to visit a board meeting, or to study minutes of board meetings. How much of what the board deals with fits the pattern suggested in the five items on pages 37–38?

Another way is to pick several leaders in your church, and sit down with them to analyze what they have done as leaders in recent weeks. List everything they have done in their role as leaders, then analyze each reported activity to see if it matches activities suggested on pages 37–38.

4. In chapter 1 you saw the value of using *models* to represent relationships and other factors in a family system. The organizational charts on pages 34–35 are also models: they graphically represent significant elements and relationships in a social system. In the space provided below, try drawing an "organic organizational model" of a local church. Study Ephesians 4 and 1 Corinthians 12 for ideas. Then try your hand at creating an organizational chart that portrays these organic relationships. (Note: The author will suggest charts later in the text, but try your own now.)

FIGURE 8
THE LOCAL CHURCH AS AN ORGANISM

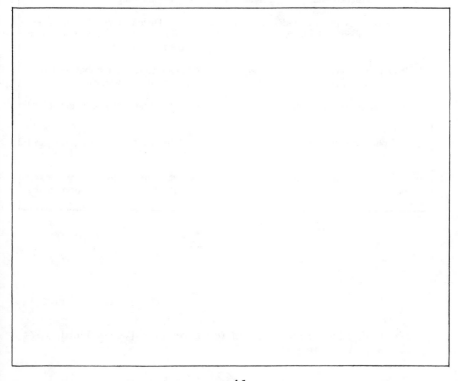

5. Some people wonder if trying to function as an organism is a viable or practical alternative. Can organic principles *work?* Bob Smith of Peninsula Bible Church in Palo Alto, California, presents the following interesting chart, suggesting that taking the body concept seriously *can* give guidelines, even in something so practical as helping Christians determine their spiritual gifts.[4]

FIGURE 9
DETERMINING GIFTS IN THE BODY

In the HUMAN BODY, how does a member of the body (e.g., a hand) know its place of usefulness?	In the BODY OF CHRIST, how do I determine my spiritual gifts?
1. It receives orders from the head.	1. Ask the Lord, "What is my place and function in the body?" Christ as head is able and responsible to answer.
2. It has inherent features that equip it for certain functions.	2. Examine inherent features, e.g., teaching—do I enjoy studying the Word?
3. It grasps existing opportunities.	3. What is obviously at hand that I am in a position to do?
4. It sees successful results. It is productive toward designed ends.	4. Do I see that God is doing something worthwhile through me?
5. It recognizes interdependence with other members of the body.	5. How do I fit in with the other members? e.g., do I find cooperative endeavor in governing ministry?
6. It supplies a need that must be met.	6. What are current needs that need to be met? e.g., music, visitation.
7. It makes progress in proficiency.	7. Do I function better with practice? I should.
8. It experiences the gratification of usefulness.	8. Do I enjoy a sense of being used as I minister?
9. It is acknowledged by the rest of the body.	9. Do others in the body recognize and appreciate my contribution to the whole?

---

[4]*When All Else Fails . . . Read the Directions* (Waco: Word, 1974), p. 125. Used by permission.

PART 1

THEOLOGICAL FOUNDATION

The Church

Christ Is Head: The Basic Reality
A Living Organism: Key to Self-Understanding
Toward Maturity: The Body Grows
Incarnation: The Church in Mission
Theological Implications of the Incarnation

Leadership

The Task of Leadership: A Healthy Body
The Identity of the Leaders: Servants
The Leader's Method: Modeling
The Leader's Method: Teaching
The Leader's Goal: Edification

A living organism, when healthy, is a dynamic system. It is in process. It is growing.

This is the New Testament's picture of the church as Jesus' body. When the church is living in intimate relationship with Christ, "from whom the whole body, supported and held together by its ligaments and sinews, [it] grows as God causes it to grow" (Col. 2:19).

TOWARD MATURITY: THE BODY GROWS

What is important to realize is that "growth" in Scripture relates almost always to internal growth toward maturity. Many will be added to the number of the church (cf. Acts 2:41).

But once in the body, it is essential that each, and all, grow.

When the New Testament speaks of the church as the body of Christ, "growth" is a repeated theme. Paul's words sum up this theme well. Gifted men are placed by Christ in the body "to prepare God's people for works of service, so that the body of Christ may be built up until we all reach unity in the faith and in the knowledge of the Son of God and become mature" (Eph. 4:12-13).

When we take seriously the teaching that the church is an organism, this theme isn't surprising. Every living being *must* grow. Development of the organism, from birth to maturity, is part of the universal process God has designed for all life.

Looking through the New Testament, we discover three words related to growth. These words, used together in Ephesians 4, give us insight into what is to be our experience in the body of Christ.

1. *Auxanō* ("increase," "growth"): In the New Testament this word is typically used of living things. It is often used of lilies or plants, and once of a child's physical growth. Only once (Acts 7:7) is the word used of numerical growth to describe the adding of converts to the Christian community. It is also used of the growing influence of the Word of God (Col. 1:6). But its main theological use in the New Testament is related to God's work in the body of Christ. Linked to Jesus, supported by the ligaments and sinews with which it has been supplied, the whole body "grows as God causes it to grow" (Col. 2:19).

As NIDNTT notes about this word, "the thought here is not solely of numerical increase, but also of maturity and the consolation of the community in Christ from which good works naturally grow."[1]

2. *Oikodomeō* ("to build up"): In its literal sense, this word is a builder's term. It refers to homes or other buildings that are erected. Used figuratively in 1 Peter 2:5, it speaks of Christians "as living stones" who are to "be built up into a spiritual house" for the residence of the Spirit of God.

By Paul the term is used in a nonliteral sense, meaning "to benefit, strengthen, establish, or edify." This term is used in the sense of "edify" some eighteen times in the Pauline Epistles. In every case Paul speaks of a ministry of believers to other believers, often specifying a reciprocal relationship. Thus, in Romans 14:19 he encourages believers to "make every effort to do what leads to peace and mutual edification"

[1]2:129

45

and in 1 Thessalonians 5:11 he says, "Encourage one another and build each other up, just as in fact you are doing."

God gives the increase *(auxanō)* as members of the body minister to each other and build each other up *(oikodomeō)*. It is particularly significant to note that in Ephesians 4 each member of the body is to serve "that the body of Christ may be built up."

3. *Teleios* ("mature"): The root meaning of this Greek word involves attaining an end or purpose, completeness or perfection. While sometimes used of moral acts to mean "fully developed" or "up to standard," normally when used of persons, *teleios* means "full-grown" or "mature." Thus in Hebrews 5:14 the writer says that "solid food is for adults," as opposed to children in the faith.

In Ephesians the process of growth in the body has this as the end in view: we are to "become mature . . . attaining the full measure of perfection found in Christ" (4:13).

It is clear from an examination of these terms and their use in relation to the body of Christ that the church *is* an organism. Like any organism, it is designed for growth. And, while God is the source of all increase *(auxanō)*, the process of growth in the body involves the mutual contribution of every member that the whole might be built up *(oikodomeō)* and achieve maturity *(teleios)*.

It is important to note that there is no implied antagonism between edification and evangelism, as some have feared. The church need not exist for either growth or service. When we examine the body internally and ask how it functions as an organism, we see that, as in any living organism, there is a dynamic growth process going on. The body, when it functions as designed, builds its members and itself toward maturity. In the next chapter we will look at the body externally and ask how it functions as the incarnation of Jesus in man's world. But for any organism to carry out its external function (e.g., life as lived successfully in its environment), it must be internally healthy. Growth toward maturity is essential for the effective functioning of the body of Christ in mission.

HOW THE BODY GROWS

Ephesians 4 not only speaks of internal growth, it also shows us clearly how internal growth takes place. We are shown a living body, supplied by Jesus Christ with leaders who are charged to prepare God's people for their work of building up the body. *It is the people of God who, in minis-*

46

tering to each other, are the agents God uses to supply all
that is needed for internal growth:

> [God] gave some to be apostles, some to be prophets, some to be
> evangelists, and some to be pastors and teachers, *to prepare God's
> people for works of service,* so that the body of Christ may be built up
> until we all reach unity in the faith and in the knowledge of the Son of
> God and become mature, attaining the full measure of perfection found
> in Christ.
>
> Then we will no longer be infants, tossed back and forth by the
> waves, and blown here and there by every wind of teaching and by the
> cunning and craftiness of men in their deceitful scheming. Instead,
> *speaking the truth in love,* we will in all things grow up into him who is
> the Head, that is, Christ. From him the whole body, joined and held
> together by every supporting ligament, *grows and builds itself up in
> love, as each part does its work* (Eph. 4:11-16, italics added).

The body builds itself up in love. Speaking truth in love, we
grow up into Jesus. And each part, prepared for its own
unique work of service, has its own contribution to the upbuilding work.

The work of each part

It is extremely significant to see that internally this body is
dependent for growth on the contribution of each part. The
church is not an association in which the role of the many is
simply to support financially the activity of the few.

Here again we see a contrast between the Old Testament
system and that of the New. In the Old Testament common-
wealth one family, and one family only, was set aside to function in priestly ministry. Priests were selected "from among
men and . . . appointed to represent them in matters related
to God" (Heb. 5:1). But only the few, from the family of Aaron
of the tribe of Levi, were permitted this representation.

Then Jesus came and initiated a new priesthood with
Himself as High Priest. This new priesthood is not closed.
Instead it is God's intention in Christ to open up the ministry
to every believer. In Jesus each believer is initiated into
priesthood, for we "are a chosen people, a royal priesthood, a
holy nation, a people belonging to God" (1 Peter 2:9). As a
priesthood, we bring our praise to God and represent each
other in matters related to God. As part of a priesthood, each
one of us is a ministering person.

This is especially important when we talk of "the ministry"
or when we struggle to grasp the role of paid and unpaid leaders in the local church. Whatever their ministry may be, it is
not to be patterned on the Old Testament priesthood in which
a few ministered to or for the many. In Christ each believer
has been initiated into the ministry, and leaders must not

accept or permit a structure modeled on the Old Testament pattern to develop.

The context of ministry

Another common emphasis of the New Testament is reflected in the Ephesians 4 passage. This emphasis is on the context in which the work of the internal "building up" ministry takes place. We are told that ministry takes place in a *relational context of love and unity.* Growth comes as we move toward deeper unity in our common experience of the faith. Growth comes as we speak the truth in love and build each other up in love.

In Ephesians, Paul stresses each of these conditions. In chapter 2 he points out that, in Jesus, persons with great racial and social differences, which had caused deep hostility, have been made one. In the one body, Christ has made peace, reconciling us to God and each other and ending the hostility (2:14-18). This supernatural act that has made us one body has also made us sharers together in the promise of Jesus, and in that great miracle of unity the complex wisdom of God will be eternally revealed to all created beings (3:6-11).

Because we are one, we are urged to build intimate relationships with each other, being "completely humble and gentle, . . . patient, bearing with one another in love." In this way we are to "make every effort to keep the unity of the Spirit through the bond of peace" (4:1-6).

Paralleling the emphasis in Ephesians on unity within the body, there are repeated references to love. Paul prays that the church might be "rooted and established in love" (for one another), and expects that in the context of loving relationships each will "have power, together with all the saints, to grasp how wide and long and high and deep is the love of Christ, and to know [by experience] this love that surpasses knowledge—that you may be filled to the measure of all the fullness of God" (3:14-19).

As God's dear children, we are to "live a life of love" and seek "in all goodness, righteousness and truth . . . what pleases the Lord" (5:1, 9).

The point of the stress on unity and love as a relational context for ministry seems to be this: in an organism, only those cells that are in intimate relationship with each other can share their resources or heal their hurts. To function as an organism, we need close and intimate relationships. If members are to perform their ministering work, the body needs to grow continually closer in unity and love.

The place of leaders

Ephesians 4 gives us a suggestive insight into the role of leaders in the body. Although we cannot identify apostles, prophets, evangelists, and pastor-teachers (4:11) with the leaders of local congregations today, we can note that even these special persons have as their mission not "to minister" but to "prepare God's people" for *their* ministry!

The word translated "prepare" is *katartizō,* which means to "put in order, restore, or put to rights." Specifically, the mission with which leaders are charged is to put the members of the body into proper condition for their works of service. In Ephesians 4:12 a related form of the word *(katartismos)* was used of the setting of a bone. Implied is the idea of setting the body in order, connecting parts appropriately so they will function as designed. It is fascinating to note in Hebrews 13:21 that it is through Christ as the Great Shepherd that God equips (prepares) His people "with everything good for doing his will." This same word is used in 1 Corinthians 1:10 where Paul exhorts the church to correct the dissension in the body and be put into proper condition by being "perfectly united in mind and thought." Part of the task of the leaders, in keeping with Christ's own commitment, is to see the body put into proper condition, with parts appropriately connected and unified, so that each part can actively engage in its ministry and thus build up the body of Christ toward maturity.

SPIRITUAL GIFTS

Whenever we deal with ministry, we are challenged to ask the source of the ability of one person to build another toward maturity. This question is answered in Scripture in the affirmation that God, through His Holy Spirit, has given each believer a "spiritual gift." The Greek word translated "spiritual gift" is *charisma* and means literally a "gracious gift," or "donation." The basic teaching is that God has, as a gracious act, given each believer a "special, spiritual endowment for service for the life of the community."[2]

What is striking as we look at passages that deal with spiritual gifts is to note the following:

1. Teaching on spiritual gifts is always associated in Scripture with teaching about the body.
2. In each context where the body and spiritual gifts are discussed, there is extensive teaching on the importance of love in the Christian community.

---

[2]NIDNTT, 2:121.

3. In each case, believers who have been given these special spiritual endowments are expected to use them in the context of the body!

While most commentators suggest that gifts listed in such passages as Romans 12 and 1 Corinthians 12 have both an inward and an outward expression, it is at least worth considering whether perhaps spiritual gifts may be in fact the endowment given believers for the building up of the body, and not primarily enablement for ministries in the world. At any rate, looking over the two basic New Testament gift/body passages, we can see a striking number of common elements that seem to suggest this view (see the chart on page 51).

Even in a passage in which gifts are merely mentioned in passing, we see many of the same themes repeated. Note how many common themes occur in 1 Peter 4:8-11:

> Above all, love each other deeply, because love covers over a multitude of sins. Offer hospitality to one another without grumbling. Each one should use whatever spiritual gift he has received to serve others, faithfully administering God's grace in its various forms. If anyone speaks, he should do it as one speaking the very words of God. If anyone serves, he should do it with the strength God provides, so that in all things God may be praised through Jesus Christ. To him be the glory and the power for ever and ever. Amen.

These observations about the New Testament's association of gifts, love, and the body's function are suggestive. We may not have explicit evidence that "gifts" are basically for the internal ministry and the upbuilding of the body. But the evidence is at least implicit. We may consider spiritual gifts as operating primarily in the context of loving relationships within the body and *not* primarily as equipment for "offices" or roles in institutional structures. The Scriptures seem to suggest that where there is love and unity, and the body is thus knit together, each member of the body will express his own unique spiritual endowment by serving others, and growth will take place as a consequence.

Yet whether or not "spiritual gifts" are related primarily to the ministry of members to the body, we can say several things with certitude.

SUMMARY AND IMPLICATIONS

What can we say about the body as an organism, and how it functions internally?

1. *In the New Testament, "growth" refers primarily to the internal development of the body toward maturity.* This is seen not only in the choice of words for growth, such as *auxanō* and *oikodomeō*, but also in the references in body pas-

FIGURE 10
PURPOSE OF GIFTS IN THE BODY

Concepts	1 Corinthians 12-14	Romans 12
Each believer given gifts	"To each one the manifestation of the Spirit is given" (12:7). "All these are the work of one and the same Spirit, and he gives them to each man" (12:11).	"We have different gifts, according to the grace given us" (12:6).
Gifts differ	"There are different kinds of gifts, but the same Spirit. There are different kinds of service, but the same Lord. There are different kinds of working, but the same God works all of them in all men" (12:4-6).	"We have different gifts" (12:6).
The body is viewed as "many parts"	"The body is a unit, though it is made up of many parts; and though all its parts are many, they form one body. So it is with Christ" (12:12).	"Just as each of us has one body with many members, and these members do not all have the same function, so in Christ we who are many form one body . . ." (12:4-5).
Gifts are given for the common good of the body	"To each one the manifestation of the Spirit is given for the common good" (12:7; (sympheron means "to help, confer a benefit").	"Each member belongs to all the others" (12:5; implies ministry to the body).
God has combined the members as He designed	"God has combined the members of the body, . . . so that there should be no division in the body, but that its parts should have equal concern for each other" (12:24-25).	"Think of yourself . . . in accordance with the measure of faith God has given you" (12:3), for "we have different gifts, according to the grace given us" (12:6).
Unity is essential for the body to function	"There should be no division in the body" (12:25).	"Love must be sincere. . . . Live in harmony with one another" (12:9, 16).
Love vital in the function of body and in the use of gifts	The love chapter (13:1-13).	"Love must be sincere. . . . Be devoted to each other in brotherly love. . . . Share. . . . Practice hospitality. . . . Live in harmony with one another" (12:9-10, 13, 16).
Ministry carried out and gifts used in gatherings of the church	1 Cor. 14:5-19 states three times in its description of gifts the location of their exercise: "so that the church may be edified" (14:5), "gifts that build up the church" (14:12), and "in the church" (14:19).	Romans 12 suggests that each member "belongs to all the others" and then describes the exercise of various gifts. The clear implication is that the gifts are used for the benefit of those to whom we "belong" (12:5-8).

sages to the maturity *(teleios)* toward which growth moves.

We are not required to reject or even discount numerical growth as vital to the life of the body of Christ. We are required, however, to be sure that in seeking to reach and win the lost we also give full consideration to keeping the body in proper condition *(katartizō)* for internal growth.

2. *In the New Testament, internal growth is presented as an organic process.* Typically in institutions "growth" is measured on some kind of numerical scale—in terms of members added, profits achieved, units constructed, etc. To facilitate such growth, leaders plan, organize, and train the members of the organization in skills related to task achievement. This whole pattern of planning, organizing, and training for tasks has been carried over into the church as the means by which church growth will be achieved.

While organic growth can often be measured—in terms of increased height, weight, etc.—it is not achieved in the same way that institutional growth is achieved. Organic growth involves changes within the organism—changes that are developmental in nature. For organic growth to take place, what is essential is the nurture of the natural processes of healthy life, which God has designed into the genetic structure of all living things. It would seem that internal, organic growth is intrinsically different from institutional growth and that very different conditions and skills are required to facilitate it.

3. *In the New Testament, growth takes place through the functioning of each member.* This is one of the basic facts about organic growth. Every cell has its role to play. Every part has its special function, and that function must be performed if the body is to be healthy.

There is no doubt, if we accept the organic nature of the church, that a primary concern of every leader and every congregation must be to help each believer make his own unique contribution to the maturing of all.

4. *In the New Testament, each believer is equipped with a special endowment by God's Spirit so that he can make his contribution "for the common good."* Spiritual gifts *(charismata)* are related to the functioning of the body and to the contribution each person makes to the growth of the whole organism. We know that gifts differ significantly and that differences in individuals are thus healthy, not detrimental. We know too that the gifts that seem "less honorable" are, according to Paul, essential to the functioning of the whole.

It follows then, that we should not attempt to force Christians into a single mold, insisting that everyone should learn a specific method of soul winning, or that all should lead home Bible classes. Since gifts are related to *organic* growth, we should take great care not to associate them in the minds of Christians with such institutional roles as "Sunday school teacher."

5. *In the New Testament, such interpersonal relationships as unity and love provide the context for organic growth.* Growth conditions are not so much a matter of classroom knowledge and skill-training experiences as of interpersonal warmth, caring, closeness, and sharing of life.

This is a very important aspect of the differences between organic and institutional systems. It is a warning to us that, in working toward the growth of Christians and the community of faith, interpersonal relationships between members of the body are of paramount importance.

6. *In the New Testament, the function of some, and possibly all, of the leaders in the body is to keep it in such a condition* (katarizō) *that each member can minister.* This striking role for leadership is very different from the role played by the leaders of many churches. Yet it is in total harmony with what we saw in the preceding chapter about the nature of Jesus' headship over the body and its implications for Christian leadership.

Whatever we discover about the role of leadership and how leaders carry out their functions in the body, we must keep in mind that spiritual leaders are "body leaders," and not merely the leaders of institutions. Leaders must then understand the nature of organic growth and know how to facilitate that kind of growth toward maturity, if they are to serve appropriately the church of which Jesus is living head.

PROBE

▶ *case histories*
▶ *discussion questions*
▶ *thought provokers*
▶ *resources*

1. In an excellent study from The Center for the Study of Church Organizational Behavior, Robert Worley argues that most congregations are organized in a utilitarian way. That is, the leaders of the church view the church as an institution that is organized to reach certain goals that they may define either biblically or politically. Worley points out that this perspective "carries with it tacit assumptions about leadership styles"—and much more:

Further, it presumes a certain stance toward other members. Under the influence of utilitarianism, leaders begin to see members as entities to be used, not as persons having moral intention or faith commitments which must find expression if they are to have dignity and integrity. Leaders expect compliance with their goals, interests, and faith commitments. No provision is made for members to express their goals, interests, and faith commitments—and act upon them. Members are useful as long as there is concurrence, compliance, and economic support. . . . Currently, no alternative perspectives exist, [but] rule in the church demands the development of alternative perspectives to utilitarianism for congregations.[3]

This quote is particularly significant. It suggests that as long as congregations are organized and the ministry of the church viewed in an *institutional* form, (1) certain leadership styles are assumed, (b) members will be "used," (3) the value of members will be measured by their function in institutional roles, and (4) no freedom will be provided to let each member operate within the context of his or her own goals, interests, or commitments—and, we might add, gifts. Think about this suggestion of Worley, and:

A. Rewrite the paragraph quoted above, stating it in your own words to expand or clarify its meaning.
B. Show how an organic rather than institutional (or, in Worley's terms, "utilitarian") perspective on the church might (1) affect leadership style, and (2) affect the behavior expected of church members.

2. Wofford and Kilinski argue that the church must be treated like an organism. When they write of selecting and training church personnel, they outline a system by which a personnel committee works to find personnel for "the jobs that are currently available" and lists these "job opportunities." Included are "elected officers, such as deacons, elders, treasurers, Sunday school superintendents, and leaders in Boys Brigade, Pioneer Girls, music ministries such as choirs and musicians, committeemen, and special forces such as vacation Bible school, gospel teams, ushers, nursery workers, and organizational officers."[4]

How would you evaluate the following statement about their approach (choosing *pro* or *con* as you wish):

---

[3]Robert C. Worley, *Dry Bones Breathe!* (Chicago: Moody, 1978), pp. 25-26.

[4]Jerry Wofford and Kenneth Kilinski, *Organization and Leadership in the Local Church* (Grand Rapids: Zondervan, 1973), p. 56.

"Wofford and Kilinski view the church as an organism, but inconsistently suggest practices in the church that treat it as an institution."

3. The following are samples of charts suggested by Wofford and Kilinski. These forms are supposed to be used by the membership committee to find and assign personnel to ministries where they will be a functioning part of the congregation. Look over these charts, then write up *an alternative plan* for helping members find their function in the body as an organism.

FIGURE 11
MEMBERSHIP PROFILE

Bible Training _____

_____

_____

_____

1. Church Offices Held:

_____

_____

_____

_____

_____

_____

2. Committees: Have Served on   Interested in
   Missionary _____
   Evangelism _____
   Publicity _____
   Worship _____
   Property _____
   Christian Education _____
   Youth _____
   Other _____

3. Would you be interested and willing to take training to equip you for a place of service?
   _____ Yes _____ Not at this time, but after _____
                                                         date

   _____No

4. Remarks and/or other ministries to which the Lord has called you to serve:

_____

_____

_____

_____

_____

SERVICE ABILITIES

Prayerfully fill out the following. Your check mark in the "willing to help" column will indicate your willingness to serve in that area for one year.

5. Christian Education

	Have Done It	Willing to Help
Teacher		
Substitute Teacher		
Clerical		
Music		
Youth Advisor		
Board of Christian Education		
Administration		

Areas of Service

Sunday School			Children's Church		
2s - 3s			2s - 3s		
4s - 5s					
6s - 8s			4s - 5s		
9s - 11s					
12s - 14s			Grades		
15s - 17s			1st, 2nd, 3rd		
Adults			4th, 5th, 6th		

Boys Brigade		
Pioneer Girls		
Vacation Bible School		
Camp		
Other		

6. Office Help

Type—at Home		
—at Church		
Dictation		
Filing, Mailing		
Telephone		
Mimeographing		
Other		

The church as the body of Christ does not exist for itself. When the church is gathered, its focus may be on the internal life and growth of the body. But when scattered—when in touch with the world—the body of Christ exists to carry out the continuing mission of Jesus. Because the church is the body of Christ and through us Jesus touches the lives of

INCARNATION: THE CHURCH IN MISSION

those we touch, the incarnation of our Lord has a continuing form. Our key to understanding the body in mission is to hear the words of Jesus to the Father: "As you sent me into the world, I have sent them into the world" (John 17:18). And "I in them and you in me" (John 17:23).

The doctrine of the Incarnation is distinct and unique to the Christian faith. Many religions speak of appearances of deities in the guise of men or animals. But these are "appearances" only. None takes the startling position of Christianity, which affirms that the God who existed from eternity and who created all things entered His creation to actually *become* a human being. Yet this is just the radical affirmation of the Christian faith. The Word, John says, "became flesh" (John 1:14).

Three key passages summarize the Christian doctrine of the Incarnation:

1. Galatians 4:4-5: "When the time had fully come, God sent his Son, born of a woman, born under law, to redeem those under law, that we might receive the full rights of sons."

2. Philippians 2:5-8: In this early expression of faith, Jesus is portrayed as One

   "Who, being in very nature God,
   did not consider equality with God something to be grasped,
   but made himself nothing,
   taking the very nature of a servant,
   being made in human likeness.
   And being found in appearance as a man,
   he humbled himself
   and became obedient to death—
   even death on a cross!

3. Colossians 1:15, 20; 2:9: "He is the image of the invisible God, the firstborn over all creation. . . . God was pleased to have all his fullness dwell in him, and through him to reconcile to himself all things, whether things on earth or things in heaven, by making peace through his blood, shed on the cross. . . . For in Christ all the fullness of the Deity lives in bodily form."

Each of these basic passages affirms that the preexisting God did in fact become true man and in His unique humanity through a real death brought redemption to mankind.

This teaching is reflected in many other passages. For instance, the following references speak of Jesus' coming "in the flesh": 1 John 4:2; Romans 8:3; Ephesians 2:15; Colossians 1:22; 1 Timothy 3:16; 1 Peter 3:18; 4:1; 2 John 7. Others speak of Jesus as having a unique relationship with the Father: Matthew 10:32; 11:27-28; 15:13; 16:17; 18:10-14, 35; Luke 2:29; 23:34, 46; 24:49. Strikingly, too, Jesus constantly affirms His identity with the Father (cf. John 5:18-23; 10:30,

CHAPTER 4

38; 14:8-11). Jesus' affirmation is "I and the Father are one" (John 10:30).

The incarnation of Christ is unique. Theologically there is and can be no incarnation other than the incarnation of Jesus. God will never again enter history as a babe, to grow up as a human being in the world. No person other than Jesus of Nazareth will ever be the preexistent God who reveals Himself to us in Scripture as Creator and Redeemer. The Incarnation was a one-of-a-kind, never-to-be-repeated event.

At the same time, it is a continuing incarnation. The Incarnation did not terminate with the death and resurrection of Jesus. Jesus, who was raised, lives today. Jesus, who was raised, lives on as God and man. Jesus, who was raised, is still God in the flesh.

In one sense, Jesus is in one place, seated at the right hand of the Father in His bodily form. One day He will return to earth and, as the promised Savior/King, rule the universe promised to Him.

Yet in another sense Jesus is *not* limited to the realm of God's throne. In this sense—and it is as real a sense as the first—Jesus lives today, in the flesh, in the members of His body. We have seen that the church *is* an organism of which Christ is head. We, the Bible tells us, are individually members of the body of Christ. Together we form that living organism. As His living body, we are in fact a contemporary expression of Jesus Christ Himself in our world. We, the church, continue His incarnation.

THE CONTINUING INCARNATION

The concept of continuing incarnation is reflected in a number of teachings of the Bible.

Likeness

This thought is stated by Jesus in Luke 6:40. Our Lord affirms that when a disciple has been put into proper condition or made complete *(katartizō)*, he "will be like his teacher" (Luke 6:40). Jesus had committed Himself to a process that would lead the Twelve, and ultimately Christians in every age, to be like Him.

Scripture states this as one of the purposes of God in bringing us salvation. The Book of Romans announces, "Those God foreknew he also predestined to be conformed to the likeness of his Son, that he might be the firstborn among many brothers" (8:29). With this commitment we have God's promise: "We shall be like him, for we shall see him as he is" (1 John 3:2).

God's commitment to make His children like Jesus is not merely eschatological. God is involved in the transformation process now. In 2 Corinthians Paul pictures us with faces unveiled to "reflect the Lord's glory," for we "are being transformed into his likeness with ever-increasing glory, which comes from the Lord, who is the Spirit" (2 Cor. 3:18).

Word written on flesh

A parallel thought is expressed in Scripture: The written Word is currently being translated into a living word "written not with ink but with the Spirit of the living God, not on tablets of stone but on tablets of human hearts" (2 Cor. 3:3). In Jeremiah, the prospect of being living expressions of the Word—and, ultimately, the Word *is* Jesus—is held out to believers. The prophet foresees a new covenant: "I will put my law within them, and I will write it on their hearts; and I will be their God, and they shall be my people" (Jer. 31:33). As living expressions of God's Word, we who "have borne the likeness of the earthly man . . . shall bear the likeness of the man from heaven" (1 Cor. 15:49).

Reflections

Scripture often says that we are to be reflections of Jesus. He is the Light of the world, and to us He says, "You are the light of the world" (Matt. 5:14). Even the name *Christian*, given to the believers in Antioch as a term of derision by outsiders, means "little Christs."

When we hear Jesus give us His new commandment in John 13 we also hear Him say, "This is how all men will know that you are my disciples, if you have love one for another." The unmistakable stamp of Jesus' kind of love on the community of faith is compelling evidence of the real presence of Jesus among His people. Even those in the world sense that love and can only explain it by admitting, "These are Jesus' people."

Walk

As we explore the Bible, we become aware that those who are called to be like Jesus are also called to live as He lived in the world. John says, "Whoever claims to live in him must walk as Jesus did" (1 John 2:6). Jesus says to His disciples: "Love your enemies." He then explains that God is the kind of Person who gives rain and sun to the evil and the good alike and that we who are sons of this Father are to be like Him (Matt. 5:43-48).

This theme is repeated in the Pauline correspondence. We are to "be imitators of God . . . as dearly loved children, and live a life of love" (Eph. 5:1-2). We are privileged to forgive "each other, just as in Christ God forgave you" (Eph. 4:32). Our life in the world is to be a practical expression of who Jesus is and how He lived when He was among us.

New man

As His new creations we who are members of Christ's body are to express Jesus in our personalities, and in our world. Paul points out that our "life is now hidden with Christ in God" (Col. 3:3). Thus all those things that belonged to our earthly or old nature are to be put away. "You used to walk in these ways, in the life you once lived," Paul points out (Col. 3:7). But now there is a new way, "since you have taken off your old self with its practices and have put on the new self, which is being renewed in knowledge in the image of its Creator" (vv. 9-10). Because we are God's people, our lives are to demonstrate Jesus to the world of men.

> As God's chosen people, holy and dearly loved, clothe yourselves with compassion, kindness, humility, gentleness and patience. Bear with each other and forgive whatever grievances you may have against one another. Forgive as the Lord forgave you. And over all these virtues put on love, which binds them all together in perfect unity (Col. 3:12-14).

Summary

While the incarnation of Jesus is a unique, one-time event, it is also a continuing event. In the idea that the church is the body of Christ, with Christ Himself its head, the Bible suggests that Jesus Christ is still present in human flesh in our world.

The idea of a continuing incarnation is supported by much New Testament teaching. God has committed Himself to bring Jesus' people to the "likeness" of their Lord. Discipling is an ongoing process, through which the Holy Spirit works to transform us from one degree of splendor to another that we might more perfectly reflect Him.

The Bible speaks of a time when the Word will be written on men's hearts. There it can be "known and read by all men" (2 Cor. 3:2). Jesus, the eternal Word, became flesh in a unique way as the God-man. Yet Jesus, the living Word, is now being engraved on the hearts of human beings and expressed through human lives in a clear and "readable" way.

Even our name, *Christians*, illustrates the fact that we are to be recognized by the world as "little Christs," lights in the world who are reflections of Him who is *the* Light.

There is, therefore, no question that believers are expected to live in this world as Jesus did. Our lives, values, behavior, attitudes, choices, even feelings, are to be in a deep and real way His. We who live in Jesus "must walk as Jesus did" (1 John 2:6).

Finally, the old elements of our personalities, warped by sin, are to be replaced by the new person who is "renewed" in the Creator's image. That renewal is expressed in the world by a life that is Christlike.

AT WORK IN MAN'S WORLD

On the eve of the Crucifixion, Jesus met the Father alone in Gethsemane. Jesus' prayer, recorded in John 17, reflects the theme of the continuing incarnation and also gives insight into our mission.

The prayer develops as follows:

vv. 1-5   The time for Jesus' glorification has come. He returns to the Father because He has completed the work the Father gave Him to do (v. 5).

vv. 6-12   That work involved the formation of a company of believers who are distinct from all others because Jesus gave them the words the Father gave Him, and they accepted them (v. 8). This believing community is the focus of Jesus' prayer. Jesus realizes that He "will remain in the world no longer, but they are still in the world" (v. 11). Recognizing the tensions life in the world will bring, Jesus prays for protection and He prays that they may be one as the Father and the Son are one (v. 11).

vv. 13-19   Jesus continues to pray that His followers might be protected from the evil one as they live in the world. Yet it is necessary that they continue in the world. While they are not of the world, even as Jesus is not of it (v. 16), they are sent on a mission to it. "As you have sent me into the world," Jesus says, "I have sent them into the world" (v. 18).

vv. 20-26   This prayer is not for the disciples of Jesus' day alone. It is for all who will, throughout history, become members of that one body. It is of deep concern to Jesus that they be brought to complete unity to let the world know that the Father has sent Him and has loved them (v. 23). How is this possible? Again we see incarnational truth. It is possible because our oneness depends on our unity as a body with a head, that all of us may be one, just as God is in Christ and Christ is in God (v. 20). Finally Jesus says, "I have revealed you to them, and will continue to make you known in order that the love you have for me may be theirs and that I may myself be in them" (v. 26).

It is because Jesus Himself is in us that we are able to do the work of God in our world. His presence in the body—a body that experiences a unity and love that bind its members to Him—is both the basis of and the answer to this prayer.

Jesus sends us into the world and lives in us to accomplish God's purposes. What, then, does Jesus want to accomplish through His body today?

THE MANIFOLD WISDOM OF GOD

The continuing incarnation of Jesus in His body, the church, is related to God's plans for the world. Through the church, God intends the "manifold wisdom of God" to be made known, not only on earth, but "to the rulers and authorities in the heavenly realm" (Eph. 3:10). God's complex and manifold plan to redeem and to glorify Himself is being worked out in a church that exists in a sin-warped world.

The following is a brief, sketchy survey of the Bible's teaching about this plan:

Witness to Jesus

"You shall be my witnesses," Jesus said as He explained His mission for the disciples (Acts 1:8). Worldwide witness is not only verbal, but also includes total lifestyle; it is not only individual, but is also a function of the Christian community. "All men will know that you are my disciples," Jesus said in John 13, "if you have love one for another."

Evangelization

The witness to Jesus is powerful, and the message brings many to a personal faith relationship with Christ. As the message is shared, God acts in the hearts of hearers. As it did in the early church, evangelism makes an impact, and those who accept the message are "added to their number" (Acts 2:41).

Physical care for others

The church has a special obligation to meet the physical as well as the spiritual needs of its members (see James 2 and 2 Corinthians 8 and 9). Yet the call to care extends beyond the members of the body of Christ. We are to serve others as well. While doing good is "especially to the household of faith," it is also to those who stand outside the door.

Worship

Jesus saw worship as intrinsic to the life of believers in God: "The Father seeks such to worship him" (John 4:23). He was speaking to a woman who was admittedly a sinner—yet she had worth and value in God's sight and was sought out by Him to become a worshiper in spirit and in truth. The church in the world is privileged to fellowship with God and to invite transformed sinners to offer worship and prayers to Him.

Good works

God acted in Christ to "purify for himself a people who are his very own, eager to do good works" (Titus 2:14). This commitment is to be a central element in the life of God's people.

The communication of hope

We live in a world marked by despair. Many have neither hope nor purpose, and, apart from a personal relationship with God, all is emptiness. Yet as God's people in the world, even in the most disastrous of circumstances, we continue confident. Our hope will puzzle those in the world around us, so we should "always be prepared to give an answer to everyone who asks [us] to give the reason for the hope that [we] have" (1 Peter 3:15).

The glorification of God

This is one of the main missions of the church, even as it was a primary concern of Jesus when He walked on earth (John 17:4). Jesus brought glory to God by completing the work given to Him. We bring glory to God in the same way. The Bible says repeatedly that the people of the world will "see your good deeds and praise your Father in heaven" (Matt. 5:16).

The revelation of God

In John 17:6 Jesus tells the Father, "I have revealed you to those whom you gave me out of the world." This revelation of God continues. As Paul explains, he needs no letter of recommendation, for those who have come to know Christ through his ministry "are a letter from Christ," revealing in themselves the living God (2 Cor. 3:1-3).

The demonstration of holiness

Jesus lived a holy life in the world. We too are called to live in holiness. Paul says to Christians, "Offer the parts of your body to him as instruments of righteousness" (Rom. 6:13).

Justice

The Old Testament places great stress on doing justice and promises that when the Messiah comes, He will establish righteousness. Modeling ourselves after God, we are to be just and to have a concern for justice in our society.

Spiritual warfare

Paul tells Christians that they do not battle against flesh and blood but against principalities and powers. The weapons of their warfare are, appropriately, not carnal but spiritual. The church as the body of Christ is engaged in this supernatural battle, even as Jesus was in His earthly life.

The exposure of darkness

We are told to have nothing to do with the unfruitful works of darkness, but rather to expose them (Rom. 13:12). When light comes, darkness is shown to be darkness. When true goodness is seen, the goodness of the unbeliever is shown to be depraved, and men whose deeds are evil can no longer pretend not to know the nature of the sin they choose.

Reconciliation

The Christian's mission involves bringing people into harmony with God through Christ and also bringing them into harmony with one another. The differences that divide people in the world—differences of race, education, birth, wealth, and social class—are seen to be irrelevant as reconciliation takes place in the one body of Christ.

The provision of a counterculture

Scripture says that we have been rescued from Satan's kingdom and translated into the kingdom of God's dear Son (Col. 1:13). In His kingdom, there is a whole new way of life to learn and to live. The church becomes the context in which Christians learn to live God's way. As a counterculture, the church demonstrates God's alternative lifestyle to the world.

God's plan has many other aspects. The church has a mission of discipling and disciplining believers. The church is to "look after orphans and widows in their distress" (James 1:27). The church is to have a deep concern for the poor and the oppressed. The church is to bring healing—both inner healing and physical healing. And so the challenge continues to expand. God's purposes for His church are almost limitless! In complex and manifold ways, God's wisdom and power are demonstrated to all beings in the world through the church.

But the greatest wonder of all is that in us Jesus Himself walks the world. In us Jesus speaks the Good News. In us Jesus clothes the fatherless and feeds the hungry. (In those of us who are destitute Jesus also *receives* the gifts of clothing and food that are given in His name.) In us Jesus exalts the Father in prayer and worship. In us Jesus continues to do good works. In us Jesus, who knew a joy untouched by circumstances, brings hope to the hopeless. In us Jesus reveals the Father and brings glory to God. In us Jesus reveals a positive and attractive holiness that exposes the darkness of sin. In us Jesus continues to show God's deep concern for justice. In us Jesus' reconciling touch is felt wherever there is division and pain. In us Jesus takes His firm stand against the powers of evil. In us Jesus is shaping a new lifestyle, a kingdom of God, a beachhead of the divine rule in the world of men. In us Jesus, the great physician, bends low to heal. In our flesh our Lord Jesus takes contemporary shape and form.

IMPLICATIONS OF THE CONTINUING INCARNATION

The vision of the body as Jesus Himself in active mission in the world is exciting. Wherever members of His body come in contact with the world, there He is present. Because He is present in us, He is able to respond through us to whatever needs may exist.

All too often church leaders attempt to organize and institutionalize programs that work toward the achievement of one or more of the listed purposes. Often the tendency is to focus on one (e.g., evangelism in evangelical circles, social programs in "liberal" groups) at the expense of others. There is also a tendency to try to organize people into task groups to meet needs or resolve problems. Organizations may be all right for the church (we'll see the limiting conditions in a later chapter). But when church leaders set goals, make plans, and design programs, they have ceased to be "body leaders" and have taken on functions that in a living organism are prerogatives of the head.

But how should the purposes of God for the body be achieved? They should be achieved through Jesus as the head, incarnated in His body. Wherever believers walk, Jesus' presence should be felt. The more Christians grow and mature into His likeness, the more His body will respond as He did to meet human needs and to accomplish the goals of God in the world.

Jesus *is* present.

Leaders do not need to organize "programs" to make His presence felt. Instead they need to concentrate on the growth that brings members to maturity and Christlikeness, confident that Jesus will express Himself through them in a dynamic and unmistakable way. Christians have been sent into the world. Because Jesus is with them, they can touch the world around them just as Jesus Christ touched His world.

PROBE

▶ *case histories*
▶ *discussion questions*
▶ *thought provokers*
▶ *resources*

1. Jesus made a big impact on His world. Yet He set up no organizations, began no programs, and recruited no workers for task or mission groups.

   How, then, did Jesus accomplish His mission? And if the purposes of God for the church parallel the purposes He had for Jesus, how should we work to carry out those purposes today?

   To explore an incarnational lifestyle, pick one of the purposes listed on pages 66–69. Study one of the Gospels to see how Jesus worked toward the accomplishment of that purpose. Using 1 John 2:6 ("Whoever claims to live in [Jesus] must walk as Jesus did") as your rationale, suggest ways in which Christians today can be used by God to accomplish the same purposes in similar ways.

2. In this chapter the authors, still building on the New Testament teaching that the church *is* the body of Christ and He is its living head, suggest that the work of the church in the world is carried out through the incarnational presence of Jesus in the believer. On the following chart jot down comparisons and contrasts between an *incarnational* and an *institutional* way of "doing justice."

   To help you think specifically, imagine the person who has this particular concern to be (1) a Christian businessman who employs several hundred persons, (2) a legislator in state government, and (3) a local church pastor or elder.

FIGURE 12
INCARNATIONAL AND INSTITUTIONAL APPROACHES
TO CARRYING OUT JUSTICE

Incarnational	Institutional

3. Don Bubna tells the following story. Read it and write a paragraph explaining how it links the concept of the internal growth of the body (explored in chapter 3) and the incarnational mission of the body (discussed in this chapter).

> *One of my good friends in Salem is a young caseworker and counselor named Dick Simpson. We met at the YMCA six years ago when my son Jeff and I were taking part in a program there. Dick knew I was a pastor when he asked me to play the role of an uptight, narrowminded religious father for a Human Relations Seminar for the Salem Police Department. I accepted, and Dick thought I did a great job. We decided to meet for breakfast one morning, and that was the beginning of a friendship that eventually brought Dick as a cautious observer to our Sunday morning worship service.*
>
> *"I can only take small doses of your preaching," he told me in his forthright way, "but I really appreciate your friendship, and I like the warm relationships in your group."*

71

He was an infrequent visitor. Months could pass between the times he darkened the door of our building. But we met for breakfast once in a while, and he accepted my invitation to a couple of men's fellowship breakfasts. By now I knew that Dick was a bright and very sensitive fellow who had been turned off by church groups during his teens, and found it difficult to believe there was a loving God who personally cared for him.

"But I'm intrigued by what I see in your fellowship," he told me. "I've never felt so accepted by a group of people before. I find myself wanting to be a part of it, and I sense that the people genuinely appreciate what I can contribute as well."

After four years, Dick began to attend the Sunday morning services regularly.

"No one tells me I have to be there, but I miss you people when I'm not there, and I get the impression you miss me." He smiled. "You know, with my sensitive ego I don't like to be always on the receiving end, but I really believe you people think I'm a person of worth."

"Even to God?"

His warm grin was Dick's way of avoiding my question. "I know what you're getting at," he chuckled. "But I'm not ready for that. Till I get there, it helps me to know that I'm appreciated by somebody."

"I hope you don't feel I'm putting you on the spot."

Dick relaxed in one of our living room chairs, sipping the coffee Dee had brought him. "You're not putting me on the spot, Don," he assured me. "That's what keeps me hanging around. No one in that church has cornered me to say I need to hurry up and get saved, but all I have to do is look at your faces. They tell me you have confidence in your God, and slowly I'm learning to have confidence in him too."

He laughed and looked at me sideways. "You people are like Cadillac salesmen. You're saying, 'Look, we've got the best in town. When you want it, come and get it. We're not going to push it on you.'"

So what are we supposed to be doing anyway, as a church? We are to be growing toward maturity in Christ, glorifying God by letting his attitudes increase in us—and thereby making him known to a world who is seeking.

That is our primary purpose—all else flows from that.[1]

---

[1] Don Bubna and Sarah Ricketts, *Building People* (Wheaton, Ill.: Tyndale, 1978), pp. 67-68. This is an excellent book.

The Scriptures are clear. The church is the body of Christ, a living organism over which He is head. We've explored some of the compelling evidence that demands we take this teaching seriously. We are not free to treat these ideas as abstract "theory." They are a reality that we who are God's people can and should experience.

THEOLOGICAL IMPLICATIONS OF THE INCARNATION

In future chapters we'll look at specific principles and practices that guide us into true "body" leadership. But first, let us examine three implications of our theology of the church: supernaturalism, release, and ministry (not administration).

Even before theology influences behavior, it has its impact on attitudes. Paul's reference in Romans 12 to the "renewing of the mind" is concerned with more than "understanding." The Greek word is *nous*, which encompasses a person's total perception of life. It includes the transformation of attitudes, values, and behavior, as well as beliefs. As we come to a deeper understanding of the church as the body of Christ, our perceptions will need to be reshaped. Our whole approach to life and leadership in His body is dynamically affected by Scripture's picture of a living organism united to Jesus Christ, who functions as our living head.

SUPERNATURALISM

The first theological implication of an incarnational lifestyle is a radical supernaturalism in our approach to life as part of the church.

One of the major drawbacks to working with the church as though it were an institution is that an institutional approach to Christian life gradually robs us of our awareness of the supernatural.

It is not hard to understand why. Leaders in an organization are always dealing with problems related to maintaining the institution and planning for the achievement of its goals. They must deal with budget and staffing. They must plan new buildings and maintain the old ones. They need to set goals and then set up committees and councils and other organizations to reach them. Even in their counseling and teaching they tend to focus on problems in their relationships with people. Even with the use of good management techniques, they come to think of the saints in relation to whether they help or frustrate the leaders' plans and hopes. The exercise of managerial skills begins to dominate more and more of their attention and demand more and more of their time. Many who entered the pastorate burdened to minister have left, discouraged by all they are required to do simply to keep the organization functioning and its agencies and activities on track.

As our focus shifts to problem solving and organizational maintenance, we feel an increasing need for better management skills. And the more managerial training we have, the more we tend to view the church of Jesus as an institution and the more we minister in the "institutional leader" mold.

But the church is *not* an institution. And we are *not* its managers.

The church is an organism.

One agonizing question that is often raised has to do with what will happen if leaders stop managing. Won't everything fall apart? After all, isn't the activity in a church directly related to the pastor "pushing" and being "behind the program"? If the elders or the board aren't in firm control of all programs, might not something go wrong? After all, someone has to be in charge, or disorganized confusion will be the result!

This kind of thinking is common. But it is possible only if we do not take Jesus Christ seriously. It is possible only if we question His power and doubt His ability to be the head in His body. It is possible only if we think of the church as an institution and doubt or deny its identity as an organism.

The first perspective that our theology must bring into focus, then, is our perspective on Jesus. When the Bible says we are *His* body, we need to see ourselves and all members of our local body in relationship to Jesus. And we need to believe that Jesus is fully capable of being our head.

Psalm 93:1-2 underlines His divine power:

> The Lord reigns, he is robed in majesty;
> the Lord is robed in majesty
> and is armed with strength.
> The world is established;
> it cannot be moved.
> Your throne is established long ago;
> you are from all eternity.

This Lord is the head of the church.

Or look at Colossians 1:15-18:

> He is the image of the invisible God, the firstborn over all creation. For by him all things were created: things in heaven and on earth, visible and invisible, whether thrones or power or rulers or authorities; all things were created by him and for him. He is before all things, and in him all things hold together. And he is the head of the body, the church.

The church of Jesus is not the brick-and-mortar buildings on the corners of our cities and towns. It is not the budgets that must be met nor the reports that must be filled out. It is not even the expectations of our congregations nor the criticisms of those who are disturbed when the leaders change the order of the Sunday-morning hymns. The church of Jesus is the men and women who, even when they are unaware of it, are linked inseparably to the living God, formed by His Spirit into one body, and who as His body are called to live increasingly in a responsive relationship with their Lord. *This* is the church true leaders serve, the church that is Christ's body. And this is the church that an adequate view of Jesus Christ in all His power and glory frees us to entrust ourselves joyfully into His care.

The church is not "our" church. It belongs to Jesus. When we have a true view of who Jesus is and a biblical vision of the supernatural reality of the body He heads, our approach to ministry in the Body will radically change.

RELEASE

When we recognize Jesus as the living head of the church, we find a great release. Most leaders in the church have taken on responsibilities that are not really theirs, so it's no wonder they feel the burden. "Release" involves simply affirming Jesus as the head of His church and giving the burdens that are His back to Him.

The principle of release is important for us in every area of our lives. Ultimately He is Lord of all, not simply head of the church. An experience of Clyde's illustrates the meaning of release, and the freedom release brings:

> As a young adult, I began to articulate my leadership style. It soon became very much a part of my total life. My leadership style was that of a domineering autocrat. It was based on a philosophy that said, *I refuse to fail.* I was so committed that I would pay whatever personal price success required. As that attitude grew, I developed a deep fear of failure. As that fear grew, my commitment to success intensified. In my business—building and developing, I buy parcels of land, develop them, build houses on them, sell the homes, and complete the community. Each new venture, each new project had an element of risk in it. I can recall telling my friends very heroically, "I will make this new project a success or I'll die out there in the sand trying."
>
> About eight years ago now our sales took off tremendously. Where at the beginning of the year I was building at the rate of four new homes each week, I had to double that production. I had to start eight new homes, and hopefully finish them, so that there were always eight being started and eight being finished. As a net result, instead of maybe having 75 homes under construction at a given time, I had 150 under construction. On a very practical level this meant bringing in a lot of new employees who didn't know the job. Soon there were many mistakes being made, and the quality of workmanship was plunging. Now add this: Each new home had a family waiting to move in, because their home was sold before I started to build. The buyers periodically visited their homes . . . and you know the rest. Soon I was filled with fear and anxiety as I dealt with people. Contractors were angry and upset with me. Buyers were complaining. My days were filled with problems I couldn't control.
>
> Let me tell you why. As a domineering autocrat I controlled everything and I made all the decisions. What this meant on a very practical level was that I often got up at 4 A.M. and spent two or three hours dictating instructions, memos, and decisions to responsible people in my company. At 8 A.M. my secretary typed the directives and distributed them to the managers. In this way I was telling them what to do.

THEOLOGICAL FOUNDATION

Another very practical aspect of my form of leadership was the type of management meetings I conducted. I would bring various top men and women together and advise them of the goals I had set. I laid out a plan for each of them to help achieve my objectives. Something very interesting used to happen in those meetings. There was one capable vice-president who would doze off. *I* was *highly excited* about these meetings and what was being discussed, and the great ideas that *I* was laying on the people. And this fellow slept!

As the business grew, I couldn't make decisions fast enough to cope with the problems. I was already getting up at 4 A.M. and I often worked till 10 at night. I realized that I could not drive myself any harder to solve the problems. Even with my strong commitment to success, I came to realize that I didn't have a choice! My reputation was being ruined. I was losing money. Things were completely out of hand, and I was faced with the very plain and blunt fact that I could do no more by the force of my personality and brute effort.

This plunged me into a state of despair and anxiety. I recall the summer that Joan and I with our girls, Kim and Sheri, took off for a month's vacation. I needed to be with the family, and I needed to pull myself together. I was intense and fearful and very depressed by what I saw happening. I was a mess as a person.

We vacationed in North Carolina's Smoky Mountains. Our lodge was completely private—the most peaceful place in the world. Yet I repeatedly exploded at the family. I had to apologize to Joan, "Honey, please be patient with me. I just need a chance to rest and get my feet back on the ground and I'll be okay."

About the third week I recall that one of the girls spilled some cereal at the breakfast table. I just came unglued and exploded. I said things that to this day I wish I'd never said. I left the table, went upstairs to the master bedroom, and closed myself in. I decided I couldn't stand to be around those kids any more. I was like a volcano looking for an opportunity to erupt. Joan and the girls were delighted to have me away from them.

I tried to pray. I tried to read my Bible. I recall sitting there with my legal pad and pencil thinking and working my way through all my problems—with no solutions coming.

During the fourth week the turmoil inside me reached a climax. I was walking alone down to the foot of the mountain, going over to the riding stable to meet Joan and the girls when the anger, anxiety, and depression got so intense I cried out loud, "God, save me from this pain. I can't take it any more."

That was a very significant point. As I look back, I see that God had my attention in a very unique way. I was worse off than when I left home.

Through friends who cared and ministered to me through books that God brought my way, I began seeing some truths about the Christian life I'd never understood before. As a result of this, for the very first time in my life I said something like this and meant it: "God, I realize that the failure and trauma that I'm experiencing is Your way of making me into the person You want me to be. So, God, if You want to bankrupt me, take away my home and all that I've accumulated in land and money and organization—if You want to take it all away as a means of making me the person You desire me to be, I want You to do that. I'm convinced now that becoming Your person is my greatest ambition and highest goal in life."

Theological Implications of the Incarnation

At the time I didn't understand all that that meant. The problems didn't go away. Some remain to this day. I can't even say that the attitude expressed was consistent. I had to pray that prayer dozens of times as the problems recurred. But today I can honestly share four very beautiful and important benefits that came to me from God as a result of that release. Here they are:

1. For the first time in my Christian life, I was able to trust God with the outcome of what I was doing. For the first time I could say, "God, I'm pouring myself into this business, into this church, or whatever. But I'm willing to trust You with the outcome, even to the extent that if You want me to fail, I want to fail. I give You the option."

2. I began to realize that failure from a human point of view might be success from God's perspective. When my friends thought, *He's failing*, God might have been saying, "Wow! I'm finally getting through to Clyde. We can make some progress now!"

3. For the first time in my life I was able to learn what it meant to live with Him as Master and me as steward. God began to teach me that when I became His son, I moved from being a slave to sin to a slave to Jesus. When I was able to give God any option in my life, even failure, it freed me for the first time in my Christian experience to be a steward of the Master.

4. When I learned to trust God with the outcome, I was liberated to begin trusting other people. In very practical ways, when we can trust the Master, Christ, as Lord and head of the church, as head of our lives, as head of any endeavor that deeply concerns us, we are free to trust others, because we're confident of God's involvement in the whole process. No longer the domineering autocrat who trusted nobody, who had to make all the decisions, I was set free to begin trusting other people to make choices. Things that used to sit on my desk regularly have now been given to somebody else.

Back in those early days of my career, I was, in a very real way, shaking my fist in God's face and saying, "God, when it comes to my success as a leader, as a businessman, I do not trust You. If I were to pass this business off to You, You might fumble the ball on me. And, I refuse to fail! I don't trust You nor anybody that works for me—only *I* can carry the ball. Keep Your hands off this part of my life; it's too important!"

Today I'm free from all that. Recognizing Jesus Christ as my Lord has brought release.

It should come as no surprise to you that in the beginning I looked for a church that operated the same way as I operated my business. It was not difficult to find. I became very deeply involved in a church where the pastor was the domineering autocrat just as I was in business. And because I was so dedicated to the idea of having one person make all the decisions and control everything, I became deeply loyal to this man and soon rose to second in command. Between the two of us we very effectively and skillfully controlled the religious life of about five hundred people. For example, within a relatively short time I was in a permanent spot on the church board. All the other elders and deacons would come on the board and then, at the end of their terms, they would have to go off. There were two exceptions. The pastor and I had permanent roles on the church board—a very important part of our control system.

I recall going to Sunday school meetings; I ran them just the way I ran meetings back at my company. I was the Sunday school superintendent and I basically told everybody what my goals were and how each one of them could fit into achieving my goals for the Sunday school. "Any questions about what you are to do?" I often asked.

It's really embarrassing to admit it now, but we never held a congregational meeting or board meeting without knowing in advance just how our ideas and plans were going to turn out in that meeting. I can recall a congregational meeting in which one dear guy raised his hand to ask a question about a proposal that the church was going to vote on. He voiced his question, and a hush came over that congregation. He was regarded as a crackpot for even questioning the recommendation. We had created a climate where people weren't to question, just do; they were not expected to think. One strong autocratic leader controlled everything. No one else ever needed to know anything.

MINISTRY, NOT ADMINISTRATION

At a recent seminar on leadership held at Honey Rock Camp, Wheaton College's northwoods camp, Clyde, who is an elder in his local congregation, shared this perspective with the pastors and elders present:

> Our church is Christ's body and not an organization requiring management. As a businessman I have been very effective in organizing people to work together to achieve corporate tasks. Helping people come together and be the body of Christ is a whole different "ballgame." My business skills don't help. However, the Bible does.
>
> First, as an elder who is gifted in pastoring, I'm learning *not to be* a manager—planning, organizing, controlling, etc.—and to be a servant instead. The Bible says, "Be shepherds of God's flock that is under your care, . . . *not* lording it *over* those entrusted to you, but being examples to the flock . . . with humility" (1 Peter 5:1-5).

This expresses the understanding that releasing involved not only his corporations but his church as well. Jesus is the living head of the church. He can be trusted with the body. With the new freedom that that trust brings, leaders discover the role God has planned for them in His church!

Ministry, not administration, is the calling of the spiritual leader.

Jesus puts it in focus in His charge to Peter as recorded in John 21:15-17:

> When they had finished eating, Jesus said to Simon Peter, "Simon son of John, do you truly love me more than these?"
> "Yes, Lord," he said, "you know that I love you."
> Jesus said, "Feed my lambs."
> Again Jesus said, "Simon son of John, do you truly love me?"
> He answered, "Yes, Lord, you know that I love you."
> Jesus said, "Take care of my sheep."
> The third time he said to him, "Simon son of John, do you love me?"
> Peter was hurt because Jesus asked him the third time, "Do you love me?" He said, "Lord, you know all things; you know that I love you."
> Jesus said, "Feed my sheep."

There can be no question that today, too, leaders in our churches have an honest love for Jesus. But perhaps many of us have forgotten our Lord's instructions to Peter. Our love for Him is not to lead us to take over the body of which He is head. Our love for Him is not to lead us to be managers of the kingdom, seeking to control and protect the work of God. Our love for Jesus is to move us to care for the sheep, to feed and nurture gently and lovingly the flock of God, building them always that they might hear and respond to the voice of Jesus, the "great Shepherd of the sheep."

PROBE

▶ *case histories*
▶ *discussion questions*
▶ *thought provokers*
▶ *resources*

1. On pages 77–80, Clyde shares his old fear of failure and the freedoms he found when he trusted God as Lord with all he possessed. Look at the four benefits Clyde lists. How might these benefits be experienced by church leaders who recognize Jesus as head of the church and release their congregations to Him?

2. In these chapters we've stated that institutional leadership styles and body leadership styles differ. The one moves toward management and control, the other toward ministry and service.

   Arn and McGavran report on the following work in San Juan, Puerto Rico. Read it and suggest how it illustrates the principles shared in this chapter.

   There had been little Protestant church growth there. In fact, it was a city where churches died. On Pearl Harbor day in 1941, a church was organized in a home, with nine members. Thirteen years later, it had grown to 627 members, a notable case of church growth.

   "How did it happen?" I asked Rev. Isidro Diaz, the pastor. "You must preach very powerful sermons."

   He replied, "My sermons have little to do with it. You see we have twelve upper rooms."

   "What do you mean?" I asked.

   "We have divided our congregation into twelve sections, and each conducts a full worship service, except for the Communion, every week," he said.

   I replied, "That must keep you busy running from one service to another."

   He said, "I never attend any of them. That's not my business. That's the business of the laymen."

   "Oh," I said, "so you have twelve branch churches, then, led by laymen?"

   He replied, "Yes! That is where the unchurched first start coming to worship. They wouldn't think of coming to the church. That's too formidable, but to a neighborhood meeting they go quite readily. These twelve house churches, each with about fifty members, give us an opportunity to grow."

That illustration is replete with lessons on church growth. Observe that, instead of one church having a relatively few people carrying the real responsibility, you now have 12 churches. In each one at least six people carry the responsibility. So you have 70 or 80 taking an active part in, and feeling the responsibility of, church growth. Each of the 12 congregations is engaged in evangelizing its neighbors. Visitors become part of a small church, small enough so real friendship can be developed, real care can be exercised, and real koinonia can be experienced. Real responsibility is delegated to laymen. They run these 12 churches, all by themselves!

The night I spoke at that church in Puerto Rico, a high school teacher confessed Christ. She had attended one of these upper rooms for over a year. After becoming a believer, she came to the main church to formally confess Christ, where later she was baptized and received her first Communion. Following this, she continued as a member of the upper room (house church) in which she had found the Lord.[1]

3. The following is an exercise in evaluating the verbal and nonverbal communication of church patterns. Place a check on the continuum to indicate what each item characterizes. Note: do not check any item which is not a valid indicator of organism or institution.

FIGURE 13
CHURCH PATTERNS

Comment—showing our church to be:	A Fine Institution	The Body of Christ
1. Recently we decided we don't need a bulletin on Sunday morning; we want to encourage spontaneity wherever possible.		_____
2. Bulletin announcement: "Our offerings last week were $750 short of our budgeted needs."		_____
3. People have become a little less concerned about starting and finishing on time.		_____
4. There seems to be a family atmosphere on Sunday morning.		_____
5. Our elders serve only three years; this assures us of always having "fresh blood" on the board.		_____
6. At church picnics our pastors and elders tend to stand around and talk while the rest of us play the games.		_____
7. In most of our church gatherings a number of people share in ministering to our group; many of them are not very good speakers, but they are very sincere.		_____

[1] Wynn Arn and Donald McGavran, *How to Grow a Church* (Glendale: Regal, 1976), pp. 95-96.

Comment   **Institution**   **Body**

8. Recently the elders of our church suggested that we send our contributions directly to the missions and ministries we feel God wants us to support. _____

9. A couple of years ago we stopped celebrating the anniversary of the founding of our church. _____

10. For our missionary conference this year our board set a much higher goal for faith pledges. _____

11. We encouraged our Sunday school teachers to conduct themselves more like friends (aunts and uncles) to the children. _____

12. Our elders often meet in one another's homes; they spend most of their time in prayer and Bible study. _____

13. Anybody standing at the door of the church greeting people should be dressed in a suit and tie. _____

14. Almost every time we meet through the week, we meet in somebody's home; it seems more and more like being together as a family. _____

15. Our missionary budget doubled in three years. _____

16. Our students are on a merit system; we reward those who memorize the most Scripture. _____

17. Almost every week a number of people in our church announce the ministries they are involved in. They often mention a need for contributions for their work. _____

18. Our board room is where our elders meet. _____

19. Our elders spend a lot of time with us; we really feel as though we know them as friends. _____

20. We chose Gothic columns for the front of our church because they provide a sense of permanence and stability. _____

21. In our gatherings, the elders often encourage us to seek God's direction in the ministries we get involved in. Many of the families in our church have share groups in their homes. _____

22. We would be better off if the Johnson family quit coming; their untidiness and relaxed mannerisms just don't fit here. _____

23. At a recent outing our elders and pastors got as dirty and sweaty as the rest of us because we all enjoyed the games and activities together. _____

24. We must protect the pulpit of this church; we don't want people to think we tolerate liberalism. _____

25. A short time back our pastor indicated he felt it was better if we didn't call him *the* pastor; he explained that God has given a number of people in our church the gift of pastoring. _____

26. Our pastor usually wears a suit and tie, especially in the church. _____

27. A short time ago one of the young Christians in our church stood up and made a rather dumb statement; he said he got the message from God. One of our elders has been meeting with him each week to pray and study the Bible. They seem to have a real fine friendship going. _____

28. We don't announce anything in our church unless it is cleared through the board. _____

29. Recently a man was embarrassed when a number of people contributed money to him to help with a serious illness. One of the elders explained that whether money comes from gifts or whether the money is earned in a job, everything he has is from God. _____

30. We are dedicating our new educational wing. _____

31. In recent years, we have had frequent "family counsel" meetings in our church to discuss matters of common concern. We no longer seem to need business meetings.   _____

32. We are having a week of special meetings to commemorate the completion of our new sanctuary.   _____

33. Our elders are very open people; they often share their shortcomings and the way in which Christ is working in their lives.   _____

34. Our board chairman is a fine parliamentarian.   _____

35. Every time a serious decision comes up that involves the whole church, the elders spend a great deal of time talking the decision over with the congregation. We always pray and try to determine what Christ's decision is on the matter.   _____

36. If our teachers can't be here on time and properly dressed, let's get some who will be.   _____

37. Recently a family in our church had a bad fire; one of the men in the church went around collecting money to replace their car, which had been destroyed.   _____

38. Elections of elders and pastors is the only orderly way to select our spiritual leaders.   _____

39. Our church is growing rapidly, but we no longer publish attendance figures; rather, there is often spontaneous sharing of what God is doing in our lives.   _____

40. We have been blessed with a very professional staff; we are buying more property all the time; soon we will own a whole city block.   _____

41. We used to have elections and each of us voted our preference; now we pray and try to sense what God would have us do. Sometimes we don't get our personal preference, but we sense that we are doing what God wants us to do.   _____

42. Our church is very progressive; we add at least one new program each year.   _____

43. We no longer consider the pulpit and the platform in our church building to be a sacred place; a variety of men and women in our church minister to us from the front of the auditorium.   _____

44. We just don't tolerate this business of bringing "dirty linen" into our meetings.   _____

45. Recently, a woman in our church was hospitalized; the elders encouraged the entire congregation to stop by the hospital to pray and minister to her.   _____

46. Our elders' meetings are boring, but we all must take our turn.   _____

47. Sometimes when our people are gathered for a time of prayer and sharing in somebody's home, they will remember the Lord with communion.   _____

48. Bronze plaques around our building help us recognize the large donors.   _____

49. Recently a young Christian in our church announced that she was separating from her husband; the elders encouraged a married couple to counsel and minister to her.   _____.

50. Our membership role is the best way to assure purity in the church.   _____

51. A man in our church feels called to start a Boy's Brigade program. A number of us contributed to give him the money he needed to start his new ministry.   _____

52. Our board of deacons always sits together as a group in the front of the church; of course, the pastors are on the platform.   _____

53. A relatively young Christian publicly expressed his desire to be an elder. A number of the people in the group encouraged him to continue his pursuit; however, it was explained that it takes time for a person to mature in his faith.
54. We just completed a thorough survey of people in our community; we are planning programs that will best bring them into our church.   _____
55. If we build a larger auditorium, the church will grow faster.   _____
56. People who don't participate in all our church programs aren't very serious about the Lord.   _____
57. Once while having dinner together, one of our families shared a serious need; everybody stopped eating and prayed regarding the matter.   _____
58. Our pastor must keep his distance from people in the congregation to protect his image.   _____
59. Some of our people enjoy singing with guitars, others enjoy more classical music; all of us are encouraged to minister with the gifts God has given us.   _____
60. Most of the elders are involved in some sort of parachurch mission; they never try to force the rest of us to contribute to the ministries God has called them to. _____
61. Our church leaders never seem to overdress in comparison to the rest of us.   _____
62. A new Christian recently made a misstatement about the Bible; none of our leaders attempted to correct him in front of the rest of us.   _____
63. At a recent party I noticed that professional as well as working class people from our church were invited.   _____
64. Recently the people of our church made a major change: they sold our building to a nonprofit corporation called "Religious Real Estate Services"; the group rents the building to us on Sunday morning, and to other groups during the week.
65. Pastors prefer to be called by their first names.   _____
66. Our Sunday morning meeting is a lot like going home to grandmother's house for Christmas.   _____
67. Our minister prefers to be called Pastor Jones.   _____
68. Our minister avoids overfamiliarity with our congregation.   _____
69. Our elders would really rather not become too strongly associated with the less mature members of our church.   _____
70. One of the women of our church runs a nursery school in our town. She now wants to start a Christian elementary school, and the elders are encouraging us to get behind her financially and give her all the help we can.   _____
71. A young couple in our church wanted to start a ministry to junior high school kids. Our elders have encouraged us to get behind them.   _____
72. We prefer all tithes and offerings be given to our church. If people get in the habit of giving to outside groups, our programs will suffer.   _____
73. Each of our elders is successful in business and well-educated.   _____
74. Our constitution requires that we have eight elders; we will never be caught short of leadership.   _____
75. Our goal is to double the number of busses every three years.   _____
76. Some of our elders are well-to-do financially and others are really quite poor; each of them seems to be settled in his relationship to God.   _____

Comment	Institution	Body

77. Our board has written a clear policy to govern who can serve in our church program. _____

78. If a man wishes to serve on our board he must have participated in all our programs and meetings. _____

79. Communion is always conducted by the same people in the same orderly way. _____

80. We like to avoid meetings in peoples' homes; it tends to hurt attendance at church meetings. _____

81. Our goal is a thousand in Sunday school by Easter. _____

82. Recent visitors to our Sunday morning service had a difficult time telling who our teaching pastor was; he always sits with the rest of us. _____

Recently a pastor friend of Clyde asked him for suggestions on how to expand his church program and outreach. The answer was simply: "Try not to plan any."

Clyde went on to explain: "Don't get me wrong. I'm not against organization and corporate goal setting. I make my living doing these things. What I really want to get across is

THE TASK OF LEADERSHIP: A HEALTHY BODY

that planning, staffing, and supervising outreach programs is a counterproductive effort for spiritual leaders in local churches. All the management techniques in the world won't get Christ's job done satisfactorily. However, the biblical approach really works."

This answer cuts to the very heart of the issue of leadership in an organism. The church, as we've seen, is the living body of the living Jesus. Since we are part of a body, not part of an institution, the task of body leaders must be distinctively different from the management tasks of institutional leaders.

In this and the next few chapters we are going to explore the New Testament's description of church leaders and their ministries.

But first, let us note that the distinction between "body leader" and "institutional leader" is a basic distinction that separates the thesis advanced in this text from the generally accepted approaches to church leadership.

Ted Engstrom and James Draper represent different expressions of the accepted institutional view. Engstrom takes a "professional management" approach in describing the role and the functions of leadership. The spirit of his view can be seen in this quote:

> Acting in our managerial capacity, all of us—presidents, department heads, foremen, supervisors, pastors, executives—do basically the same thing. We are each and all engaged in part in getting things done with and through people. Each of us must, at one time or another, carry out all the duties characteristic of managers. Even a well-run household uses these managerial functions, though in many cases they are used intuitively.
>
> Today's effective leader gets things done because he utilizes a workable style and has the ability to motivate others highly. He also becomes successful when he is task oriented. This means he must learn the resources available to his organization and study the means to arrive at goals. He must have the ability to define policies and procedures to organize the activities of his people toward the common goal.[1]

CHAPTER 6

A rather more authoritarian view is taken by Draper in his study of Titus for "Patterns for Church Living." He interprets the term *elder* as "bishop" or "pastor" and goes on to suggest:

> The church is a divine institution, and God planned that men of God would lead the church. This does not mean that the people in the church have no voice, but the church is not a pure democracy. It is a theocracy, a government under God. The people are led by the men of God whom God has placed over them. The pastor has a responsibility under God that must not be discarded. He must be the spearhead for what God is doing. . . .
>
> Are ordained men to be dictatorial? Not at all! However, they have a responsibility under God to lead. Without someone to lead or make binding decisions, we would spend all of our time discussing and not

---

[1]Ted Engstrom and James T. Draper, Jr., *The Making of a Christian Leader* (Grand Rapids: Zondervan, 1976), p. 138.

89

doing. There has to be some authority placed by God in the church. The pastorate is a sacred trust. God says in effect, "You are responsible to lead my people. If one of these little ones falls by the wayside because of your neglect, you must answer to me."[2]

Both Engstrom and Draper present church leaders as "getting things done through people." Both see spiritual leaders as motivators who lead. Both, however, see the key to this kind of leadership in terms of *power to make decisions.* Engstrom's approach is more sophisticated and gracious, as his "task oriented" leader "defines policies and procedures to organize the activities of his people." Draper's blunt approach, which in two brief paragraphs transforms the biblical term *elder,* first into "pastor" and then into "ordained men," suggests that, while the responsible leader should not be dictatorial, he still must be the "some*one*" who makes "binding decisions." For the pastor is the "authority placed by God in the church."

Yet, this is just the issue! If we are a body, and Jesus is head over all things for us, then policy making, goal setting, organizing, decision making, and all the other roles of management cannot be the responsibility of the human leadership of the body. We may not yet know how spiritual leaders *do* function. But if we are committed to Scripture's portrait of what the church is, we know that somehow the usual approach to leadership fails to reflect the realities portrayed in the Word of God.

WHO ARE THE LEADERS?

Before we go further, it will be helpful to raise a question about what spiritual leaders God has placed in the church. Here, too, there is much debate and some confusion. In our English versions, terms such as *apostle, pastor, teacher, deacon, bishop,* and *elder* are all found, along with designations such as *overseer, guardian,* and *shepherd.* Many of these terms are used interchangeably, and some are different English translations of one Greek word.

When they are looked at functionally, there seem to be some distinctions. For instance, Paul and Peter as apostles had an itinerant "church planting" or missionary ministry to the whole church and world. Timothy and Titus, who seem to be almost apostolic legates, also had a relationship to the church at large. Other leaders—identified as deacon, elder, and bishop—seem to function within larger or smaller local

---

[2]James T. Draper, Jr., *Titus* (Wheaton: Tyndale, 1978), pp. 24-25.

90

congregations. Yet both Peter and John refer to themselves as elders as well as apostles.

Certainly no biblical evidence can conclusively defend contemporary church structure. We can't even choose decisively between "congregational," "episcopal," and "presbyterial" titles for spiritual leaders. Stewart suggests, "In the local churches it seems probable that prophets, pastors and teachers were all appointed to the single office of leader."[3] Another article in the same encyclopedia sums up much of the biblical evidence:

> The question over which the Church has been divided throughout her history is the relationship of the office of elder to the total ministry of the Church. First, it should be noted that in several important ecclesiological passages the office of elder is not specifically mentioned. The office of deacon *(diakonos)*, bishop or pastor *(episkopos)*, as well as elder are noticeably omitted (1 Cor. 12:4-11, and vv. 28-30). . . . In a somewhat more definitive listing of church offices in Ephesians 4:11, "pastors" *(poimēn)* and "teachers" *(didaskalos)* are among the titles used to describe these leaders. Second, the pastoral epistles refer to only two offices: pastors or elders and deacons. In 1 Timothy 3:1-13, the text uses *episkopos* and *diakonos;* whereas Titus 1:5-9 seems to use the terms *episkopos* and *presbuteros* almost interchangeably: "I left you in Crete . . . [to] appoint elders *(presbuteros)* in every town. . . . For a bishop *(episkopos)* . . . ." In the letter to the church at Philippi, the salutation mentions only "bishops" *(episkopos)* and "deacons" *(diakonos)*, and it should be noted that both terms are pl.[4]

From the above discussion, two things seem particularly significant. First, there is some distinction between local ministry roles and broad, "whole church" ministry roles. The apostles, who had the broad ministry role and who shared it with legates such as Timothy and Titus, were also elders. But they were also something more than, and distinct from, elders. The elders, bishops, pastors, and deacons referred to had ministry roles in local congregational settings.

Second, the interchangeability of titles for local leaders suggests that no sharp distinction between their tasks was made in New Testament times. It seems likely that the "job description" for an elder or bishop or pastor would be the same, although there may have been distinctions between theirs and the ministry of deacons. This in turn suggests that the ministry of these leaders was not primarily institutional in character. Instead, the terms chosen reveal something about

[3]D. G. Stewart, "Bishop (elder)," in *Zondervan Pictorial Encyclopedia of the Bible*, ed. Merrill C. Tenney, 5 vols. (Grand Rapids: Zondervan, 1975), 1:618.
[4]Donald M. Lake, "Elder in the NT," ibid., 2:267.

the function and personality of the leaders in the congregation that is not institutional in character. For instance,

elder *(presbyteros)* literally speaks of individuals who are older and who in biblical cultures had earned respect by virtue of their character, experience, and years.

bishop *(episkopos)* speaks of individuals who oversee, take care of, care for, and visit. The picture is of a very person-oriented individual, who stays in close touch with and cares for others.

pastor *(poimen)* is literally "shepherd." Used of church leaders, it again focuses attention on close relationships and care for the growth and well-being of members of the body.

The emerging picture of the local church leader, then, is not that of the manager of an enterprise or a decision maker, but of one who with the wisdom gained by personal experience builds an intimate relationship with others whom he cares for and tends with a view toward their growth and maturity.

THE MISSION OF THE LEADERS

The responsibility of leaders is not to manage the church. They are not to be God's voice of authority in the body. The responsibility of leaders is the care and nurture of believers. Human leaders in the church use their wisdom and maturity to guide the congregation and individual members into growing ways of life so that when Jesus speaks, His body will be healthy and responsive.

Ephesians 4:12 reflects this concept of the leadership role in the term chosen for ministry—"equipping" *(katartismos)*. Leaders are to "straighten out the disjointed" and put the body in order for growth and service. And the leaders spoken of in this passage are both the "whole church" and "local church" leaders (apostles, prophets, pastors/teachers)! There is no distinction between the goals of spiritual leaders in their ministry to the body, even though there may be differences in gifts and differences in areas in which their ministries are carried out. Even the apostle Peter, we recall, was charged by Jesus to feed His lambs and tend His sheep (John 21:15-17).

Whatever titles we give leaders in churches today, and whatever roles they play, their common mission is an equipping, shepherding one.

The management of the body is the prerogative of the head, but the care of the members is the mission of human leaders, that the body might be healthy and responsive.

This fundamental conclusion leads to some very basic questions, which will be answered thoroughly later as we explore how leaders carry out their mission in the church. The questions are: What is it that makes for bodily health? What are the necessary conditions for growth in the body of Christ? What processes must leaders be sensitive to, guard against, and guide through, if God's goal of a healthy body is to be achieved?

While these questions will be examined in detail later, it is appropriate to give an initial survey here. Essentially, the conditions necessary for growth in the body must be conceived of as *relational*. Any living organism functions properly only when its parts are in intimate and harmonious relationship with each other and with the total organism. So the body of Christ "grows and builds itself up in love" as each part does its work," when the whole is "from the head . . . joined and held together" by each supporting part.

Spiritual leaders in the church not only have personal ministries to other believers (as do *all* Christians, for every believer possesses at least one spiritual gift), but they also have the ministry of tending the relationships between members of the body and themselves, and between members of the body and God.

Let's look briefly at the central relationships for which leaders are responsible as overseers.

To one another

The first relationship that is necessary for bodily health and is thus the responsibility of spiritual leaders is interpersonal. Jesus made it clear that the church is to express in its lifestyle what He called His "new commandment." "You are to love one another," Jesus said, "just as I have loved you."

The New Testament repeatedly emphasizes this vital relationship. Now that you have been made alive, Peter says, "so that you have sincere love for your brothers, love one another deeply, with all your hearts" (1 Peter 1:22). John adds, "Dear children, let us not love with words or tongue, but with actions and in truth"; for "this is how we know what love is: Jesus Christ laid down his life for us. And we ought to lay down our lives for our brothers" (1 John 3:16, 18). The writer of Hebrews is concerned that we "spur one another on toward love and good deeds" (Heb. 10:24), while Paul suggests that "over all these virtues put on love, which binds them all together in perfect unity" (Col. 3:14).

The overwhelming testimony of the New Testament is that

love, expressed and experienced among members of the body of Christ, is absolutely essential if it is to be healthy and alive. Thus the development of love within the body is a primary concern of those spiritual leaders who guard her health.

To the Spirit

Our relationships in the body of Christ are not only horizontal, between persons, but also vertical, between believers and God. Strikingly, Scripture makes clear the relationship of each Christian individually and the church corporately to each of the three persons of the Godhead.

Our relationship to the Spirit as it relates to bodily health focuses on giftedness. In chapter 3 we saw that spiritual gifts are given to each Christian "for the common good." Our gifts are to be exercised primarily, if not exclusively, to bring the body and its members to a shared maturity. In our service to one another, God the Holy Spirit expresses Himself through us, and His supernatural working makes possible a transformation that can come only from God (2 Cor. 3:18).

The relationship of the believer to the Spirit exists, whatever the activity of leaders. But the relationship of the believer is experienced as ministry to and from others takes place. Observing the development of Paul's argument in 1 Corinthians 12 and 14, we see that the context for the use of gifts is the gathered church (14:26-33). Love is to mark that coming together (1 Cor. 13), for it is love that moves us to reach out and serve one another and frees us to share burdens with one another (12:25-26).

When spiritual leaders in the church oversee the building of the capacity of members to exercise their spiritual gifts, they (1) develop the context of love that is the normal interpersonal climate of the church and (2) provide opportunity, when the body gathers as well as through individual involvement, for all to minister.

To the Father

Individually and corporately the body of Christ is to express its relationship to the Father through worship and prayer. This relationship is made possible by our growing awareness of who God is by nature. It is because of who He is that we worship, praise, and honor Him. It is because of who He is that we find confidence to bring our requests, our needs, our disappointments, our expectations, our sins, our fears, and our joys to Him.

Both prayer and worship are deepened as we focus attention not on ourselves or our experiences but on God Himself and see Him in relationship to our experiences. This is one of the great missions of spiritual leaders in the church: to help the members of the body come to see and know God as He is, and to guide the corporate experience of the church so that the whole body responds to Him appropriately.

To Christ Himself

Jesus is the living head of the church, and our Lord. Our relationship to Him is to be one of obedience, for He said, "If anyone loves me, he will obey my teaching. My Father will love him, and we will come to him and make our home with him" (John 14:23).

As living head of the church, Jesus is to be recognized as the responsible manager of each life and of the teams He calls together for special ministries or tasks. Spiritual leaders are themselves to be committed to seeking His guidance and will and to training each individual and group within the body to function with full awareness of and in full responsiveness to the Lord as sole head of the church.

There is still much to say about these relationships and how, in practice, leaders minister in the body to enrich them. But for now, it is enough to suggest that the role of all leaders is related to the health of the body. A healthy body is one that maintains

1. a warm, loving relationship among its members;
2. a ministering relationship with others in expectation that the Spirit will supernaturally use the gifts He has given to each one;
3. a dependent relationship with God the Father, based on a growing understanding of who He is by nature and expressed in worship and prayer;
4. a responsive relationship with Jesus Himself, who is recognized and responded to as sole head of the church, which is His body.

THEOLOGICAL FOUNDATION

PROBE

▶ case histories
▶ discussion questions
▶ thought provokers
▶ resources

1. The authors suggest that the terms used to designate church leaders in the New Testament are basically descriptive of personal qualities and ministries and are not really "titles" or organizational positions.

One such term *(deacon* or *deaconess)* was not discussed in the chapter. The following lists give all occurrences of this designation in the New Testament. Look up the references and study them. Do you think it most likely that they refer primarily to a position in an organization or to personal qualities/ministries?

diakonos (deacon, deaconess)
Matthew 20:26; 22:13; 23:11
Mark 9:35; 10:43
John 2:5, 9; 12:26
Romans 13:4; 15:8; 16:1
1 Corinthians 3:5
2 Corinthians 3:6; 6:4; 11:15, 23
Galatians 2:17
Ephesians 3:7; 6:21
Philippians 1:1
Colossians 1:7, 23, 25; 4:7
1 Thessalonians 3:2
1 Timothy 3:8, 12; 4:6

diakonia (service)
Luke 10:40
Acts 1:17, 25; 6:1, 4; 11:29; 12:25; 20:24; 21:19
Romans 11:13; 12:7; 15:31
1 Corinthians 12:5; 16:15
2 Corinthians 3:7-9; 4:1; 5:18; 6:3; 8:4; 9:1, 12-13; 11:8
Ephesians 4:12
Colossians 4:17
1 Timothy 1:12
2 Timothy 4:5, 11
Hebrews 1:14
Revelation 2:19

diakoneō (to serve)
Matthew 4:11; 8:15; 20:28; 25:44; 27:55

Mark 1:13, 31; 10:45; 15:41
Luke 4:39; 8:3; 10:40; 12:37; 17:8; 22:26-27
John 12:2, 26
Acts 6:2; 19:22
Romans 15:25
2 Corinthians 3:3; 8:19-20
1 Timothy 3:10, 13
2 Timothy 1:18
Philemon 13
Hebrews 6:10
1 Peter 1:12; 4:10-11.

2. The chart on pages 98-99, suggests contrasts between leadership in Christ's body and leadership in a well-run institution. Glance over the lists and decide which tasks imply an intimate relationship between leaders and people and which involve activities that imply management functions.

(Later in the book items on the left will be more fully discussed and explored.)

FIGURE 14
BODY LEADERSHIP VERSUS INSTITUTIONAL LEADERSHIP

IN CHRIST'S BODY (THE CHURCH)

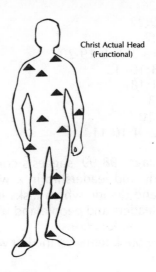

Christ Actual Head
(Functional)

LEADERS (▲) AMONG THE PEOPLE

OBJECTIVE SET BY THE BIBLE—To sustain and nurture *LIFE,* to equip, to allow Christ to transform lives and lead people into ministry.

BUILDING PEOPLE RELATIONSHIPS—Guiding people into loving, supportive relationships, utilizing small gatherings to help people learn "one-anothering" skills.

BUILDING MUTUAL MINISTRY—Persuading believers that the Holy Spirit is transforming their lives and empowering them to minister to each other, equipping them to serve one another's needs.

DEVELOPING A PRAYER-AND-WORSHIP LIFE STYLE—Encouraging prayer and worship in the group, providing nonthreatening, intimate occasions where people can learn together to tell God they love Him, affirm Him, and need Him.

ENCOURAGING ALLEGIANCE—Building allegiance in the group to Jesus Christ, head of the church and functional leader of the local congregation, rather than encouraging allegiance to a pastor, a teacher, or a board.

PROVIDING AN EXAMPLE—Building close and open friendships with people, allowing them to see strengths as well as weaknesses in our lives.

EXERCISING BIBLICAL AUTHORITY—Leading from weakness, always building up people, and using the Word of God to encourage, exhort, confront, and teach, depending totally on Christ to work in people's lives in a powerful way.

COMMUNICATING CONFIDENCE—Demonstrating strong confidence in people, thereby showing assurance that Christ is at work in people's lives even when it doesn't look as though He is.

PRESERVING FREEDOM—Helping people to look to Christ for their leadership and decisions; refusing to plan and organize the ministries of people in the congregation; limiting influence to teaching, exhorting, and persuading; never exercising organizational controls.

IN A WELL-RUN INSTITUTION (ORGANIZATION/ENTERPRISE)

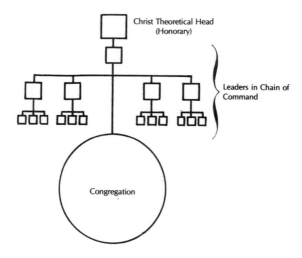

Christ Theoretical Head
(Honorary)

Leaders in Chain of
Command

Congregation

LEADERS <u>OVER</u> THE PEOPLE

OBJECTIVE SET BY LEADERS—To accomplish *tasks,* to provide programs and services (youth, music, evangelistic, discipleship, platform performances, outreach, etc.).

PLANNING—Setting goals, budgeting, planning facility and staff needs, setting quotas, and deciding equipment needs.

ORGANIZING—Desiging a pyramid organizational chart to show lines of responsibility and authority, writing job descriptions, developing procedures and systems to control the organization.

STAFFING—Selecting people on the basis of aptitude, technique, education, and professionalism; weeding out those who are weak performers.

CONTROLLING—Following the chain of command carefully, establishing policies that require each person in the chain to function within the scope of his responsibility and authority. Having regular performance reviews and salary reviews. Requiring regular progress reports, inflicting penalties, and rewarding with incentives.

DIRECTING—Making decisions and managing the decisions of others, maintaining communications systems, and leading others in the organization.

Paul's words to Timothy in 2 Timothy 2:24-25 highlight a critical aspect of the identity and the ministry style of spiritual leaders: "The Lord's servant must not quarrel; instead, he must be kind to everyone, able to teach, not resentful. Those who oppose him he must gently instruct, in the hope that God will give them repentance leading them to a knowledge of the truth."

THE IDENTITY OF THE LEADERS: SERVANTS

Leaders in the body of Christ should never forsake the role of servants. Even when they are opposed to a plan or program, they are not permitted to demand, but must remain gentle in instruction and rely on the head of the body to change the hearts of their opponents (or their own).

As leaders, they are called to be servants.

In our culture "servanthood" is not highly respected. People strive to be possessors, not the possessed. We want others to serve our needs; we aren't enthusiastic about setting aside our own concerns to serve them. *Servant* and *slave* are equally terms of denigration, words that seem to demean and to imply a diminishing of personal worth and value.

Against the background connotations of these words as they are perceived in our culture, it is helpful to develop a biblical perspective. For the New Testament sets the servant in a very different light.

SERVANTHOOD IN SCRIPTURE

In the Old Testament

There are two primary "servants" identified in the Old Testament. One is the nation of Israel itself; the other is the promised Deliverer.

The picture of the nation as a servant is related in part to the purpose for which God chose Israel. But what is important for us is to realize that to be named "servant" is to be recognized as one whom God has shaped with special care and to whom He is personally committed. We see both these themes in Isaiah 44:1-2:

> But now listen, O Jacob, my servant,
>   Israel, whom I have chosen.
>   This is what the LORD says—
> he who made you, who formed you in the womb,
> and who will help you:
> Do not be afraid, O Jacob, my servant,
> Jeshurun, whom I have chosen.

To be named a "servant" by God is no invitation to an inferior calling! God's servants are always special to Him. Even when Israel failed in her calling as a servant, God's commitment was never shaken, and He has promised to restore.

The dominant Old Testament servant figure in the Old Testament is not Israel however. It is the Messiah. One day, the Old Testament documents promise, a Man will come who will *be* the Servant of the Lord. He will perfectly perform the will of God, and through His obedience win freedom for the captives. Isaiah 42:1-4 gives a beautiful picture of this Servant, highlighting His relationship to God and His attitude as He goes about His ministry:

> Here is my servant, whom I uphold,
>   my chosen one in whom I delight;
> I will put my Spirit on him
>   and he will bring justice to the nations.

He will not shout or cry out,
 or raise his voice in the streets.
A bruised reed he will not break,
 and a smoldering wick he will not snuff out.
In faithfulness he will bring forth justice;
 he will not falter or be discouraged
till he establishes justice on earth.
 In his law the islands will put their hope.

The Servant portrayed here is a source of special delight for the Lord. He is gifted with the Spirit, adopts a gentle and quiet lifestyle, and works for the birth of justice. Although He meets with resistance, He is neither discouraged nor fails but succeeds in carrying out the purpose to which He is called.

To Christ the Servant and to all servants for whom Jesus is the example, God's promise comes:

I, the LORD, have called you in righteousness;
 I will take hold of your hand.
I will keep you and will make you
 to be a covenant for the people. . . .
(Isa. 42:6)

Servanthood as pictured in the Old Testament is not an attractive way of life. There is a high cost. This is highlighted in the following sketch of Christ the Servant as portrayed in Isaiah:

The Servant was chosen by the Lord (42:1; 49:1) and endued with the Spirit (42:1); He was taught by the Lord (50:4), and found His strength in Him (49:2, 5). It was the Lord's will that He should suffer (53:10); He was weak, unimpressive, and scorned by men (52:14; 53:1-3, 7-9), meek (42:2), gentle (42:3), and uncomplaining (50:6; 53:7). Despite His innocence (53:9), He was subjected to constant suffering (50:6; 53:3, 8-10), so as to be reduced to near-despair (49:4). But His trust was in the Lord (49:4; 50:7-9); He obeyed Him (50:4-5), and persevered (50:7) until he was victorious (42:4; 50:8, 9).[1]

Even so, servanthood is a high and special calling that involves a covenantal relationship with God. It is not a forced obedience to a thoughtless master. There is instead a willing commitment by the servant to a Master who fully commits Himself to the servant as well.

Leviticus 25 and Exodus 21 give us the controlling Old Testament image of the servant/master relationship. Leviticus shows us a brother Israelite who becomes poor and sells himself to a more prosperous countryman. In that re-

---

[1]Robert T. France, "Servant of the Lord," *The Zondervan Pictorial Encyclopedia of the Bible,* ed. Merrill C. Tenney, 5 vols. (Grand Rapids: Zondervan, 1975), 5:361.

lationship he must never serve as a slave: "He is to be treated as a hired worker or a temporary resident" (Lev. 25:40). Even then his service is limited. In the year of Jubilee (the seventh year in this case) he is to be freed to return to his own land and family. But, as Exodus points out, such a servant may develop key relationships during his service. So "if the servant declares, 'I love my master and my wife and children and do not want to go free,'" then by the servant's own free choice "he will be his servant for life" (Exod. 21:5-6).

The parallel here is beautiful. Out of the emptiness and poverty of the life we once lived for ourselves, we have come to One who has unlimited resources. We choose to serve Him. After a time sufficient to experience what that servitude really means, we seem to face a new choice. Will we trust in our own resources or will we bind ourselves even more firmly to the Master whom we love? Having chosen servanthood, believing Christians—the spiritual leaders not the least—make a free commitment to serve God for life.

This is the covenantal nature of our relationship to God as servants. He has shaped and called us to be the leaders of His body and committed Himself to be with us always. In return, we commit ourselves to serve Him within the body wherever He chooses to place us.

Like our Lord, we have been selected to live and to give ourselves for God's people.

In the New Testament

Our primary insights into servanthood in the New Testament are provided in the Gospels and in the example of Jesus. Jesus is in fact our greatest example of servanthood: "Even the Son of Man did not come to be served, but to serve, and to give his life as a ransom for many" (Mark 10:45). We are called to His lifestyle.

"But you are not to be called 'Rabbi,'" Jesus instructed the Twelve and the crowds, as He exposed the false spiritual leadership of the Pharisees. "You have only one Master and you are all brothers." No, "the greatest among you will be your servant. For whoever exalts himself will be humbled, and whoever humbles himself will be exalted" (Matt. 23:8-12).

In private, Jesus went beyond words with His disciples. In the intimacy of the upper room, Jesus knelt before them and with a towel and basin of water cleansed the dust from their feet. The Twelve were deeply embarrassed. It wasn't right that their Lord should stoop before them. But Jesus insisted. Then when He had finished, He asked them:

> Do you understand what I have done for you? You call me "Teacher" and "Lord," and rightly so, for that is what I am. Now that I, your Lord and Teacher, have washed your feet, you also should wash one another's feet. I have set you an example that you should do as I have done for you. I tell you the truth, no servant is greater than his master, nor is a messenger greater than the one who sent him. Once you know these things, you will be blessed if you do them (John 13:12-17).

In the kingdom of Jesus, and in the fellowship of His living church, leaders are servants who stoop to minister from the servant's position and bring cleansing to the body of our Lord.

SERVANT LEADERSHIP

The basic attitude of the servant-leader is sketched in both the Old and the New Testaments. Yet in a striking incident, reported in two of the Gospels, Jesus goes beyond attitude to define more clearly the servant's leadership style. More than a servant's heart is required. There is also to be a servant's *method.*

James and John provoked the incident by encouraging their mother to ask Jesus for key power positions in Jesus' coming kingdom. When the other ten disciples heard about this request, they were very indignant at the two brothers. Taking this teachable moment, Jesus called them together to speak of the nature of leadership in the fellowship of the church. Jesus contrasted the leadership style and method of secular rulers against the leadership style and method of those called to lead in His body.

> You know that the rulers of the Gentiles lord it over them, and their high officials exercise authority over them. Not so with you. Instead, whoever wants to become great among you must be your servant, and whoever wants to be first must be your slave—just as the Son of Man did not come to be served, but to serve, and to give his life as a ransom for many (Matt. 20:25-28).

This passage attacks many of our ingrained presumptions about leadership and helps us define *how* a servant leads. In the paragraphs below are a few of the contrasts that are explicit or implied in the illustration Jesus uses. There is space on the chart on page 108 for you to fill in a number of additional contrasts. From my workshop experiences, at least thirty contrasts and comparisons can be found. Here are several:

Relationship with the led

The passage states it clearly: the ruler is "over" those he leads. But the servant is "among." We cannot be servant-leaders if our position or role or our own attitude tends to lift us above others and makes a distinction between us and the rest of the people of God.

Command

Rulers "lord it over" and "exercise authority" over the led. Here is a command-type of authority, which tells others what to do and demands conformity of behavior. But we cannot even imagine that a *servant* entering a household where he is assigned would issue commands! To attempt to use such a command authority calls forth one of God's most powerful rebukes: "Not so with you."

Mode

Command authority tells others what to do. The leadership mode involves issuing orders, passing on decisions the leader has made. Servants have one role in the household—to serve. Rather than *tell*, the servant *shows*. Example, not command, is the primary mode through which the servant leads.

Effect

The command authority of the secular ruler does lead to behavioral change. There are all sorts of sanctions that secular leaders—be they in the military, in government, or in business—rely on to obtain the behavior they require. But servants must rely on an inner response in those they influence. Without the power to coerce behavior, servants must seek the free choice of the ones being led. The one style achieves behavioral conformity; the other style achieves heart commitment.

Power

The secular leadership style has a wider range of coercive means to enforce response. In business, raises or denial of raises and many other symbols of approval and disapproval are used to coerce behavior. But in the church of Christ no such means of coercion are available. All such methods are decisively rejected!

Compile as many additional contrasts and comparisons between the "secular ruler" and "servant-leader" styles of leadership as you can.

There are many more contrasts implicit in the illustration Jesus chose to use. There are implications about the attitude and character of the leaders. There are implications about where authority resides. There are implications about the re-

FIGURE 15
COMPARING AND CONTRASTING STYLES OF LEADERSHIP

SECULAR RULER	SERVANT LEADER

lationship and attitude of the leader toward others. But the most striking and significant element of the passage is seen in the simple words: "Not so with you." In these words Jesus once and for all cuts us off from all those approaches to leadership that are implied in the ruler style. Jesus limits us to a leadership that finds expression in servanthood and relies on a servant's seeming weakness.

Yet it is the servant style that brings victory. The servant-leader will bring the body into a harmonious relationship and will lead its members toward maturity. The living Lord will act through His servants to work out His own good will.

But commitment to servant leadership carries with it a high cost. By forsaking the world's kind of leadership, the body leader is sure to be misunderstood. He will seem unimpressive. He will suffer under misunderstanding and may be reduced at times to near-despair. And it takes so much longer to gain heart response than behavioral conformity. His gentleness itself, in a world where decisive and competitive men are admired, will lead to charges of weakness. But if he retains a total commitment to servanthood and all it implies, the spiritual leader will be used by God in the body, and through his ministry Jesus *will* build His church.

A TEST CASE

A passage in Scripture that gives us further insight into how servanthood is to find expression under pressure (a theme that will be further developed in chapter 10, in which we explore the issue of goals) is in 2 Timothy. Here Paul shows his younger assistant how to deal with those who become involved in false teaching and quarrelsomely turn against others in the household of God (2 Tim. 2:14-19). Timothy is urged to cleanse himself from all that is ignoble so that he will be useful to the Master (2:20-21) and resist passions that would lead him to battle. He is instead to follow righteousness, faith, love, and peace (2:22). Then Timothy is given this specific instruction on how to deal with the "foolish and stupid arguments" that produce quarrels:

> The Lord's servant must not quarrel; instead, he must be kind to everyone, able to teach, not resentful. Those who oppose him he must gently instruct, in the hope that God will give them a change of heart leading them to a knowledge of the truth, and that they will come to their senses and escape from the trap of the devil, who has taken them captive to do his will (2:24-26).

What! Timothy isn't to "contend for the truth"? He isn't to throw himself into battle?

No, Timothy *is* to engage in battle, but *as a servant.*

A servant "must not quarrel" (RSV has "must not be quarrelsome, or contentious") but, instead, he is to "be kind to all" and "to gently instruct." These phrases in the original are very revealing:

"To be kind to all" is *ēpion einai pros pantas.* The word translated "to be kind" means "to be gentle, or mild" toward all. We approach everyone with an unthreatening and unattacking attitude, never resentful, never responding with antagonism to those who are antagonistic to us.

"To gently instruct" is *en prautēti paideuonta.* The word translated "gently" means to act or speak with gentleness, humility, courtesy, consideration, and meekness. The word *instruct* suggests correcting or giving instruction to a youth who is growing toward maturity.

Finally, the servant never relies on himself to achieve success but always remembers that the only hope of effectiveness for his ministry rests in God. We who are leaders in the body of Christ are engaged in a supernatural struggle, not a natural one. The distortion that comes into the thinking and attitude of our brothers and sisters, like the distortion that has captured the non-Christian, is a trap set by the devil, who tries to warp our lives to do what he wants us to do. In this kind of struggle, God must give the change of heart that will bring freedom and lead others to an experience of His truth. Only a change of heart and behavior, never a change of behavior alone, will mark the victory God seeks to win in the lives of His people.

Here then we see the commitment of the servant to remain a servant always and to reject totally the leadership style of the world.

- Our attitude is a servant's attitude, one of gentleness and humility.
- Our resource is the quality of our own lives, and gentle instruction in the truth.
- Our expectation is that God will act to change hearts.

Within this framework, God can and will use body leaders to build a healthy and strong body, one that is responsive and obedient to Jesus Christ.

The Identity of the Leaders: Servants

PROBE

▶ *case histories*
▶ *discussion questions*
▶ *thought provokers*
▶ *resources*

1. In a group with several others, make as thorough a list of contrasts and comparisons between servant and secular ruler styles as you can. Use a chart like the one on page 108.

2. The following list is both humorous and helpful. It indicates ways that a person without the power of a secular ruler can still try to manipulate and control others from a supposed "servant" stance.

TWELVE WAYS TO DOMINATE INSTEAD OF LEADING

1. *Use your superior knowledge of Scripture to snow the opposition.*
2. *Wrest Scripture out of context to use as a club.*
3. *Intimidate by a display of temper, shouting, pouting and other such kid stuff.*
4. *Threaten to quit if they don't do it your way.*
5. *Seek support for your position by privately persuading other elders.*
6. *Be stubborn and hold out for your way until everyone gets tired and gives in.*
7. *Sneak the action through when some of the opposition is out of town.*
8. *Make public announcement of a decision before it's made by the board; then they will have to do it your way.*
9. *Cut down those who disagree with you in your messages from the pulpit.*
10. *Pull your rank; tell them, "The Lord told me this is the way we do it."*
11. *Think through all the answers, plan all the programs, and just tell them what we're going to do. Don't ever open the door for them to think, make suggestions or plan with you.*
12. *Be the whole show on the platform at every meeting. That way nobody else can get a word in. Don't ever ask your men to lead a meeting, pray, read Scripture, teach or anything like that. After all, they've never been trained and you have (beyond your intelligence).*

"But the wisdom from above is first pure, then peaceable, gentle, open to reason, full of mercy and good fruits, without uncertainty or insincerity" (James 3:17 RSV).[2]

3. Is it enough to have a "servant's heart"? Some feel that this is the issue in servanthood. Yet, as the following chart shows, there must be both a servant's attitude and a servant's leadership style if spiritual leadership in the church is to be effective. For details on the style, refer to pages 106–10.

Problems are fewer when the leader's basic attitude is reflected in his leadership style. The autocratic leader feels comfortable with a

---

[2]Bob Smith, *When All Else Fails . . . Read the Directions* (Waco: Word, 1974), p. 138.

command leadership style. The servant-leader grows more and more comfortable with the servant leadership style. Yet at times real problems are caused because a person with a servant attitude finds himself functioning in a command or control system and is pressured to adapt a command leadership style (the "secular ruler" approach of institutional organizations).

FIGURE 16
CORRESPONDENCE BETWEEN THE LEADER'S ATTITUDE
AND HIS STYLE

BASIC ATTITUDE	LEADERSHIP STYLE
Autocratic	Command
Open	Sharing
Servant	Servant

Have you ever experienced this tension? What problems has it caused you? How did you handle them?

And have others ever wanted to press you into a leadership style that does not reflect your own sense of identity? What happened? How did they feel? And why?

What can leaders who are servants do to touch the hearts of those they are called to lead? There are two primary and compelling roots of the servant-leader's power to influence. Paul links them together when he says to Timothy, "Watch your life and doctrine closely. Persevere in them, because if

THE LEADER'S METHOD: MODELING

you do, you will save both yourself and your hearers" (1 Tim. 4:16). The root of the servant-leader's power is the reality of the Word of God, expressed through lifestyle and teaching.

The spiritual leader who is a servant does not demand. He *serves*. In his service the spiritual leader sets an example for the body—an example that has compelling power to motivate heart change. In this chapter we want to survey the impact of the servant as a model or example of the Christian life on the church and see how, through serving, leaders motivate others to choose to follow Christ.

THE PRINCIPLE ILLUSTRATED

Paul and Timothy clearly illustrate the modeling principle. Paul often refers to Timothy's opportunity to observe his life and teaching closely and to the necessity for Timothy also to lead by example and instruction. Note the interplay of these factors in these two representative passages:

> Command and teach these things. Don't let anyone look down on you because you are young, but set an example for the believers in speech, in life, in love, in faith and in purity. Until I come, devote yourself to the public reading of Scripture, to preaching and teaching. Do not neglect your gift, which was given you through a prophetic message when the body of elders laid their hands on you. Be diligent in these matters; give yourself wholly to them, so that everyone may see your progress. Watch your life and doctrine closely. Persevere in them, because if you do, you will save both yourself and your hearers (1 Tim. 4:11-16).

And

> You, however, know all about my teaching, my way of life, my purpose, faith, patience, love, endurance, persecutions, sufferings—what kinds of things happened to me in Antioch, Iconium and Lystra, the persecutions I endured. Yet the Lord rescued me from all of them. In fact, everyone who wants to live a godly life in Christ Jesus will be persecuted while evil men and imposters will go from bad to worse, deceiving and being deceived. But as for you, continue in what you have learned and have become convinced of, because you know those from whom you learned it, and how from infancy you have known the holy Scriptures (2 Tim. 3:10-15).

This is the practical outworking of the incarnational principle we explored in earlier chapters. Paul says that believers are "a letter from Christ" that is written "with the Spirit of the living God . . . on tablets of human hearts." What is more, the living letter can be "known and read by everybody" (2 Cor. 3:2-3). As Jesus, the living Word, writes God's truth on the personalities of believers, the validity of the written Word is compellingly demonstrated to all.

Scripture indicates that Christian growth and learning involve (1) hearing the Word, (2) seeing it expressed in others' lives, and (3) *then* choosing to do the Word, with (4) a personal experience of God's presence as the outcome. We see this pat-

(marginal text alongside the first quotation)
CHAPTER 8

tern in Philippians: "Whatever you have learned or received or heard from me, or seen in me—put it into practice. And the God of peace will be with you" (4:9). Thus the biblical pattern of communication can be diagramed as follows:

FIGURE 17
THE BIBLICAL PATTERN OF COMMUNICATION

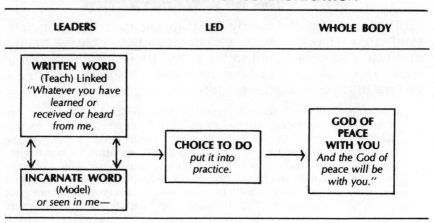

LEADERS	LED	WHOLE BODY

WRITTEN WORD
(Teach) Linked
"Whatever you have
learned or
received or heard
from me,

INCARNATE WORD
(Model)
or seen in me—

CHOICE TO DO
put it into
practice.

GOD OF
PEACE
WITH YOU
And the God of
peace will be
with you."

All too often we attempt to communicate the written Word only in verbal form. And we are amazed when so many believers fail to make the choice to obey the Word and put it into practice. But the error is ours. For verbal communication is to be accompanied by a lifestyle demonstration of the realities taught. When the Word is taught *and* lived by the spiritual leader, then responsiveness comes and choices to obey are made.

Spiritual leaders must model the truths they teach. We are to lead others to a deeper commitment to Christ, the head of the body, by our example as well as our instruction. No wonder leaders like Timothy must "set an example for the believers" and "watch [their] life and doctrine closely."

Robert Coleman makes a similar point:

Leadership must be public in doing good if it is to gain confidence, trust, and legitimacy from volunteers. Confidence and public trust are the basis of legitimacy and have their own power which is given to leaders. Leadership which is public models for a congregation a style of being responsible and accountable to God and His people. Public activity is visible. It demonstrates that some are active. Activeness based on Christian commitments creates the possibility for members with a new energy to align themselves with that which is visible. Persons and

116

groups can identify with values that are producing the activity among leaders. Public activity makes it possible to gather and focus the energy and commitments of persons and groups within the congregation. Achievement of a broad range of goals and objectives is made possible when a congregation is active."[1]

QUALIFICATIONS FOR LEADERS

The affirmation of public and visible leadership is good, but it misses the main point stressed in the New Testament. Leadership is not so much to be public in its *activity* as in its *character*. It is the character, values, attitudes, behavior, and commitment of the leaders, as these reflect Christlikeness, that provide the compelling model.

This emphasis is reflected in the passages of Scripture that give the qualifications for spiritual leadership. There is no mention here of seminary degrees or ordination. There is no mention of possession of this or that particular spiritual gift, or even of great public activity in various "ministries." Instead, the spotlight is placed squarely on the character of leaders. Simply put, those recognized as leaders in the body of Christ are to be those whose lives publicly and visibly provide a Christlike example. Leaders are selected on the basis of the kind of model they are of what each Christian should become. Bob Smith has summarized these qualifications in a clear way in the outline on pages 118-19.

To *be* this kind of person is essential, because a leader's spiritual power to motivate heart changes is rooted in his incarnation of the Word that he teaches. How impossible it would be for a materialistic person to share Jesus' instructions on trust in a Father who cares for the lilies of the field. How impossible for a contentious and angry person to teach the peaceable wisdom described in James 3 and 4! How impossible for a domineering person to successfully teach that we are to be "subject to one another" and to adopt the attitude toward others that is taught in Philippians 2. Such a person teaching such truths would rob the learner of the compelling sense of reality that the Word of God must have if we are to entrust ourselves to it.

No, the basic qualification for spiritual leaders has nothing to do with skills or training or even the possession of particular spiritual gifts. The basic qualification for spiritual leaders is that they be living demonstrations of the reality of all that they teach!

---

[1]Robert E. Coleman, *Dry Bones Can Live Again* (Old Tappan, N.J.: Revell, 1969), p. 29.

FIGURE 18

QUALIFICATIONS FOR LEADERSHIP

SCRIPTURE	QUALIFICATION	EXPLANATION
	1. Above reproach	Not open to censure, having unimpeachable integrity.
	2. Husband of one wife	A one-wife kind of man, not a philanderer (doesn't necessarily rule out widowers or divorced men).
	3. Having believing children	Children are Christians, not incorrigible or unruly.
	4. Not self-willed	Not arrogantly self-satisfied.
	5. Not quick-tempered	Not prone to anger or irascible.
	6. Not addicted to wine	Not overly fond of wine, or drunken.
	7. Not pugnacious	Not contentious or quarrelsome.
Titus 1:5-9	8. Not a money-lover	Not greedy for money.
	9. Hospitable	A stranger-lover, generous to guests.
	10. Lover of good	Loving goodness.
	11. Sensible	Self-controlled, sane, temperate.
	12. Just	Righteous, upright, aligned with right.
	13. Devout	Responsible in fulfilling moral obligations to God and man.
	14. Self-controlled	Restrained, under control
	15. Holding fast the Word	Committed to God's Word as authoritative.
	16. Able to teach sound doctrine	Calling others to wholeness through teaching God's Word.
	17. Able to refute objections	Convincing those who speak against the truth.
	18. Temperate	Calm and collected in spirit, sober.
	19. Gentle	Fair, equitable, not insisting on his own rights.
Additional from 1 Timothy 3:1-7	20. Able to manage household	A good leader in his own family.
	21. Not a new convert	Not a new Christian.
	22. Well thought of by outsiders	A good representative of Christ among non-Christians.

SCRIPTURE	QUALIFICATION	EXPLANATION
	23. Willingly, not under compulsion	Not serving against his will.
	24. According to God (in some Greek texts)	By God's appointment.
Additional from 1 Peter 5:1-4	25. Not for shameful gain	Not money-motivated.
	26. Not lording it over the flock	Not dominating in his area of ministry (a shepherd is to lead, not *drive* the flock).
	27. As an example	A pleasure to follow because of his Christian example.
	28. As accountable to the Chief Shepherd	Motivated by the crown to be gained—authority to reign with Christ.

AMONG THE BRETHREN

One foundation of the influence possessed by servant-leaders is found in the example they set. Yet not even the most mature of leaders will set an example of perfection. The more closely we live among the brethren, the easier it will be for them to see our weaknesses. How closely among body members should we live? And how open must our lives be to have a servant's impact on our brothers and sisters?

Second Corinthians 3 gives us special insight into the need for a public life and into the dynamic power of such a life. In the context Paul is speaking of the incarnation of the Word in our lives: we are living letters (3:1-3). Paul then points out that the ministry of a Word that so infuses life and brings righteousness is a truly glorious ministry. Yet by God's work in our lives we are enabled to be ministers of such a covenant (3:4-11). Paul says a striking thing in his application of this belief: "Therefore, since we have such a hope, we are very bold. We are not like Moses, who veiled his face to keep the Israelites from gazing at it while the radiance was fading away" (3:12-13). No, because of the presence of the Spirit of God in our lives, we have a unique freedom. *We take the veil off!* "And we, who with unveiled faces all reflect the Lord's glory, are being transformed into his likeness with ever-increasing glory, which comes from the Lord, who is the Spirit" (3:18).

This outline is from Bob Smith, *When All Else Fails . . . Read the Directions* (Waco: Word, 1974), pp. 29-30. Used by permission.

Paul is referring, of course, to the time when Moses came down from Mt. Sinai with the Ten Commandments. He had been with God and his face glowed with such brilliance that the people of Israel could not look at him. But it was not then that Moses put the veil over his face. No, he put the veil on when he noted that the splendor was *fading!* He did not want the Israelites to gaze at his face when the radiance had disappeared!

It is totally different for the believer. Paul says we exercise boldness and remove the veil. This does take boldness. When we open our lives to others, they see the blemishes and weaknesses that appear. But Paul says they see more! What they see in our unveiled face is a reflection of the Lord's own glory. Looking at our lives, they see Jesus!

How can this be? Again Paul explains. God the Holy Spirit is present in our lives and He is working in us a transformation that reshapes us into Jesus' likeness. We are undergoing that transformation "with ever-increasing splendor." Over a period of time, as leaders live among the people of God and unveil their lives to the people of God, the reality of Jesus' presence is seen in His transforming work in them.

Spiritual leaders must be chosen by the standards given in Scripture. Persons who are clearly "in transformation" are those in whom others will see Jesus and, seeing Him, will hope to risk obedience to His Word.

Hope, then, is the motivating power of the leader's example. If I can see progress toward the promised goal in the lives of those with whom I identify—those I know well and trust— then hope frees me to risk obedience to the Word of God too. And it is in obedience that I find the fulfillment of my faith and the prize of the presence of the God of peace.

THE IMPACT OF MODELS

The New Testament's picture of the servant as one who *does*, rather than one who adopts the leadership style of the world and *tells*, has a unique integrity. The Christian both hears the Word from his spiritual leader and sees the Word expressed in his person. The open life of leaders among—not over—the brothers and sisters is a revelation of the very face of Jesus. And to see Jesus expressing Himself in a human being brings the hope that transformation might be a possibility for me too.

Leaders, then, must be chosen carefully for the very qualities of Christlikeness that they are to demonstrate as examples. It is no wonder that the writer to the Hebrews urges the church, "Remember your leaders, and imitate their faith" (Heb. 13:7). It is no wonder that Paul, speaking of attitude, can say to the Corinthians that they should follow his example (1 Cor. 11:1), or, speaking of the deepest motives that guided his choice, can remind the Thessalonians that he does not try to please or manipulate men, but always to please God, "as you know" (1 Thess. 2:1-5). As the leaders live among God's people, their total character is to be open and exposed.

Such openness is understandably threatening to some. But it is the only way to have the servant's impact on the hearts of others. In another book Larry has discussed factors in interpersonal relationships that facilitate or make more powerful the impact of a model on others:

1. There needs to be frequent, long-term contact with the model(s).
2. There needs to be a warm, loving relationship with the model(s).
3. There needs to be exposure to the inner states of the model(s).
4. The model(s) need to be observed in a variety of life settings and situations.
5. The model(s) need to exhibit consistency and clarity in behaviors, values, etc.
6. There needs to be a correspondence between the behavior of the model(s) and the beliefs (ideal standards) of the community.
7. There needs to be explanation of life style of the model(s) conceptually, with instruction accompanying shared experiences.[2]

As we live open, sharing lives among members of the body of Christ—building warm relationships, opening up our lives to others, explaining the biblical principles on which our values and choices are made—and demonstrate in our character the trustworthiness of God's promise to make each of us more like Christ, the hearts of believers *will* be touched and we *will* see them respond.

The world's way of leadership may seem safer. We can hide behind the facade of power, issue instructions, and demand conformity. But in the church of Jesus Christ this approach will never achieve the goals that God has in mind. No, we must take the risk of leading as servants. We must expose ourselves to misunderstanding and doubt until the integrity of our lives and the supernatural work of God in the hearts of His people brings response to Him.

---

[2]Lawrence O. Richards, *A Theology of Christian Education* (Grand Rapids: Zondervan, 1975), p. 84.

THEOLOGICAL FOUNDATION

PROBE

▶ case histories
▶ discussion questions
▶ thought provokers
▶ resources

1. Adopting a servant-leader style is dangerous. It tends to create misunderstandings and leads to different kinds of suffering. The following is a report of the experience and feelings of someone who has pastored four churches in thirteen years and now hesitates in fear at taking the stance of openness recommended in this chapter. Can you identify with his feelings? How might you help him take the risky steps he fears, but yearns to take?

> Probably 98 percent of my ministry can be summed up in the phrase "formal traditional structure." This is the easiest and most comfortable way for me to share what I believe to be the truth. However, it is neither rewarding nor fulfilling. People's lives have not been changed! They come with needs and leave with needs. Furthermore, both my wife and I are hurting in the ministry. Because we've been hurt and wounded, we are gun-shy as to being open and honest with others. Because we have not fostered growing, affirming relationships within the church, we have no one to "tell it like it is." We have found that whenever we have been honest and open, it has been used against us later.
>
> For instance, we recently spent a couple of services discussing our church. The final point of the discussion was that we need to get to know each other more fully and work together to see our church grow. Several days later one of our church leaders said that he took it that I was backing away from my responsibilities and dumping it all on the church members. All I was doing was encouraging the body-life concept.
>
> Quite frankly, I am presently afraid of open and honest communication with some of my church leaders. Nothing hurts like being misjudged about something that is from the depths of your being. I'd rather work in a factory and point people to Christ than sit around in a church board meeting with suspicious, nonloving, misjudging people and a lot of hurtfulness going on. I don't know how much more my wife and I can take. I am concerned that we do not get permanently, irreparably hurt. I am especially concerned for her. We have been hurt so often that we have become very protective of ourselves. It is not what we want, but it has come to that. I am not sure at this point what I am able to do or what I will do! I need help!!!

2. On pages 118–19 is a list of the scriptural qualifications for spiritual leaders. We suggested one reason for presenting them: there are many truths that a leader who lacks these qualifications simply cannot communicate as realities to the people of God.

 For an interesting exercise, take each of the twenty-eight qualifications on the list and beside each one jot down at least two scriptural teachings that a person who lacked it could not communicate as livable truth.

3. One of the students in the Wheaton College Graduate School did an interesting study of a discipleship-training process used in South America. She took each of the seven "facilitating factors" listed on page 121 and, using questionnaires and interviews and recall of her own experiences, explored the impact of their presence or absence in discipling groups led by two different leaders. Her conclusion:

> *It was easy to see a qualitative difference between the two groups. I had no idea before that these two groups were so very different. The coordinator of discipleship also had no idea.*
>
> *What made the difference? The presence or absence of these seven factors! M—— made the giving of her life an integral part of discipleship. The other teacher views herself as just a teacher. She is not a model for her group. Since sharing real problems is not a priority for this teacher, her students do not share and therefore do not incorporate God's dealings into their real-life situations.*
>
> *A personal-time commitment is different in each teacher. M—— gives each student personal time each week, but the other teacher finds very little time to give individual attention. This factor reinforces the teaching situation. The only opportunity for establishing a friendship is at scheduled meetings.*
>
> *Knowledge of the inner states of members is important in a leader's efforts to explain God's ways of dealing with our problems. M—— shared herself with her students so they felt a part of her life and they saw her grappling with reality before their eyes. The other teacher shared with others but not with her group. By this action, she always kept her pupils at the level of students. Her remoteness did not encourage the development of their spiritual gifts. Nor did she give the group members a chance to minister to her.*
>
> *The current group had difficulty in knowing if her behavior was consistent with her teaching. The reason for this is that members saw the teacher only at meetings, which are often artificial situations. M——, however, encouraged observation of her life in almost every situation. The students could easily see that her life was consistent with her teaching and therefore gave credibility to the Christian faith.*

Questions:
a. Which of the two situations is *most like* one of the settings in which you communicate Scripture to others?
b. What would you have to do to minister more in the pattern of M——?
c. Look over the "educational ministries" of your church. Are the teachers in your Sunday school and other educational groups more like M—— or more like the other teacher?

4. Who, in your experience, is most like a servant, as described in this book? Write that person a note, sharing your appreciation for him and his lifestyle. It's likely that, like the pastor in Probe 1, he has suffered misunderstanding for his commitment, so your note of appreciation would be a real blessing.

Paul's instruction to Timothy was twofold: "Pay attention to your life and your teaching." The leader's lifestyle is one key to his influence in the body of Christ. But so is the way in which the leader verbally communicates the Word.

THE LEADER'S METHOD: TEACHING

Life and teaching are to correspond. Yet it is important when we read this statement in Scripture that we have a biblical, not a cultural, idea of what "teaching" really is.

The unabridged edition of the *Random House Dictionary of the English Language* gives this definition of the word *teach:* "1. to impart knowledge of or skill in; give instruction in . . . ; 2. to impart knowledge or skill to; give instruction to . . . ; 3. to impart knowledge or skill; give instruction. . . ." Synonyms listed are "coach . . . , instruct, tutor, educate, inform, enlighten, discipline, train, drill, school, indoctrinate."

In our culture, there is no doubt that the primary meaning of teaching is imparting knowledge. For Timothy to pay attention to his teaching (cf. 1 Tim. 4:11-16) brings to the mind of most people a picture of Timothy expounding biblical doctrine in a sermon or classroom setting.

Most teaching in the church today is done in a formal setting. Sunday schools are organized, church buildings are built with classrooms, pews are arranged in rows so that all can look toward the pulpit where the sermon is given in lecture form. Verbal transmission of the content is given within a specific time frame (usually one hour) and within the walls of a set-apart building. All of this is involved in the typical process of Christian education.

C
H
A
P   9
T
E
R

But the concept of teaching as shaped by our culture is not the only possible one. Throughout most of human history and in most cultures, in fact, other ways have been more prominent in building beliefs and values. Anthropologist Fortes suggests that education in the widest sense "is the process by which the cultural heritage is transmitted from generation to generation" and that thus the basic task of education is the "moulding of individuals to the social norm."[1]

This surely is the basic task of Christian teaching. We seek to communicate a whole new way of living. Since we have been raised with Christ, Paul argues in Colossians 3, we are to put off the old man and the ways in which we used to walk. We reject the evil aspects of the life we once lived. Now as God's chosen people, we put on a new life marked by "compassion, kindness, humility, gentleness and patience" (v. 12). In behavioral science terms, we seek to communicate a new cultural heritage—that of members of God's kingdom on earth—and for this lifestyle we too require the "moulding of individuals to the [new] social norm."

Formal classroom instruction has been shown to be in-

---

[1]Meyer Fortes, "Social and Psychological Aspects of Education in Taleland," in *From Child to Adult: Studies in the Anthropology of Education,* ed. John Middleton (Garden City, N.Y.: Natural History, 1970), p. 15.

adequate to accomplish such a molding. It is effective in transmitting a set of beliefs as concepts. But mastery of faith's intellectual content will not automatically be translated into lifestyle (see the first ten chapters of Richards' *Theology of Christian Education* for a thorough discussion of this issue). How do we communicate the belief content of God's kingdom culture in such a way that the culture infuses all of life and shapes the personality of the learner?

In his monograph, Fortes describes a socialization process in Taleland in which "teaching" comes through real situations into which children are drawn by life itself. And he compares this with the artificially created "training" setting of the Western-school approach:

> Corresponding to this contrast in method we can observe a contrast in psychological emphasis. The training situation demands atomic modes of response; the real situation requires organic modes of response. In constructing a training situation, we envisage a skill or observance as an end-product at the perfection of which we aim, and therefore arrange it so as to evoke only motor or perceptual practice. Affective or motivational factors are eliminated or ignored. In the real situation, behavior is compounded of affect, interest and motive, as well as perceptual and motor functions. Learning becomes purposive. Every advance in knowledge or skill is pragmatic, directed to achieve a result then and there, as well as adding to a previous level of adequacy.[2]

The chart on page 129 tabulates the contrasts that Fortes is making.

Not *all* Christian teaching was done in nonformal, life-structured situations, of course. But not all Christian teaching (indeed not *much* of it) was done in a formal setting. There were no educational wings on church buildings in the first centuries of the church; in fact, there were no church buildings! So without making any commitment at this point to nonformal teaching as "the" way to communicate biblical truths we can say that it would be a mistake when we read of "teaching" in the New Testament to automatically read into that word our Western culture and twentieth-century connotations.

To say that the spiritual leader reaches others by lifestyle and teaching does not necessarily suggest that all spiritual leaders must stand for sixty minutes a week before a group or class or congregation and talk about the Bible. There may be other ways to do what the Bible refers to as "teaching."

---

[2]Ibid., p. 38.

FIGURE 19

CONTRASTS IN LEARNING
IN ARTIFICIAL AND IN REAL SITUATIONS

ARTIFICIAL SITUATIONS (Schooling, Education)		REAL SITUATIONS (Socialization)	
Psychological factors in schooling model		**Psychological factors in socialization model**	
atomic:	Response desired is to learn specific content (perception) and be able to restate it.	organic:	Response desired is integration of specific content (perception) into life pattern.
	Perception learned is not associated with motives and feelings.		Perception is learned in association with motives and feelings.
isolated:	Content learned is not integrated with present experience.	integral:	Content learned is immediately integrated with present experience.
	Content learned is not immediately useful.		Content learned is in useful and useable form.
	Content learned is not related to adéquacy or competency of individual to live successfully in his culture.		Content learned is directly related to adequacy and competence of individual to live successfully in his culture.
Characteristics of schooling/ educational model		**Characteristics of socialization/ educational model**	
place:	special place and time, apart from the sphere of life in which the learner lives, set aside for learning	place:	in the normal processes and experiences of daily life (non-formal setting, close association with others in the social group)
teacher:	viewed as one who "knows" and passes on knowledge	teacher:	a person (or persons) who shares the situation and is viewed as a model who lives the content
content:	organized logically, with system imposed by the things being taught	content:	organized by applicability to the life situation in which it is taught
learning:	demonstrated by the ability of the learner to accurately repeat the content communicated	learning:	demonstrated by the ability of the learner to live a life appropriate to the content (beliefs) taught

TEACHING IN THE NEW TESTAMENT

One chapter of the Book of Titus, Paul's instructions to another young New Testament leader, helps us see the range of ideas involved in the biblical concept of teaching. The passage is reproduced below, with key words and phrases boxed in. These key words and phrases, when examined closely, give us a helpful picture of how leaders "taught" the body as they lived a servant life among the early Christian brothers and sisters.

FIGURE 20
TITUS 2 (RSV)

But as for you, ⎣teach⎦ what befits sound doctrine. ²⎣Bid⎦ the older men be temperate, serious, sensible, sound in faith, in love, and in steadfastness. ³⎣Bid⎦ the older women likewise to be reverent in behavior, not to be slanderers or slaves to drink; they are to ⎣teach what is good⎦, ⁴and so ⎣train⎦ the young women to love their husbands and children, ⁵to be sensible, chaste, domestic, kind, and submissive to their husbands, that the word of God may not be discredited. ⁶Likewise, ⎣urge⎦ the younger men to control themselves. ⁷⎣Show yourselves in all respects a model⎦ of good deeds, and in your ⎣teaching⎦ show integrity, gravity, ⁸and sound speech that cannot be censured, so that an opponent may be put to shame, having nothing evil to say of us. ⁹⎣Bid⎦ slaves to be submissive to their masters and to give satisfaction in every respect; they are not to be refractory, ¹⁰nor to pilfer, but to show entire and true fidelity, so that in everything they may adorn the doctrine of God our Savior.

¹¹For the grace of God has appeared for the salvation of all men, ¹²⎣training⎦ us to renounce irreligion and worldly passions, and to live sober, upright, and godly lives in this world, ¹³awaiting our blessed hope, the appearing of the glory of our great God and Savior Jesus Christ, ¹⁴who gave himself for us to redeem us from all iniquity and to purify for himself a people of his own who are zealous for good deeds.

¹⁵⎣Declare⎦ these things; ⎣exhort⎦ and ⎣reprove⎦ with all authority. Let no one disregard you.

"Teach what befits sound doctrine": the Greek is *lalei ha prepei tē hygiainousē didaskalia.* "Teach" is *laleō*, "to speak, or to express oneself." In transitive uses it means "to assert, proclaim, communicate."

What is to be communicated here? Not "sound doctrine" itself, but what befits or is in harmony with sound doctrine. The teaching ministry of Titus involves holding up a lifestyle that is in harmony with the revealed truths that comprise the content of our faith.

"Bid the older men be. . . ." There is no separate word for "bid" in the Greek. The construction uses the verb *to be (einai)* both in verse 2 and in verse 10. This is a common usage, which here not only describes what Titus is to teach but also implies the imperative communication of the need to adopt the special lifestyle required.

"Teach what is good." The term *kalodidaskalous* is used only here in the New Testament. It is composed of two words, *kalos* ("good") and *didaskaleō* ("teach"). The older women are to be regularly involved in teaching or instructing the younger women.

"Train the young women." The Greek verb here is *sōph-*

130

ronizō. It means "to encourage, advise, urge." In secular and classical Greek, it implied the teaching of morality, good judgment, and moderation. It was in effect advice focused on personal moral improvement.

"Urge the younger men." The Greek verb is *parakaleō* which means "to encourage or exhort." Close personal involvement with personal exhortation and encouragement to adopt a godly lifestyle is in view here.

"Show yourself in all respects a model" *(Seauton parechomenos typon).* The teacher is to make himself visible to others as a model. "Model" is *typon,* which is not only a "visible impression," but "a pattern or example to follow."

"Teaching" in verse 7 is *didaskalia,* "the act of instruction."

"Training us" (v. 12) is *paideuousa.* This word is related to the bringing up and guidance or education of a child. We can view it as giving parental guidance and daily correction to bring a youth to maturity.

"Declare" in verse 15 is again *laleō,* "to speak."

"Exhort" is again *parakaleō.*

Finally, "reprove" in the last verse of the chapter is *elenchō,* which means "to bring to light, expose," and, in this context, "to point out, convince, reproving if necessary to convict."

What picture do we have, then, of the "teaching ministry" of the spiritual leader in Titus 2?

First, the teaching ministry of the leader focuses on shaping lives that fit the doctrines of Scripture, not simply on the repetition, drilling, or mastery of the doctrines themselves. Christian doctrine has life impact; therefore the lifestyle into which leaders guide believers is to be one that "befits" sound doctrine.

Second, the teaching ministry of the leader involves him in every dimension of the life of the body member. A listing of *what* is to be taught (e.g., temperateness, soundness in faith, love, honesty, caring deeply for husbands and children, self-control, and submissiveness to masters) indicates that spiritual leaders are to be in close touch with the daily experiences of believers. The tensions and problems of daily life, reactions to pressures, relationships with others—all these are the concern of spiritual leaders who seek not so much to inculcate beliefs as to build Christlike men and women.

Third, the terms used reflect a very broad concept of teaching. Teaching is *not* merely classroom instruction; it is, in fact, difficult to see classroom instruction in this passage at all. Instead, "teaching" means bringing Scripture's insights into the nature of reality to bear on the lives of body members by instruction, encouragement, advising, urging, exhorting, guiding, exposing, and convincing.

The emergent picture is simply this: The spiritual leader incarnates the Word of God in his relationships among the people of God and in the context of that relationship also gives verbal guidance and encouragement, focused on helping the members of the body live life in harmony with divine revelation.

REFLECTIONS

In this picture from Titus, we have a clear reflection of what the Old Testament says about the communication of the written Word of God. The Word will have a life-changing impact and lead the believer to love and experience God (Deut. 6:4-5) when the following principles from Scripture are followed:

FIGURE 21
PRINCIPLES OF COMMUNICATION

PRINCIPLE	PASSAGE FROM DEUTERONOMY
The Word is lived out by the model. who is its teacher,	These commandments that I give you today are to be upon your hearts
A close, "among" (=family) relationship exists between the teacher and the learner.	Impress them on your children.
The context of teaching is a daily life shared by teacher and learner alike.	Talk about them when you sit at home and when you walk along the road, when you lie down and when you get up (Deut. 6:6-7).

In a biblical sense then, to be "apt to teach" does not presuppose teacher training, or seminary education, or ordination. It does not imply clear lectures, good sermons, or even well-designed textbooks. The biblical phrase "apt to teach" indicates a capacity to guide others into godly living by an application of the Word of God to the practical issues of life. And the goal of teaching is that each member of Christ's body adorn the doctrine of God and lead a life worthy of the God who calls us into His kingdom and His glory (1 Thess. 2:12).

PROBE

► case histories
► discussion questions
► thought provokers
► resources

1. Exploring the training of a disciple in the Talmudic age, Moses Aberbach points out that discipleship included much more than academic study:

> Disciples were expected not only to study the law in all its ramifications, but also to acquaint themselves with a specific way of life, which could be done only through constant attendance upon a master. . . . The rabbis taught as much by example as by precept. For this reason the disciple needed to take note of his master's daily conversation and habits, as well as his teaching.[3]

The relationship between master and disciple was no formal one. Aberbach shows that the teacher cared for his disciples as sons, usually providing for them at his own expense and praising and admonishing them. An intense, father-son kind of love developed.

It is this kind of training and teaching, not the formal schooling approach of our day and culture, that reflects the background against which the New Testament was written. To catch the impact, try

a. writing out a definition of "teaching" as a rabbi or disciple in the relationship Aberbach describes might write it;
b. imagining a way to structure a local church in the twentieth century in which this kind of teaching/learning might take place for the whole body.

2. In this chapter the authors suggest that teaching in a New Testament sense will
a. include basic doctrinal content
b. stress application of truth to shape lifestyle
c. take place in nonformal locations
d. arise out of specific circumstances and needs
e. take place in the context of warm interpersonal relationships
f. involve a variety of verbal styles (instruction, encouragement, exhortation, etc.)
g. have *practicing* the Word as its clear goal

---

[3]Moses Aberbach, "Relations between Master and Disciple in the Talmudic Age," in *Essays Presented to the Chief Rabbi Israel Brodie,* Jews' College Publications, New Series, no. 3 (London: Soncino, 1968), p. 318.

This picture of teaching contrasts with more formal teaching, which tends to
  a. concentrate primarily on content
  b. make applications as an afterthought, if at all
  c. take place in formal settings set apart for instruction
  d. arise out of a "curriculum," which structures learning by a logical development of the content taught
  e. limit the openness of relationships between teacher and student
  f. focus on a single verbal style (lecture and instruction)
  g. have *knowledge* of the Word as its clear goal

3. One interesting way to check out these differing perceptions of what teaching in the body of Christ is to involve may be to look at some of the teaching incidents recorded in the New Testament and see which of the characteristics listed are reflected there. Here are several possible studies you may want to make yourself:
  a. Pick *any* incident in which Jesus instructs or teaches.
  b. Study Peter's sermons in Acts 2 or 3.
  c. Look at Philip's time with the Ethiopian eunuch (Acts 8:26-40).
  d. Examine Paul's Letter to Philemon.
  e. Read Jude.
  f. Observe Paul's ministry style as revealed in 1 Thessalonians 2.
  After doing one or more of these studies, how do *you* think spiritual leaders are to "teach" in the body?

Of all the words associated with leadership that have cultural connotations not in harmony with biblical usage, "authority" is perhaps the most significant. Just as "leader" in our society speaks of a control position, and "teach" speaks of the transmission of information, so "authority" seems necessarily to imply power.

THE LEADER'S GOAL: EDIFICATION

God gives human leaders authority. But it is a unique authority. It does not rest on power in any way. Most importantly, it does not imply a right to control the behavior of others. The authority of Christian leaders is an authority granted to build up brothers and sisters so they will be able to live out the will, not of men, but of God.

Engstrom introduces his discussion of authority this way:

First we have to understand authority. A common but well-reasoned definition is this: "Authority is whatever you possess at the moment that causes someone else to do what you want him to do at the moment." In other words, any leader who is able to get done what he wants has all the authority he needs at the moment.[1]

This concept of authority as something that causes another person to "do what you want him to do" is reflected in most definitions. For instance, the *Random House Dictionary of the English Language* speaks of authority as "a power or right to direct the actions or thoughts of others. Authority is a power or right, usually because of rank or office, to issue commands and to punish for violations." Again the root idea seems to be control or direction of the actions of others.

We see this same idea even in sophisticated examinations of authority. For instance, William Oncken, Jr., in a 1970 *Colorado Institute of Technology Journal,* gives an analysis of authority that suggests it is comprised of four elements:

CHAPTER **10**

1. The Authority of Competence: the more competent the other fellow knows you are, the more confident he will be that you know what you are talking about and the more likely he will be to follow your orders, requests, or suggestions. He will think of you as an authority in the matter under consideration and will feel it risky to ignore your wishes.

2. The Authority of Position: This component gives you the right to tell someone, "Do it or else." It has teeth. "The boss wants it" is a bugle call that can snap many an office or shop into action.

3. The Authority of Personality: The easier it is for the other fellow to talk with you, to listen to you, or to work with you, the easier he will find it to respond to your wishes.

4. The Authority of Character: This component is your "credit rating" with other people as to your integrity, reliability, honesty, loyalty, sincerity, personal morals, and ethics. Obviously you will get more and better from a man who has respect for your character than from one who hasn't.[2]

In this quote we see certain key phrases emphasized: ". . .

---

[1]Ted Engstrom, *The Making of a Christian Leader* (Grand Rapids: Zondervan, 1976), p. 112.

[2]William Oncken, Jr., *Colorado Institute of Technology Journal* 22 (July 1970): 273.

likely to follow your orders, requests, or suggestions . . . the right to tell someone . . . respond to your wishes . . . get more and better from. . . ." The assumption is that the goal of one who has authority is to cause others to do *his* will. *But this is never the goal of the spiritual leader in the body of Christ.* The Christian leader always seeks to bring others, and the whole local body, to a responsive relationship with Jesus Christ. Our goal is to help others seek, come to know, and do *His* will.

This is a very basic and utterly jolting notion. The Christian leader does not try to protect his power; he wants no power. Yet the Christian leader speaks and acts with an authority given by God. That authority is exercised, as Paul puts it, "to build you up, not tear you down" (2 Cor. 10:8; 13:10). Christian leaders seek to free and lift up members of the body to the place of personal responsibility to Jesus, not to place them *under* their own authority or control. As Paul argues in Romans 14, "Who are you to judge someone else's servant? To his own master he stands or falls. And he will stand, for the Lord is able to make him stand" (14:4). Indeed, "for this very reason, Christ died and returned to life so that he might be the Lord of both the dead and the living. You, then, why do you judge your brother?" (14:9-10). It is Jesus who is Lord, and it is to Him that each of us must look. Only Jesus has the right to command or to control, and it is to His wishes we are to be responsive.

This same warning against usurping God's authority over our brothers is given in James: "Anyone who speaks against his brother, or judges him, speaks against the law and judges it. When you judge the law, you are not keeping it, but sitting in judgment on it. There is only one Lawgiver and Judge, the one who is able to save and destroy. But you—who are you to judge your neighbor?" (4:11-12). Spiritual leaders are not lifted up above their brothers to judge them and their behavior. Indeed, like our brothers, we have only one responsibility: to be obedient and responsive to Jesus Himself. No, the Christian leader's authority is something drastically different from authority as understood in the world.

TWO OBJECTIONS

This view of authority is open to two immediate objections. What about church discipline? And what about those passages that tell believers to "obey your rulers" (Heb. 13:17)? Let's look at the two issues separately.

Discipline

Discipline is to be exercised in the church. When a brother or sister adopts a sinful lifestyle, the church is told to follow a procedure that aims at his or her restoration to holiness. After a series of confrontations, if the sinning person refuses to repent, then the church refuses to fellowship with that person. Through this isolation, the body acts out on earth the reality of loss of fellowship with God that Scripture says comes when a believer walks in darkness.

Discipline therefore seems to involve (1) judging or evaluating behavior and (2) attempting in unmistakable ways to influence or control behavior. How then can we suggest that Christians are neither to judge their brothers nor attempt to bend them to their wills? How can we suggest that Christian "authority" is something different from the secular understanding of it?

First, it should be clear that the church—leaders and people—does *not* judge the behavior of a person under discipline. The church simply agrees with God, who has already judged that behavior and revealed His judgment on it in Scripture. This is why church discipline is reserved strictly for matters of sin. Discipline is not to be used to enforce the decisions or suggestions of body leaders.

Second, the purpose of discipline is not to bend sinning brothers to our wills. It is to let them realize by experiencing ostracism from the body that sin has broken their fellowship with the Lord. We may deceive ourselves about our fellowship with God. But there can be no self-deceit when dearly loved friends separate themselves from us.

The purpose of discipline is to help the one under it discover the reality of his position, face that reality, and make a personal decision to reject his sin and return to fellowship. In this sense, discipline is designed not to pressure but to reveal the reality of the sinner's condition, so that the choice to be made is unmistakable and clear.

Commands for obedience

There *is* a bond of obedience laid on members of the body in their relationship to leaders. But that bond of obedience is as different in Scripture from our usual impression as the biblical idea of headship is different from the distorted relationships that have developed from misunderstanding it.

As we saw in earlier chapters, the idea of "submission" in Scripture is, first, mutual and, second, cast in terms of the freely chosen response of love to love. There is a similar loving tone to "obedience."

For instance, the Book of Hebrews first exhorts believers, "Remember your leaders, who spoke the word of God to you. Consider the outcome of their way of life, and imitate their faith" (13:7). Shortly after, the writer says, "Obey your leaders and submit to their authority" (v. 17). It would seem that here we have a clear-cut case of the very kind of authority that this chapter suggests spiritual leaders must reject. Here is a demand for obedience. Leaders seem to have at least some right to control. And here is a reference to an "authority" that leaders have.

But let's look more closely at this verse. In the original the phrase reads, *Peithesthe tois hēgoumenois hymōn kai hypeikete*. Each word here is significant and conveys a much different message from its English equivalent.

Peithesthe is from *peithō,* which literally means "let yourselves be persuaded, or convinced." A fair translation would be, "Be open to the persuasion of your leaders."

Tois hēgoumenois hymōn is translated "your leaders." It is a term used of rulers and princes, but the original word means "to lead, or guide." Here we see the spiritual leader in the church as one who has traveled along the road toward godliness and, as a valid model, is able to point out that way to others.

Hypeikete is the single word translated by the English phrase "submit to their authority." The word is at times so translated. Originally, however, it was used, as in classical Greek, to describe soft and yielding substances.[3] The root idea is not "give in" but "be disposed to yielding."

The whole instruction, therefore, focuses on the attitude that members of the body are to maintain toward their leaders. We can paraphrase the instruction and so capture the underlying thought of the verse as it would have been understood by a Greek reader of the New Testament: "In your relationship with those who are your leaders and guides to godliness, be sure you maintain a yielding disposition, and remain open to their persuasion." The passage goes on, "For they keep watch over you as men who must give an account. Be responsive to them so that their work will be a joy, not a burden, for that would be of no advantage to you."

With this insight, the whole tone of *obey* changes. The "authority" of the leader is seen not to be some right to control, but only a right to influence the choices of brothers

---

[3]See Liddell and Scott, *Greek-English Lexicon,* p. 1954.

140

and sisters over whom the leader keeps watch. No wonder the "servant of the Lord must not quarrel but be gentle." Without power to demand response, with only the servant's resources of a godly life and a living Word to share, the servant-leader must do nothing to make it more difficult for one instructed or corrected to yield. Ultimately the choice to respond is entirely that of the person being ministered to. The leader has no "authority" as men know authority and he seeks no such power over others. The servant of the Lord, the spiritual leader in the body of Christ, seeks only to woo and win each person to obedience to the one Lord and sole head of the church, Jesus Christ Himself.

THE AUTHORITY WE HAVE

What, then, is the nature of the authority that leaders in the body of Christ have? Where does it reside and how is it exercised?

A striking passage from 2 Corinthians helps us understand, although at first it seems to call into question all that we've been exploring in this chapter. Paul is writing to the Corinthians with a warning, and here is what he has to say:

> I already gave you a warning when I was with you the second time. I now repeat it while absent: On my return I will not spare those who sinned earlier or any of the others, since you are demanding proof that Christ is speaking through me. He is not weak in dealing with you, but is powerful among you. For to be sure, he was crucified in weakness, yet he lives by God's power (13:2-4).

At first the passage seems to portray Paul threatening his readers and demanding obedience. He does warn them. He states that he will not spare. Surely, it seems, when Paul comes again, some terrible sanctions will be imposed on those who refused to bend to the apostle's will.

But read the passage more closely. What is the issue, and how will Paul exercise discipline?

Christ is speaking through me

The Corinthians in rejecting the guidance of the apostle were making a dangerous claim. They were saying, "Jesus is *not* speaking through you." And yet Jesus *was.* The apostle had been called by God, gifted, and then given to the church (Eph. 4:11-12). What's more, Paul's calling was well known by the body in Corinth. Paul had established the church and probably spent three years teaching among them. The impact of his world-wide ministry was known, and his letters may already have been given the standing of "the other Scriptures"

141

that Peter gives them (cf. 2 Peter 3:16). Paul's life clearly demonstrated the work of God: he could without hesitation present himself as an example to the Corinthians, and he had done so (1 Cor. 4:10-11).

By lifestyle and by teaching, the Word of Christ *was* revealed to the men and women of Corinth by Paul the apostle.

It was here, in both *life* and *teaching,* that Paul had demonstrated his authority as a spiritual leader. There is no other basis on which we can claim spiritual authority today. It is because Jesus *is* speaking through us, both through our lives and through words that are in full harmony with sound doctrine, that we have spiritual authority.

Jesus said, "My sheep hear my voice, and they know me." God's people hear the voice of the Shepherd, and they follow, not the man, but Jesus who speaks through him.

He is not weak but is powerful among you

What can Paul do to enforce his authority when it is rejected by the body of believers? He first warns the Corinthians that Jesus *is* speaking through him. They must be yielding and responsive to the Lord's voice. Paul explains that when he comes he will not spare them. But, strikingly, *Paul himself will do nothing to "enforce" his spiritual authority!* How then will it be enforced? Look at the words again. "Christ is speaking through me. He is not weak in dealing with you, but is powerful among you." Simply put, Jesus Himself, resident in each believer and the community, will act to vindicate His spokesman. Because Jesus lives and is powerful among His people, the authority of Christian leaders can and will be vindicated *without their action.*

SUMMARY

While Christian leaders do have authority, it is very different from secular authority. First, by it the leaders never seek to bend others to their will, but to bring them to responsiveness to Jesus. Second, the Christian leader rejects power and position as a basis for authority. The sole claim to any authority the spiritual leader has is that Jesus speaks to the community through him, both through his lifestyle (incarnating the Word) and his teaching (communicating the Word). Finally, this kind of authority rests on a purely supernatural base. It is only because Jesus lives and is powerful in the lives of His people that the voice of the servant-leader is heard. It is God's work that causes believers to open themselves to persuasion. In full confidence that as Jesus speaks His people will

hear, leaders in the body of Christ are free to set aside all the trappings of power, and to live humbly among the brethren.
As servants.
And nothing more.

PROBE

▶ case histories
▶ discussion questions
▶ thought provokers
▶ resources

1. The New Testament describes false leaders in contrast to spiritual leaders. They are recognized by the distortions that appear in their lifestyle and teaching. Read what is said about them in 2 Peter, Jude, and 2 Timothy.

2. Wofford and Kilinski catalog some of the advantages and disadvantages of power-based types of authority in the church. Study the summary carefully. Then answer the questions listed below the quotation.

ADVANTAGES

   – The use of authority facilitates the coordination of activities. If two or more persons or groups must carry out functions which must be phased together, a direct command or at least a strong influence is usually required to blend the functions. Suppose a special program is to be held on Wednesday night, and it is very important to the church that all other activities be suspended so that all the members may be able to attend this program. There is no other method worth consideration than the use of some type of power.

   – The use of authority assures that there will be a minimum of confusion. The leader makes his point and the decision is clearly transmitted. There is comparatively little wasted effort or disorder.

   – The use of authority assures uniformity. If you wish to have a consistency in educational materials, a decision to use material from a single press for the entire Sunday school can gain this end. Failure to use direct authority here leads to a wide range of approaches and quality of material.

   – The use of authority provides security to the leader. With direct authority there is little questioning or disagreeing. The leader can get his decision accepted with little open argument.

   – The use of authority is relatively simple. One doesn't need to be a psychologist to figure out how to give an order. Little understanding of people is required.

143

THEOLOGICAL FOUNDATION

From these advantages it is apparent that the use of authority is an important tool in every leader's bag. He must use authority in many situations in order to accomplish a desired end.

DISADVANTAGES

– Authority tends to be met with resistance. Since the use of power places the person being led in a dependency role, he often resents this position. His self-worth is threatened. Although not exhibiting open hostility, he may often resolve to do no more than the minimum. In some cases, the member will even sabotage the operation because of his resentment. It is regrettable when sabotage occurs in the church, for it is directly contrary to scriptural principles.

– Reliance on authority also results in a stagnation of members. The dependency fostered by authority tends to cause the members to sit back and wait for orders or suggestions. Thus they lose confidence in their own ability and certainly do not grow in their ability to assume greater responsibility.

– Although conformity is desirable in certain situations, it is undesirable in many others. If there is excessive conformity, the creativity and spontaneity of the organization is lost.

– The use of authority can thwart or distort communication. The member may begin to feel pressured and will not feel free to state his position. He often states one position but believes another, contrary to indication.

– The full human potential is not being utilized. As authority is abused, a leader may exercise his power for the sheer desire to dominate. He assumes that he knows best how to do the workers' job. A caste system does not recognize the potential of most of the members.

– The authority system is not responsive to change. Since the members do not have a part in initiating change, they tend to be fearful of its consequences.[4]

Questions to discuss:

a. How many of the supposed *advantages* of authority relate to issues about which Jesus Himself as head of the church reserves the right to decide?

b. How many of the supposed advantages of authority relate to *short-term goal achievement?* How many of these short-term goals, if achieved, might fight against the long-term or basic goal of directing believers into a life of personal responsibility to Jesus Christ?

---

[4]Jerry Wofford and Kenneth Kilinski, *Organization and Leadership in the Local Church* (Grand Rapids: Zondervan, 1973), pp. 157-58.

c. Look over the disadvantages. How might the use of authority make it hard for believers to be "yielding and open to persuasion"? Can you see how "authority" might actually fight against the effectiveness of servant leadership?

d. How many specific problems in a body context might be created or made worse if spiritual leaders were to adopt a "secular ruler" style of leadership, as opposed to a "servant" style?

3. Below are the key concepts advanced in the five chapters in this section of the text. First, summarize each concept in your own words and explain its implications. Second, in a brief paragraph indicate which of the concepts is most significant to you personally, and explain why.

- Leaders are called to build a healthy and responsive body, over which Jesus is to be head.
- Leaders are servants in the body.
- Leaders lead by modeling for the body a Christlike lifestyle.
- Leaders lead by teaching the Word of God to the body.
- The authority of church leaders rests in the fact that Jesus speaks to the body through their lives and teaching.

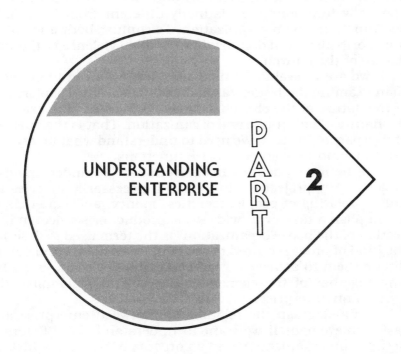

UNDERSTANDING
ENTERPRISE

PART 2

In part 1 of this text we have argued that the church of Jesus Christ is an organism and that its leaders must therefore function in the church in unique ways. Body leadership and body functions are distinctly different from leadership and functions in an organization. To confuse body and enterprise, organism and organization, is to do violence to the very nature of the church.

If we are to evaluate this contention, we need to do more than examine the issues raised by our theological exploration of the nature of the church as body. We also need to examine the nature of enterprise and organization. That is the purpose of this part of the text. We need to understand what an organization is and how an enterprise functions.

The dictionary defines an enterprise as "an undertaking or project." Any project or undertaking necessarily involves an orderly relating of people, facilities, money, and materials to accomplish a task or provide some product or service. In this section of the book "organization" is the term used to describe the kind of order required to relate these elements and subordinate them to achieve a goal. Organization, then, is the fitting together of the elements necessary to accomplish the goals of an enterprise.

We must grasp the relationship between enterprise and task achievement if we want to understand the differences between an organization and an organism. We need a historical overview of the issues that have concerned the management of enterprise. We also need to understand the nature of a successful enterprise.

Ten years ago as a local church leader, Clyde was prompted to examine the meaning of enterprise. In his church and in his corporations he was committed to the achievement of goals. A friend suggested that he was too much a project man. In return Clyde suggested that perhaps his friend spent

A DESCRIPTION OF ENTERPRISE

too much time talking to people and generally looking out for their welfare. One was a project person, the other was a people person. That was the issue.

After ten years of exploration, experience, and research, this remains the basic issue. Projects—or people.

To suggest that there is a project-versus-people issue in any enterprise is not to suggest that an enterprise is necessarily a bad or immoral thing. Let's realize right away that the objective of any enterprise is to provide products or services *for* people. The leadership of an enterprise is just as much a vocation, a calling from God, as is leadership in the church. The leader of an enterprise can equally seek to glorify God as he serves people.

However, the quality of service provided through an enterprise is directly related to the accomplishment of tasks. The priority in an enterprise must always be the successful accomplishment of tasks.

We can easily see why this is so. Imagine that someone purchases a new home. The builder has promised to have it completed before Christmas. But the promise goes unfulfilled; the disappointed family finds construction workers finally finishing their new home around Easter. Or imagine a traveler arriving at an airport in one city and discovering that his bags are on the way to another city. Or suppose that the

 objective of an enterprise is to teach children arts and crafts for two weeks during the summer break. If the craft materials arrive four days after the class has started, the promised service cannot be provided.

In any enterprise the goal must be reached and the task that was set accomplished if people are going to be served responsibly.

In the management of an enterprise, then, it is a good manager's primary *moral* responsibility to accomplish tasks. The project itself, not the people working on the project, is necessarily his first concern.

What is involved in a well-run enterprise—one that fulfills its moral obligations to those it serves by achieving its goals? It involves effectively managing the four basic resources any enterprise must utilize. These resources are (1) people, (2) money, (3) facilities, and (4) materials. Each of these four resources must be of the right type, and be delivered in the right quantity at the right place and time.

Let's say, for instance, that the objective of a particular enterprise is to make a good choir available for a convention, including three men able to sing tenor. It will be easy for the enterprise to hire three male singers. But if one is a bass, another sings in a monotone, and the third never shows up for practices, the enterprise will be a failure because of inadequate manpower.

Again, the children's arts and crafts class is a clear case of the right type of materials in the right place and in the right quantity but at the wrong time. A single failure frustrates the whole enterprise.

Or suppose the objective of an enterprise is to provide good medical treatment. At the completion of a new clinic, doctors, nurses, medicines, machines, beds, and supplies may all be in the right place, but suppose the administrator overlooked appropriate electrical outlets for special equipment and that half the treatment rooms are too small to be functional.

In each of these instances resources were improperly managed and the objectives of the enterprise were affected. And because the enterprise failed to accomplish its objective, the people for whom its services were intended were deprived.

The very reason for the existence of any enterprise is the accomplishment of its task objectives. Part of a leader's moral obligation is to give the *project* his highest priority. His resources include people as well as facilities, money, and materials.

There is therefore a very basic difference between leadership in an enterprise and leadership in the body of Christ. The body is a living organism, with each member a vital part of Jesus Himself. The moral obligation of the leader in Christ's body is to give *people* his highest priority. God has committed Himself to transform believers into the likeness of Jesus Christ. He has shared His own life with us; each one is in Christ forever linked with God. The primary objective of a leader in the body is the health of the organism and all its parts, for unless an organism is healthy the head is unable to work through it. No wonder, then, that Paul sees the focus of the ministry of leaders as the preparation of God's people for their works of service, with the implication that "the body of Christ may be built up, until we all reach unity in the faith and in the knowledge of the Son of God and become mature, attaining to the whole measure of the fullness of Christ" (Eph. 4:12-13).

ORDER IN ORGANISM AND ORGANIZATION

We have just characterized an enterprise as of necessity giving priority to projects, and the church (an organism) as of necessity giving priority to its members. This is one important way to distinguish between an enterprise and a local church.

Yet to many this contrast seems relatively unimportant. Can't an enterprise be concerned about people? And shouldn't a church be concerned about such tasks as evangelism and social service? The answer to each of these questions is, of course, yes. But the questions miss the point. The point is that an enterprise *by its very nature* must give priority to tasks, and thus be organized primarily for task accomplishment. The church of Christ on the other hand *by its very nature* must give priority to its members and be organized to build believers.

If an enterprise fails to accomplish its tasks, its income is lost and its people must be laid off. The needs of the people involved in an enterprise can be met only if its goals are achieved. Tasks are its first priority. If, on the other hand, the body fails to nurture and build its members, Christ will have an immature and unresponsive body through which to express His life in the world, and His purposes will not be fully achieved. The mission of Jesus to the world can be carried out effectively only if Christ's life is communicated to the members of His body.

In other words, an enterprise and an organism have by their very natures two different priorities.

There is another vital comparison. All systems, whether living organisms or multiperson organizations, do have order. They are organized; there is a systematic relationship between their parts.

Some management theorists have noted this systematic relationship or order and have suggested that multiperson organizations should be organized like an organism. Organization theorists, particularly those who take a systems approach to enterprise, have used biological systems metaphorically to explain organizational and social systems.

This approach has, however, encountered serious criticism. Kast and Rozenzweig make the following distinction between organisms and social organizations:

> General systems theory emphasizes that systems are organized—they are composed of interdependent components in some relationship. The social organization would then follow logically as just another system. But we are perhaps being caught in circular thinking. It is true that all systems (physical, biological, and social) are by definition organized, but are all systems organizations? Rapoport and Horvath distinguish "organization theory" and "the theory of organizations" as follows:
>
> > We see organization theory as dealing with general and abstract organizational principles; it applies to any system exhibiting organized complexity. As such, organization theory is seen as an extension of mathematical physics or, even more generally, of mathematics designed to deal with organized systems. The theory of organizations, on the other hand, purports to be a social science. It puts real human organizations at the center of interest. It may study the social structure of organizations and so can be viewed as a branch of sociology; it

UNDERSTANDING ENTERPRISE

can study the behavior of individuals or groups as members of organizations and can be viewed as a part of social psychology; it can study power relations and principles of control in organizations and so fits into political science (30, pp. 74-75).

Why make an issue of this distinction? It seems to us that there is a vital matter involved. All systems may be considered to be organized, and more advanced systems may display differentiation in the activities of component parts—such as the specialization of human organs. However, not all systems consist of separate, purposeful entities. Can the heart or lungs be considered as purposeful entities in themselves or are they only components of the larger purposeful system, the human body? By contrast, the social organization is composed of two or more purposeful elements. "An organization consists of elements that have and can exercise their own wills" (1, p. 669). Organisms, the foundation stone of general systems theory, do not contain purposeful elements which exercise their own will. This distinction between the organism and the social organization is of importance. In much of general systems theory, the concern is primarily with the way in which the organism responds to environmentally generated inputs. Feedback concepts and the maintenance of a steady state are based on internal adaptations to environmental forces. (This is particularly true of cybernetic models.) But what about those changes and adaptations which occur from within social organizations? Purposeful elements within the social organization may initiate activities and adaptations which are difficult to subsume under feedback and steady-state concepts.[1]

The major point the authors make is a vital one. Organizations consist of members with independent wills, each of whom can and does exercise his separate will independently. Organisms, on the other hand, are not made up of individual, purposeful entities or members. Only in the supernatural relationship existing between Christ, the head, and the church, His body, to which He is linked by the Spirit, can human beings be found together in an organism relationship.

The apostle Paul in 1 Corinthians 12 does not feel any tension between the church as a multiperson entity and the church as an organism because each member in the body will, when mature, subject his or her will to the will of the Lord,

---

[1]Fremont E. Kast and James E. Rozenzweig, "General Systems Theories: Applications for Organizations and Management," *Academy of Management Journal*, vol. 15, no. 4 (December 1972), pp. 447-65.

154

thereby satisfying the requirement that the members of an organism not exercise their independent wills.

We can only conclude that the *kind* of order in an organization and the *kind* of order in an organism are intrinsically and essentially different. Thus not only is the first priority of an enterprise/organization in essential contrast to the first priority of the church as a body/organism, but there is also an essential difference in the way the members must be organized to function effectively in each type of structure.

THE WATERSHED DECISION

Typically, local churches are ordered and organized as multiperson organizations. And church leaders function in the same way as enterprise leaders, organizing and using people as resources to reach the goals they set. Thus the institutional church tends to give priority to tasks, and its human leaders utilize principles for ordering the members to accomplish tasks that are utilized in enterprise management.

Typically, too, the leaders of the church operate with only the best of motives, but with little or no awareness that "organization" order and priorities conflict with "organism" order and priorities. Yet an understanding of enterprise makes that contrast clear. We cannot be both enterprise and body. We must be one—or the other.

The reasons why this choice must be made will be developed more fully in the next chapters.

PROBE

▶ *case histories*
▶ *discussion questions*
▶ *thought provokers*
▶ *resources*

1. On the chart on page 156 is a list of the characteristics of an enterprise, ordered to deal with "independent wills" so as to achieve task-oriented goals. In the spaces provided, list the contrasting characteristics of an organism.

2. Restate the following quotation in your own words. Then state the implications of the restatement for those who tend to mix features of organisms with those of organizations.

> *General systems theory would have us accept this analogy between organism and social organization. Yet we have a hard time swallowing it whole. Katz and Kahn warn us of the danger:*
>
> > *There has been no more pervasive, persistent, and futile*

155

FIGURE 22
CONTRASTING CHARACTERISTICS
OF ENTERPRISE AND OF ORGANISM

ENTERPRISE	ORGANISM
1. *Participants.* An exclusive group of people, selected on the basis of aptitude, technique, education, and ability to contribute to the completion of the task.	
2. *Termination.* People are terminated when their performance is unsatisfactory or their abilities are no longer needed. For example, the objectives of an enterprise may change, and a particular employee's talents may no longer be required.	
3. *Relationships.* The relationship of one person to another is generally characterized by control; the one with greater responsibility controls the other for the purpose of completing tasks. The subordinate always has less at stake and less responsibility with regard to the objective.	
4. *Compensation.* People involved are usually compensated in an amount directly related to the market value of their contribution (sub-task) to the completion of the overall task objective.	
5. *Resources.* The resources of an enterprise are people, money, material, and facilities, related in an appropriate mix for the completion of the task.	
6. *Priorities.* Completion of the task generally will take priority over the welfare of the people contributing to the task.	

fallacy handicapping the social sciences than the use of the physical model for the understanding of social structures. The biological metaphor, with its crude comparisons of the physical parts of the body to the parts of the social system, has been replaced by more subtle but equally misleading analogies between biological and social functioning. This figurative type of thinking ignores the essential difference between the socially contrived nature of social systems and the physical structure of the machine or the human organism. So long as writers are committed to a theoretical framework based upon the physical model, they will miss the essential social-psychological facts of the highly variable, loosely articulated character of social systems.[2]

3. The following "watershed diagram" suggests critical differences between organizational and organismic leadership approaches. Look over this chart, and try to determine where on this chart your church would fall.

FIGURE 23
CONTRASTING OBJECTIVES: PEOPLE OR TASK ACCOMPLISHMENT

"God has called me to help this group be Christ's body	"God has called me to accomplish a divinely appointed task with this group."

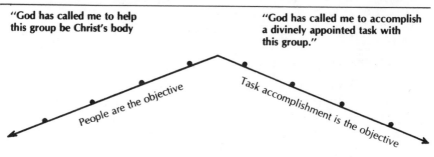

BODY	**ENTERPRISE**
• A person's needs are primary, his contributions secondary.	• A person's contributions are primary, his needs secondary.
• People are valued as brothers and sisters in Christ.	• People are valued for their performance and responsibility in the "ministry."
• People are included in interdependent relationships.	• People are included or excluded on the basis of their ability, aptitude, education, and necessity to the efficiency of the enterprise.
• The development of people is the ultimate goal of the body's existence.	• People are *used* to reach the goal of the existence of the enterprise.

4. For your information, Dynamic Church Ministries (DCM) is an enterprise whose objective is to develop, produce, and distribute ministry tools for use by local church leaders to help them help their group be the body of Christ. Beacon Homes, Inc. (Beacon) is an enterprise whose objective is to develop and produce shelter products (homes) and render associated services to people. Clyde's local church is an organism whose objective is to experience life in a healthy way and to allow Christ to transform individuals and guide them individually and in groups to accomplish God's purposes in the world.

---

[2]Daniel Katz and Robert L. Kahn, *The Social Psychology of Organizations,* 2nd ed. (New York: Wiley, 1978), p. 31.

157

UNDERSTANDING ENTERPRISE

A Description of Enterprise
The Great Conflict
The Manager's Dilemma
Enterprise as a Ministry Tool

During the Industrial Revolution there was no question of the way in which an enterprise viewed its workers. Workers were necessary elements in the production of goods. People, like raw materials, were to be used to produce those goods.

But with the twentieth century came an awareness of workers as persons. Many people became aware of the fact

THE GREAT CONFLICT

that achieving the objectives of an enterprise might at times conflict with the welfare of the workers.

The result has been a great deal of speculation about the best means and methods of business management. But the fundamental question still remains unchanged: Do people or projects have ultimate priority?

The intent of this chapter is to provide an overview of the thinking that has been done on the leadership of an enterprise, or management. This overview will tend to focus on the "people" side of enterprise.

The foundations of management theory in America were laid in the early 1900s (1910-1920). They began with a concern for efficiency, with an analysis of the exact elements in a task that were necessary for work to be done more effectively.

One of the earliest writers on the theory of management, Frederick W. Taylor, is often regarded as the father of scientific management. He would, for example, attempt to build a "science of shoveling." Pollard describes his method: "The actual movements of shoveling, the use of hands, arms and legs were studied in detail, as were the different types of base on which material could lie, for example, earth, wood, metal, and so on."[1] Based on the results of this study, the correct methods, tools, and amounts to be shoveled could all be determined.

Frank Gilbreth, co-author of *Cheaper by the Dozen*, and his wife were concerned about the "one best way" of working, and are remembered almost entirely for the development and perfection of the time-and-motion study approach.[2]

CHAPTER 12

At the same time that these and other American authors were looking at management from the standpoint of work, French executive Henri Fayol developed a "process approach" to management. From his experience and observations, Fayol isolated the five basic functions of a manager, functions we still work with some fifty years later. The functions Fayol defined are:

1. foresight and planning
2. organization
3. direction
4. coordination
5. control

As scientific management theory developed, a major conflict emerged. Efficiency and effective management might conflict with the highest good of the people involved in the enterprise. Fundamental psychological needs might not be met—they might indeed be violated—by stressing the most "effective" way of working. On the other hand, meeting the psychological needs of workers might jeopardize the highest

---

[1]Harold R. Pollard, *Developments in Management Thought* (New York: Crane, Russak, 1974), p. 10.
[2]Ibid., p. 18.

good of the enterprise. And to maximize profits an enterprise must accomplish tasks with the highest degree of efficiency.

EMERGING CONCERN FOR WORKERS

In the 1920s and 1930s the welfare of the worker was first articulated as a necessary concern of those managing an enterprise. Mary Packer Follett raised important questions regarding a person's hopes, fears, and aspirations. She first suggested an idea Chris Argyris would stress some forty years later: giving orders does, or can, demean the person to whom the orders are relayed. She asks, "What happens to a man, *in* a man, when an order is given in a disagreeable manner? . . . He loses his temper or becomes sullen or is on the defensive; he begins thinking of his 'rights.'"[3] On the other hand, a supervisor who is so close to his workers that he can't give orders is equally unable to motivate good performance.

It was becoming increasingly clear that people's needs had to be considered if an enterprise was to utilize to the fullest the potential of its workers.

It was a Quaker, Seebohm Rowntree, who addressed the issue of the morality (not just the efficiency) of managing a business. His family had founded a cocoa industry in York, England, and was still running it in the 1920s and 1930s. As a Christian, he had high ethical and humanitarian standards. Yet he was also a practical idealist and a keen businessman. In the democratic spirit Rowntree established employee councils. Pollard describes Rowntree's philosophy and his business policy as follows:

> He maintains that, one way or the other, workers desire two things from industry: better material conditions and improved status. The company's labour policy was framed deliberately "to introduce into the management of the business, in *all matters directly affecting the workers*, as great a measure of democracy as possible *without lowering efficiency.*" Two fundamental points are raised here. Democracy would improve status and self-respect for the worker, but it was not to interfere with the prerogative of management to manage the business; it was limited to aspects affecting the workers, and here control would be shared between management and workers. Secondly, it must not interfere with the efficient running of the business. Indeed only if the business was efficiently run could it afford to carry out such policies.
>
> Behind the policy lay the question "Could capitalist industry do these things for workers at least as well as socialist or communist systems?" Rowntree throught that it could (italics his).[4]

Another theorist, Oliver Sheldon, went beyond this con-

---

[3]Ibid., p. 165.
[4]Ibid., p. 123.

clusion to introduce concern for people in the community and marketplace as a moral obligation of management. Pollard summarizes as follows:

> Management must control not simply the production of goods, but the production of goods which have value to the community, at a price the community can afford to pay, and of a quality which reasonably satisfies the needs for which they are designed. In a broader sense he gives " 'service to the community' as the primary motive and fundamental basis of industry," and such service "may be economic in character, but must be ethical in motive."[5]

As moral issues were defined, tensions between the well-being of the workers and the community and the well-being of the enterprise were increasingly recognized.

The pressure to deal with the human dimension of enterprise came, however, not so much from Christian theorists like Rowntree as from the practical realities of life in the twentieth century. Great social changes swept the Western world, and it became increasingly clear that to be successful an enterprise must gain the willing cooperation of its employees. People's needs *must* be addressed or the enterprise would fail!

Elton Mayo, in the later part of the 1930s and 1940s, set management thought off on a new trail. He focused on the importance of systems and the need to gain the cooperation of subordinates. At the same time, J. A. C. Brown was dealing with group dynamics and exploring the impact of a manager on the work group. Brown made a distinction between "leadership" that really worked, and "headship" as a position in the hierarchy, which may or may not be effective. However, his approach was one sided: he tended to oversimplify as though by changes in management approaches all tensions could be resolved.

In 1957 Chris Argyris made a great contribution to the personal side of management. He pointed out that a basic conflict will always exist between an organization and the individuals working in it. He argued that psychological maturity and development is a basic human need and demonstrated ways in which management systems by nature conflict with that need. Argyris assumes that this conflict will arise "where the individual finds he cannot at the same time fulfill his personal needs and meet those of the organization. For example, the organization requires him to be dependent and submissive, while he wishes to exercise his independence and use his own intelligence"[6] in his quest for psychological maturity.

---

[5]Ibid., p. 108.
[6]Ibid., p. 213.

Argyris emphasized the need for management to assess its own approach as well as the behavior of employees. In essence he was suggesting that management tended to treat employees as though they were lazy, uninterested, apathetic, money-hungry, and prone to errors and waste. This kind of thinking tended to view poor performance as a reason to increase pressure and install tighter management controls. But the addition of controls served only to increase the sense of psychological failure. Perhaps what management needed to do to improve performance was to provide greater freedom and responsibility!

This management approach seemed to support J. A. C. Brown's concept of a "primary [social] group," which the author said existed to serve the social needs of individuals. He described the primary group as an informal organization that exists in addition to the formal organization shown on organizational charts. Brown believed that "if the aims and objectives of the primary groups coincide with those of the formal organization there will be a well-integrated, effective firm, achieving its objectives with a minimum of internal friction and difficulties."[7]

Douglas McGregor has made a significant contribution to management by his reexamination of the control processes in management. McGregor points out that "control action must, if it is to be effective, be appropriate to the situation in which it is to operate. Much management action is ineffective because it runs counter to human nature, which is an essential factor in the total situation."[8] In his exploration of control in management, McGregor propounded two theories of behavior. The first, Theory X, is the traditional view of management's need to direct and control. This theory assumes that:

1. The average human being has an inherent dislike of work and will avoid it if he can.

2. Because of this human characteristic, most people must be coerced, controlled, directed, and threatened with punishment to get them to put forward an adequate effort toward the achievement of organizational objectives.

3. The average human being prefers to be directed, wishes to avoid responsibility, has relatively little ambition, and above all wants security.[9]

---

[7]Ibid., p. 195.
[8]Ibid., p. 223.
[9]Ibid., p. 225.

McGregor concludes that data from experience does at times tend to support these assumptions, *but only because of their response to mismanagement!* They are reacting to a management that utilizes control, threat, punishment, and coercion to get people to put forth the effort needed to reach organizational objectives.

In contrast to this theory, McGregor put forward a new theory, Theory Y. Its assumptions are based on information about behavior gained from the social sciences. According to this view, management should assume that:

1. The expenditure of physical and mental effort in work is as natural as play or rest.
2. External control and the threat of punishment are not the only means of bringing about effort toward organizational objectives. A person will exercise self-direction and self-control in the service of objectives to which he is committed.
3. Commitment to objectives is a function of the rewards associated with their achievement.
4. The average human being learns, under proper conditions, not only to accept but also to seek responsibility.
5. The capacity to exercise a relatively high degree of imagination, ingenuity, and creativity in the solution of organizational problems is widely, not narrowly, distributed in the population.
6. Under the conditions of modern industrial life, the intellectual potentialities of the average human being are only partially utilized.[10]

Where did McGregor find the "new information" on which he based his Theory Y? Undoubtedly from the studies of Maslow and Herzberg.

Abraham Maslow's work in social psychology led him to develop the now-famous idea of a "hierarchy of human needs." Maslow sees an order in human needs (from basic needs for food and shelter to "higher" needs for self-actualization). McGregor picks up on this theme and points out that the more elementary of human needs are generally being met in industrial societies, but the higher ego and self-actualization needs are generally *not* being met. This is significant, because when basic needs are satisfied, people concentrate on the higher needs. If work can be organized to meet these higher needs (for achievement, recognition, use of potential, development of capabilities, etc.), it becomes pleasant, and people

---

[10]Ibid., p. 226.

will seek responsibility and will become personally committed to the objectives of the organization.[11]

Herzberg argues that when a job satisfies one's needs, it will also improve his performance.

In summary, prior to 1900, managers of an enterprise generally saw no compelling reason to be concerned about the personal needs of workers. Since 1900, however, personal needs have loomed larger as a management concern. On the theoretical level there is the moral obligation to serve the highest good of the worker. On a very practical level there is the fact that a demonstrated concern for the needs of workers tends to enhance their performance. For the good of the enterprise, managers need to care about what is happening to their employees.

Much early thinking about human relationships in an enterprise focused on the need for the individual interests of the worker to be subordinated to the general interest of the enterprise. Thus when companies in the 1960s were concerned about "company-employee relations," the desire of management was to make sure that the workers would "feel good about the company" or "cooperate with the boss."

But in the 1970s much broader and more sophisticated concerns emerged. Greater reliance was placed on the behavioral sciences, and complex assumptions about relationships between the individuals and the organization were made. McGregor's principle, derived from Theory Y, suggested that there must be a true integration of organizational needs with the needs of persons in the organization if optimal productivity is to be achieved.

Yet, though these theories had been formulated, no one had yet suggested *how* managers could implement them.

MODELS OF ORGANIZATIONAL DESIGN

In looking at various models of organizations, it is important to remember that we are dealing with a business enterprise. They cannot be judged simply on how well they meet the psychological needs of workers and provide for their well-being. They must first of all be judged as to how well they order people, money, facilities, and materials for the optimum achievement of a company's objectives.

Yet it is clear that one of the reasons for the pressure to rethink organizational theory today is that within an enterprise human needs must be considered, not only from a moral point of view but also with the benefit of the enterprise in mind.

---

[11]Ibid., p. 227.

The Great Conflict

The classical model

This model represents the traditional approach to organization, with its concentration of authority and its pyramidal structure. This structure is still common in most enterprises, and an analysis of management tasks within its framework will be provided in detail in the next chapter. Here in overview is how Shetty and Carlisle describe it:

Early in the twentieth century the great German sociologist Max Weber, noting common elements in different types of organizations (business, government, and military), called this form of organization bureaucracy. In his bureaucratic system, Weber placed very heavy emphasis on a hierarchical structure, position, authority, and rules for solving repetitive problems. Functionaries with specialized training learn their tasks better by practice. "Precision, speed, unambiguity, knowledge of the files, continuity, discretion, unity, strict subordination, reduction of friction and of material and personal costs—these are raised to the optimum point in the strictly bureaucratic administration, and in its monocratic form." It could be said that Weber tried to promote efficiency through technical proficiency, a disregard for personal feelings, and governance by rules and regulations. As bureaucracy develops towards perfection, the more it is dehumanized and the more completely it succeeds in eliminating from official business all purely personal, irrational and emotional elements. Weber said that bureaucracy was succeeding because of its machine-like qualities.

Around the same time, Frederick W. Taylor popularized "scientific management" in which man is thought of as mechanical and motivated by economic considerations. Though Taylor was primarily concerned with the production aspects of an organization, some of his proposals, such as functional foremanship and separation of planning and doing, had indirect implications to organization structure. The classical organization theory was further developed and refined by Mooney and Reiley, Fayol, Gulick, Urwick and others. They based their theory of departmentalization on the assumption that an organization, given an overall mission, will be able to identify the required tasks, allocate and coordinate these tasks by giving jobs to sections, place the section within units, unite the units within departments and coordinate departments under a board, all in the most economic manner. They thought of an organization as a rational instrument for implementing objectives and policies.[12]

The Behavioral Model

This model grew out of the increasing awareness of the role and needs of the person in an enterprise. Shetty and Carlisle describe this kind of organization primarily in terms of the way people function in it. Here is their summary:

The behavioral theory reacts to the excessive mechanistic structure and argues that an industrial organization should be viewed as a social

---

[12]Y. K. Shetty and Howard M. Carlisle, "A Contingency Model of Organization Design," *California Management Review*, vol. 15, no. 1, pp. 38-45.

system with at least two objectives: producing the product and generating and distributing satisfaction among employees (achieving both economic effectiveness and job satisfaction). Hence, an organization should be considered a social system which has both economic and social dimensions.

Behavioralists argue that effectiveness is achieved by arranging matters so that people feel that they count, that they belong, and that work can be made meaningful. The behavioralists do not necessarily reject the classical doctrine, but they feel that more goes into an organization design than rules, regulations and strict rationality. For instance, every member of any organization is unique to some degree, and all actions are not necessarily explained rationally. There is the element of subjectivity to an individual's actions: they are based on his perception and personal value system.

Behavioralists, at least the earlier ones, do not necessarily prescribe any one form of organization structure but believe it can be improved by modifying it in accordance with informal structure—through less narrow specialization and less emphasis on hierarchy, by permitting more participation in decision-making on the part of the lower ranks, and by a more democratic attitude on the part of the managers at all levels.[13]

The organic model

The struggle to integrate organizational needs more fully with the needs of human beings has led to another theory of organization. This attractive concept seems to provide for the maximum achievement of human potential, though how to manage such a system or ensure that an enterprise so designed reaches its objectives is yet uncertain. Shetty and Carlisle summarize:

> Recent years have seen the development of a form of organization structure based on behavioral theories called the organic organization—a structure in which there is a minimum of formal division of duties. According to this view, organizations should be composed of temporary task forces in which membership will shift as needs and problems change. Warren Bennis argues that bureaucracy (the classical structure) is too rigid to be serviceable in the time of rapid technological change and that it will therefore be replaced by the task-force type of organization. He says:
>
> First of all, the key word will be temporary. Organizations will become adaptive, rapidly changing temporary systems. Second, they will be organized around problems-to-be-solved. Third, these problems will be solved by relative groups of strangers who represent a diverse set of professional skills. Fourth, given the requirements of coordinating the various projects, articulating points or "linking pin" personnel will be necessary who can speak the diverse language of research and who can relay and mediate between the various project groups. Fifth, the groups will be conducted on organic rather than on mechanical lines; they will emerge and adapt to the problems, and leadership and influence will fall to those who seem most able to solve the problems rather than the programmed role expectations. People will be differentiated, not ac-

---

[13]Ibid.

cording to rank or roles, but according to skills and training. . . . Though no catchy phrase comes to mind, it might be called an organic-adaptive structure.[14]

Each of these three models of organization is an attempt to describe *order* (the relationships between people) in an organization. But none satisfactorily resolves the tension we have traced between the needs of people in an enterprise and the necessity for the enterprise to achieve its objectives. The classical model seems to ignore personal needs, but over the decades it has proved to be an effective way to organize an enterprise for the achievement of task objectives. The behavioral model is not really an ordering system at all; it is simply a series of affirmations about how people should be treated and involved. It is expected even by behavioral theorists that human concerns will be introduced into a bureaucratic organizational structure. The organic model is the most amorphous of them all. It is as yet still only theoretical; no body of knowledge growing out of actually running an organization as an organism has yet developed. As noted in the last chapter, the whole analogy between an organism and a social system is, at best, doubtful. The analogy between an organism with a single will and an organization composed of multiplied individuals with independent wills simply cannot be validly maintained.

But the struggle to find some integrative principle continues. Why?

Because, *in the world of enterprise, there is always tension, and usually conflict, between the priority an enterprise must give to achieving its objectives and the needs of its members for personal growth and well-being.* No system for resolving this conflict has been devised. It is in the nature of an enterprise to have task objectives, and for an organization to be successful these objectives must be reached. It is in the nature of human beings to have personal, psychological, and other needs that will to some extent conflict with the need of the enterprise to accomplish its tasks successfully.

Persons, or projects? That is the question.

While struggling to find a way to affirm *both* persons *and* projects, no one in the fields of the behavioral sciences or management theory has yet resolved the conflict. Nor has anyone been able to deny convincingly that, in the case of a conflict between the two, the nature of an enterprise demands that it favor the project.

---

[14]Ibid.

UNDERSTANDING ENTERPRISE

An enterprise exists primarily to achieve some task objective. It does not exist basically to meet the growth or psychological needs of its employees.

PROBE

▶ case histories
▶ discussion questions
▶ thought provokers
▶ resources

1. The survey given in this chapter leads the authors to the following simple conclusion: In an enterprise, people are necessarily a resource to be used. Workers in an enterprise can be viewed as means to an end, but never as the end itself.

   Do you agree or disagree? Give reasons for your answer.

2. Here are several other conclusions the authors might or might not draw from the discussion of enterprise to date:
   a. A Christian in an enterprise does not need to be concerned about the psychological needs of his employees.
   b. Treating people in a Christian manner in an enterprise would in fact make a manager less effective.
   c. Christians should be deeply concerned about the moral issues raised by this chapter.
   d. The church is different from all enterprise organizations because all its members are in fact *ends;* none are to be "used" by leaders as means.
   e. Behavioral scientists will probably one day find some organizational scheme that fully integrates projects and people and gives equal priority to each.

   With which of these conclusions do you think the authors would *not* agree? Revise them to express conclusions with which they might agree. With which of the above conclusions would you agree and why?

3. Contemporary management theory, especially in the 1970s, does suggest other directions not encompassed in our survey of the historic, or process, approach. Some of these are the quantitative approach, the behavioral approach, and the systems approach. Working to resolve the tensions that exist between proponents of these new approaches, Fred Luthans has suggested a "contingency theory" of management, which management practitioners have developed:

   Certain quantitative approaches worked in some situations with some types of problems but not in others. The same was true for behavior approaches. For example, job enrichment

170

seemed to work well with skilled technicians but not skilled machine operators.

Two of the difficulties encountered in practice were that the quantitative people could not overcome behavioral problems and the behavioral people could not overcome operations problems adaptable to quantitative solutions. In the 1970s it is becoming more and more apparent that neither the quantitative nor the behavioral approaches have all the answers for all situations.

Many of today's management theorists believe that a systems-based theory can solve the quantitative/behavioral dilemma.[15]

Luthans continues:

For example, bureaucracy was not able to cope with a highly dynamic situation; decentralization did not work well in a highly cybernated situation; and the free-form, matrix designs were not adaptable to a situation demanding cutbacks and stability. Even Warren Bennis, who has been a leading advocate of discarding classical, bureaucratically organized structures and replacing them with modern free-form, behaviorally oriented structures has recently retrenched. Ironically, because of his actual experience as a practitioner, he now admits that bureaucratic structures may be appropriate in certain situations.

The contingency designs are conditional in nature. The bureaucracy may work best in a stable situation and the free form in a dynamic situation. Technology, economic and social conditions, and human resources are some of the variables that must be considered in a contingent organization design.[16]

Luthans sounds optimistic as he highlights three contingency concepts developed by Fred Fiedler that appear to be helping pave a path out of the theory jungle:

Luthans comments:

In simple terms, the model states that a task-directed leader is most effective in very favorable and very unfavorable situations, but that a human relations-oriented leader is most effective in moderately favorable and moderately unfavorable situations. Of special interest, however, is his ability to classify situations according to the three dimensions of position power, acceptance by subordinates, and task definition. This type of classification is the necessary goal of any contingency approach.[17]

---

[15]Fred Luthans, "The Contingency Theory of Management: A Path Out of the Jungle," *Business Horizons*, 16 (June 1973): 70.

[16]Ibid., p. 71.

[17]Ibid.

FIGURE 24
THE CONTINGENCY MODEL OF LEADERSHIP

Task-Directed Leader	Human Relations-Oriented Leader		Task-Directed Leader
very favorable	moderately favorable	moderately unfavorable	very unfavorable

SITUATIONS

Three Classifications for Situations:
1. Position-power dimension
2. Acceptance-by-subordinate dimension
3. Task-definition dimension

—Fred Fiedler, *A Theory of Leadership Effectiveness* (New York: McGraw, 1967).

Luthans also suggests a model of behavioral change that he hopes will move management toward a contingency approach. Here he describes Organizational Behavior Modification (O.B. Mod.):

It can be used to train industrial supervisors through a process method of instruction to be contingency managers of their workers. Preliminary results of this program are very encouraging. The study has demonstrated that when first-line supervisors apply O.B. Mod. techniques to their subordinates, desirable job behaviors leading to improved performance can be accelerated through the use of reinforcement and undesirable behaviors can be decelerated through the use of punishment.

However, the key to the success of the approach depends upon the worker's ability to perceive the contingency that if he behaves a certain way, then his behavior will result in a certain consequence. The if-then contingency pattern used in O.B. Mod. is similar to the contingency approaches used in organizational design and leadership style.[18]

The third concept relating to this issue is quantitative, and involves its movement toward contingency. Here Luthans quotes Stanley Young, who says,

We must know under what conditions it is advisable to move from Linear Programming to rule of thumb and then back to Linear Programming. There is an over-concern with single decision rule, and we must learn how to use different combinations of rules under a variety of operating conditions.[19]

[18]Ibid., p. 72.
[19]Ibid.

172

In summary, Luthans looks back at what has happened in recent years with competing views of organizational management and then looks ahead optimistically.

The process path was split by the behavioral and quantitative paths. However, neither of these approaches by itself seems capable of leading management out of the jungle. Currently, the systems path seems to be drawing them together toward a unified theoretical development, but by the time the juncture is reached in the future, something may emerge which differs from the sum of the parts. This outcome is predicted to be the contingency theory of management.[20]

Look back over this brief discussion of contingency theory. Do you see any way in which it in fact resolves the essential conflict between the project and personal needs? Or is the contingency theory simply a model that promises managers a better way to use people and other resources that have always been subordinated to objectives in every organization?

---

[20]Ibid.

The traditional or "process" approach to management is often criticized by management theorists. Yet it is the system most used and most tested. It is, in a word, a system that incorporates the practical experience of decades of enterprise leadership and that has been refined and fine-tuned. It has weaknesses. But it works.

THE MANAGER'S DILEMMA

What's more, the approach is comprehensive and seems to cover most of the demands facing a manager.

Working within the framework of the process approach, let's see if we can understand the tasks facing the manager of any enterprise and see why "project versus people" places managers in such a terrible dilemma.

The process approach finds its roots in Fayol's five functions of management.[1] Today these five functions are generally identified as: planning, organizing, directing, controlling, and staffing. Let's look at each function separately and see the complex problems any manager must solve.

PLANNING

A good picture of the future gives managers a sense of security. They have some idea of what is likely to happen in and to their enterprise. All good managers struggle to build a picture of the future. Even a poor picture is better than no picture at all.

Some of the elements involved in planning the future are:

1. Corporate objectives
2. Company goals
3. Short range (usually one year) plans
4. Long range (usually three to five year) plans
5. Quantitative plans involving dollars or units produced
6. Narrative plans involving more subjective goals
7. Project matrices (see figure 25, page 178)
8. Plan integration
9. Involvement of executives as planners
10. Organization of plans for comparison with actual results
11. Corporate planning facets
12. Strategic planning process
13. Anticipatory decision making
14. Systems analysis and planning
15. Mathematical planning models
16. Internal and external environmental factors
17. Marketing plans
18. Planning staff
19. Personnel planning
20. Manufacturing-and-facilities planning
21. Financial planning (budget)

In working on all these plan elements, there are many issues that must be constantly kept in mind. Recently at the "Management Course for Presidents" sponsored by the Presidents Association, affiliated with the American Management Association, David S. Atkinson presented the following brief but helpful overview of the planning and preplanning process. He suggests that managers must constantly ask and seek to answer these questions:

_____
[1]See p. 161.

177

FIGURE 25
THREE MATRICES SHOWING PLANNING GRIDS[2]

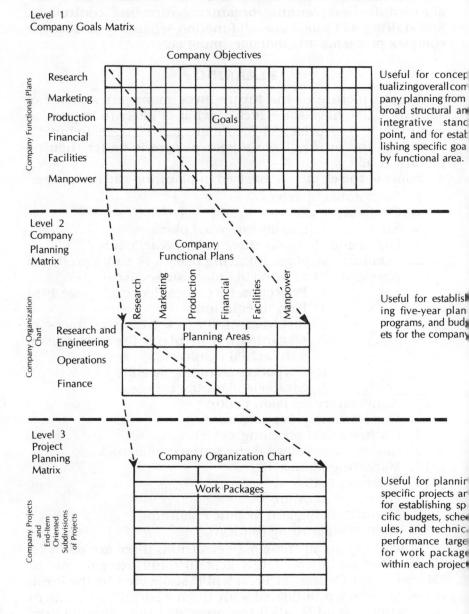

Level 1
Company Goals Matrix

Company Objectives

Company Functional Plans

Research
Marketing
Production
Financial
Facilities
Manpower

Goals

Useful for concep
tualizing overall com
pany planning from
broad structural an
integrative stand
point, and for estab
lishing specific goa
by functional area.

Level 2
Company
Planning
Matrix

Company
Functional Plans

Company Organization Chart

Research
Marketing
Production
Financial
Facilities
Manpower

Research and
Engineering

Operations

Finance

Planning Areas

Useful for establish
ing five-year plan
programs, and budg
ets for the company

Level 3
Project
Planning
Matrix

Company Organization Chart

Company Projects
and
End-Item
Oriented
Subdivisions
of Projects

Work Packages

Useful for plannin
specific projects ar
for establishing sp
cific budgets, sched
ules, and technic
performance targe
for work packag
within each project

[2]Bruce N. Baker, "Improving Essential Facets of Planning Integration."

178

1. Where are we?
2. Where are we going as we are?
3. Where do we want to go?
4. What may get us there?
5. How are we going to get there?
6. When will results be achieved?
7. Who is going to do it?
8. How much will it require of our resources?
9. Reassessment—can we do it?[3]

Certainly the planning dimension of a manager's responsibility is complex and difficult!

ORGANIZING

As we saw in the preceding chapter, organizational theory is changing very rapidly to adapt to changes in society and to integrate a growing body of behavioral science knowledge. The upshot has been the development of a number of ways in which to organize tasks and responsibility.

The classical system, represented in the typical pyramidal organizational chart, is only one option. It is, as Pastore suggests, "oriented toward control and stability, advocating such concepts as 'authority should equal responsibility,' 'line and staff,' 'functional division of labor,' 'unity of command,' and 'chain of command.'"[4]

What kind of organizational structure might a manager choose in a setting in which there was rapid change? Pastore describes the systems approach:

> The other half of the dichotomy is based mostly on an orientation toward change rather than control and stability. Rather than the classical "divisions of labor," this theory stresses the "integration" of knowledge; rather than rigidly defined authority-responsibility relationships, the systems theory imposes a participatory or "bargaining" organizational environment in which one's responsibility may purposefully exceed one's authority.[5]

Both approaches sound simple. But when we look at the patterns by which they are implemented, we realize how complex organizing can become. For instance, following the relatively simple chart below, showing how the classical system might be designed, is a somewhat more complex chart showing a possible design of the systems approach.

---

[3]David S. Atkinson, "Planning—Long and Short Range," from the Management Course for Presidents (The Presidents Association, affiliated with the American Management Association), pp. 11-12.

[4]Joseph M. Pastore, "Organizational Metamorphosis: A Dynamic Model," *Marquette Business Review*, vol. 15, no. 1 (Spring 1971), pp. 17-30.

[5]Ibid.

FIGURE 26
CLASSICAL STRUCTURE OF ORGANIZATION[6]

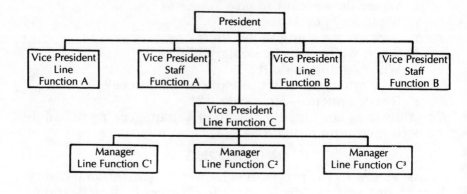

FIGURE 27
SYSTEMS STRUCTURE OF ORGANIZATION[7]

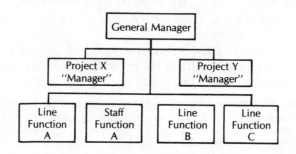

The manager soon realizes, however, that there are many more people and functions to integrate into his organization than are shown on these simplified charts. As specific projects are undertaken in an enterprise, the organization of its personnel and resources for the task can become tremendously complicated. For instance, a matrix-type project structure is shown in the figure below. (*Matrix* here simply means "the rectangular arrangement into rows and columns.") See how complicated the interrelationships have become.

[6]Ibid.
[7]Ibid.

FIGURE 28
MATRIX-TYPE PROJECT STRUCTURE OF ORGANIZATION[8]

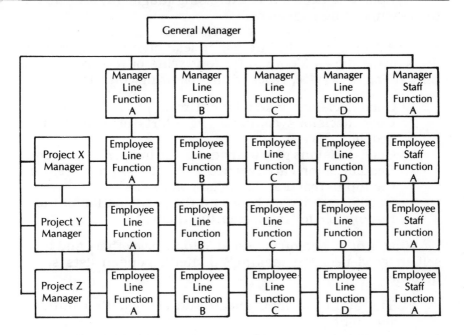

Much could be said about the weakness of each of these and other structures currently in vogue. But what is significant is that the manager is faced with complex decisions in the exercise of his responsibility. Typically, managers tend to follow the traditional structures and to choose the weaknesses with which they are familiar. But they must make a choice.

DIRECTING

Directing is related to making choices or decisions. In any situation the manager must either make decisions or involve others in the process of decision making so as to achieve company objectives.

Lawrence Appley has described "the truly desirable leadership situation" as one in which "a strong individual who is fully conscious of the values of and earnestly seeks the thinking and contributions of other people, has the courage to make a decision when it should be made even if it is contrary to the opinion of the group.[9]

---

[8]Ibid.

[9]Lawrence A. Appley, "Decision Making," from the Management Course for Presidents, p. 1.

181

To Appley "a decision is exercising judgment, and this is the essence of management."

Actually, a manager needs the ability not only to make good decisions himself, but also to lead others to make good decisions. Charles Moore, after four years of research at the United Parcel Service, reached the following conclusions:

1. Good decisions take a lot of time.
2. Good decisions combine the efforts of a number of people.
3. Good decisions give individuals the freedom to dissent.
4. Good decisions are reached without any pressure from the top to reach an artificial consensus.
5. Good decisions are based on the participation of those responsible for implementing them.[10]

What kind of person is best able to involve others and himself in good decision making? J. Keith Louden lists seven qualities:

1. The ability to look ahead and see what's coming— foresight
2. Steadiness, with "patience and persistence and courage"
3. A buoyant spirit that in spite of cares generates confidence
4. Ingeniousness, the ability to solve problems soundly yet creatively
5. The ability to help others
6. Righteousness, the willingness to do the right thing and speak the truth
7. Personal morality of a quality that commands the respect of others[11]

Yet even this paragon cannot function well without person-to-person and group skills, through which he develops skills in and an understanding of communication.

CONTROLLING

D. A. Jaquith defines control as "the procedures used to assure that performance conforms to plan." It is "the means by which delegation is possible while retaining responsibil-

---

[10]Charles W. L. Foreman, "Managing a Decision Into Being," from the Management Course for Presidents, pp. 3-4.

[11]J. Keith Louden, "Leadership," from the Management Course for Presidents, pp. 10-11.

ity."[12] This definition of control rests on the reality that a manager can delegate authority to somebody else, allowing him to accomplish tasks and carry out duties. But the manager will always retain ultimate responsibility for the tasks being satisfactorily completed and the objectives being reached.

How can the manager carry out this responsibility? It is best exercised when planning, organization, and control functions are interrelated. So the manager must design delegation, feedback, and corrective action systems that operate in a constant circular flow.

There are a number of types of control systems available to the manager. Jaquith lists some of the types of control that can be used:

A. Continuing controls—designed to keep effort on the track:
   1. Objectives should be clearly defined.
   2. Policies—rules or laws to be followed en route toward objectives—should be in writing and should clearly specify intent, not detail.
   3. Procedures should specify the manner in which an activity should be accomplished—the best practice known at the moment, developed through activity analysis with the objective of doing what is needed and not one thing more:
      a. Does the specific action contribute toward the goal?
      b. Is it necessary?
   4. Position descriptions—in writing—should define responsibility, authority, and relationships.
   5. An agreement between a manager and an individual subordinate as to what performance will be satisfactory should also be in writing. Such an agreement:
      a. assures common understanding
      b. promotes a balanced effort
      c. provides a basis for review
      d. stimulates self-appraisal
      e. improves attitudes and relationships
   6. Budgets or financial plans should be geared to individual responsibilities.
   7. Reporting procedures should be created to identify deviations from the plan.

---

[12]D. A. Jaquith, "Control" from the Management Course for Presidents, p. 1.

   8. Incentive systems should be designed to reward
      good performance.
B. Warning controls—designed to alert the manager to
   the need for action—should be provided.
   1. Controls that are primarily numerical:
      a. timely and adequate data on results
      b. reports on deviations from the plan
      c. progress reports on specific programs
      d. critical item tabulations—orders received,
         backlog, inventory levels, rejects, accidents, etc.
   2. Other warning controls:
      a. performance reviews
      b. progress reports
      c. personal observation[13]

These disciplines are essential to a well-run enterprise. All
too often the delegation of authority and the moving of tasks
from the superior's desk to the subordinate's desk is not followed up with appropriate supervision—supervision based on
sound, easy-to-follow, and simple information.

Unfortunately most control systems have an unavoidable
gap between the time a problem appears and the time it can be
corrected. Yet, as Koontz and Bradspies note, relatively few
future-directed control systems have been devised. They
suggest that

> perhaps the most widely used is the continual development and revision
> of various kinds of forecasts, utilizing current expectancies to forecast
> probable results, comparing these with performance desired, and then
> developing programs to avoid undesired events.[14]

Once again the complexity of the manager's task is at least
glimpsed as we see a few of the issues related to control in an
enterprise.

STAFFING

Many top managers feel that their most important resource is people. Therefore selecting and training the people
in an enterprise is perhaps the most significant of all management functions. It has been said that if a company has the
right people, the other resources come more easily.

The complexity and importance of this task is shown in
the chart on page 185, which gives an overview of the relationship between manpower planning and corporate planning as
a whole.

---

[13]Ibid., p. 3-5.
[14]Harold Koontz and Robert W. Bradspies, "Managing Through Feedfor-
ward Control," *Business Horizons*, vol. 15, no. 3 (June, 1972), pp. 25-36.

CORPORATE MANPOWER PLANNING CYCLE[15]

Corporate Policy

Corporate objectives and goals (direction of movement)
Strategic timing
Condition of the market
Availability of product
Readiness of process
Availability of manpower
Availability of financial resources
State of the technology

Corporate Planning

Economic Forecasts
Market Forecasts
Facilities Planning
Research and Development
Investment Planning
Systems Planning

Manpower Requirements (Forecasts)

Expected occupational mix (range and distribution of skills)
Capital substitutions and product and process adaptation to manpower supply and cost
Changes in organizational arrangements
Productivity forecast

Converted into budget

Manpower Management to Meet Requirements

Utilization of current work force for maximum current efficiency and capacity to meet future needs.

Organizational Arrangements	Manpower Allocation Procedures	Aids to Sustained High Performance

a. Optimal placement of man in job
   Union-management relations (shop rules)
   Effective leadership
   Adaptation of organization and leadership to interaction of technician and workers
   Cooperative work relationships
b. Vertical and lateral organizational mobility
   Wage and salary flexibility
   Adaptable job ladders and seniority provisions
   Up-to-date skills and knowledge of work force (job and man information)
c. Training and education; personal and organizational adaptability to change
   Reward systems consistent with organizational goals and individual needs and aspirations
   Optimal turnover and absenteeism rates

Developing work force needed in future through human resource development and recruiting.

Internal Supply	External Supply
Hiring criteria	Hiring criteria
Wage required	Wage required
Cost to train	Cost to train
Screening procedure	Screening procedure
Search cost (locate and select)	Search cost (locate and select)
Time to locate and make ready	Time to locate and make ready
Availability for the job opening	Availability for the job opening
Quality and skill	Entry occupation
Shop rules	Quality and skill
	Shop rules
Make	Buy

Performance and budget review

[15]Frank H. Cassell. "Manpower Administration: a New Role in Corporate Management." *Personnel Administration*. vol. 34. no. 6 (November-December 1971). pp. 33-37.

In many companies personnel selection is becoming a more central and involved part of the total corporate operation. Sensitivity to human development, lagging quality in performance, absenteeism, and carelessness—not to mention expanding federal requirements—have made top management conscious of the need to be concerned about its employees.

Personnel groups were long regarded as a kind of second cousin among corporate departments. They are increasingly being staffed by highly competent leaders and highly qualified assistants.

WHAT IS THE MANAGER'S TASK?

Put most simply, "managing" (the act of leading an enterprise) can be defined as getting things done through another person in the most efficient way. I am managing well when I am able to get accomplished by other people subtasks that, when completed, constitute the completion of that whole for which I am responsible. Doing the task myself is not good management.

Management can be defined more gently. But ultimately it means the use of other people to reach my objectives.

My use of others need not be unchristian. In fact I may and should operate, as Louden insists, in a fully "righteous" and completely "moral" way. But at the same time I need to face the fact that in managing I am unquestionably subordinating people to projects. I am ordering their efforts, not for their own personal growth or development, but for the achievement of the objectives of the enterprise.

I need to face one other fact, demonstrated fully in this chapter's review of management functions. Management is a demanding and complex task. If I am to manage well, I must be responsible for planning, organizing, directing, controlling, and staffing. Yet each of these areas of management is complex. *There are so many factors involved that it is inconceivable that I should be able to deal with them all and not, in at least some cases, come into conflict with some worker's personal psychological needs.* And this is the manager's dilemma.

In spite of the insistent voices of the behavioralists that personal needs be fully integrated with the operation of an enterprise and in spite of a Christian concern for individuals in the organization, I will certainly find at times that my responsibility to manage effectively conflicts with the real or perceived needs of others.

186

The dilemma comes when I face this conflict and am forced to decide. When the conflict is irreconcilable, what do I do? Do I act in the best interests of the enterprise (and of all the people within and affected by it)? Or do I act in the best interests of the individual(s) whose needs are not being met, or who may even be to some extent harmed by acting in the best interests of the enterprise? It is idealistic and admirable to say that we must synthesize the well-being of both project and people. But it is at the same time unrealistic. In the real world, the nature and complexity of enterprise management and the nature and complexity of humankind simply do not blend.

PROBE

▶ *case histories*
▶ *discussion questions*
▶ *thought provokers*
▶ *resources*

1. If you were the manager in the dilemma stated in the last paragraph, how would you decide? For the project? Or for the employees? Why?

2. In several earlier chapters we have insisted that the church is not an organization but an organism, and that its priority therefore is its people.

   Suppose that you are the pastor or a board member of a local congregation. You attend a seminar in which the management principles surveyed in this chapter are presented as "the scientific way to administer a local church." Tell how you would evaluate what the seminar leaders are advocating in regard to the following:
   a. Its short-range impact on the numerical growth of the congregation
   b. Its short-range impact on the relationship of the leaders of the congregation to its members
   c. Its short-range impact on the attitude of the members of the congregation toward the leaders
   d. Its long-range impact on the ministry of the leaders to the people of the congregation
   e. Its long-range impact on the ministry of members of the congregation to its leaders and other members
   f. Its long-range impact on the awareness of all in the congregation that Jesus Christ is the living head of the church

PART 2

UNDERSTANDING ENTERPRISE

A Description of Enterprise
The Great Conflict
The Manager's Dilemma
Enterprise as a Ministry Tool

We have argued that organizations and enterprises are intrinsically different from organisms and have insisted that the body of Christ must be led as an organism and organized on organismic principles.

Does this mean that Christians can never use enterprise theories? Is there something morally "wrong" about the enterprise approach?

ENTERPRISE AS A MINISTRY TOOL

We want to make a recommemdation that may be somewhat surprising: While we must always protect the body nature of the church itself, we will also want to encourage Christians who are called to ministry tasks to utilize the disciplines of enterprise! How to do this and still protect the integrity of the body is the major concern of this chapter.

Let's begin by exploring a myth. It's a myth perpetuated by a number of Christian writers, including Engstrom and Dayton in their book on management. It's a myth summed up in the heading of the first section of their first chapter, "Christian Organizations Are Different." Here's what they say:

Christian organizations *are* different—or at least they should be! They are different because they have a higher allegiance than the basic purpose of the organization. They work on the assumption that they are doing something, are part of something, that has an eternal value. They are different because the individuals in the organization share this common allegiance to a "God who is there." And because they have this higher and common purpose, they assume a moral and ethical level which should always transcend their short-term goals."[1]

In a later chapter, the authors quote from a letter by David Secunda, vice-president of the American Management Association, who seems to agree that organizations and management itself can take on a moral or immoral quality, a Christian or non-Christian character:

Management, as I see it, contains nothing that is incompatible with Christian principles or beliefs. It is a means to an end—not an end unto itself—and does not pursue an agreement on ends. At its core is the effort to enhance the human potential and without this, it becomes a box of tools and techniques, useful but also subject to good intelligent misuse. Likewise there is no excuse to justify bad or ill-managed Christian organizations. Believers have no more license to be ineffective when dealing with human resources than does a surgeon. Lives are at stake in both cases. But management as a process can benefit from change or an additional dimension. One such is a sounder being that would emerge from a blending of management and Christian fundamentals. We have not done this but there is no reason why you shouldn't try. However, it can't be done from books and computers, even though they have a place. The understanding of each alone takes much of a man—to do both demands unusual commitment, but the prize may be worth the try.[2]

CHAPTER **14**

Engstrom and Dayton seem to suggest that *organizations* are Christian or non-Christian and can take on a moral or immoral quality. Secunda seems to say that *management as a system* can do the same. This is the myth. It's a myth rooted in attributing the qualities that describe persons to organizations and systems.

In point of fact, it is only persons who are Christian or non-Christian, moral or immoral. "Organizations" have no moral or Christian qualities; the people who run them do.

[1]Ted W. Engstrom and Edward R. Dayton. *The Art of Management for Christian Leaders* (Waco, Texas: Word, 1976), pp. 15-16.
[2]Ibid., pp. 37-38.

Organizations have no objectives; the objectives are those of the leaders. Management is neither moral nor immoral. It is the manager to whom such terms can apply. Organization and management are in essence amoral.

Historically the term "Christian organization" has been used to describe organizations whose stated objectives are evangelistic or in some other way Christian. For instance my objectives may be to provide Christian education for future church leaders. I set up an organization designed to help me reach that objective. To many it is this objective that makes my organization "Christian."

But this is a serious confusion. Suppose that in the process of building a school and staffing it I become involved in lying and breaking securities laws. In that case the means I chose to use would be immoral, or unchristian. Is my organization still a "Christian" organization?

Or suppose that as a Christian I am led by God to establish an organization whose objective is to provide shelter (build homes). Is my organization "secular" or "non-Christian" in spite of the fact that I was led by God into the undertaking and my objectives involve serving people and meeting basic needs? Or is my management "secular" if I use good management principles and in the process treat people according to every biblical principle governing interpersonal relationships?

These illustrations should make it clear that organizations and the management processes used to run them are neither "Christian" nor "non-Christian," "moral" nor "immoral" in themselves. It is the people who set the objectives of the organization and the people who choose the means to reach those objectives who behave in Christian or non-Christian, moral or immoral, ways.

It should be clear that there is nothing intrinsically wrong in a Christian's use of the *tools* of management to set and achieve ministry objectives. We cannot and do not dismiss management processes and organizational structures because they are "secular" and somehow "unspiritual." Like any tool, be it ax or automobile, enterprise theory can be used rightly or wrongly. What makes the use right or wrong is not the system itself but the way in which it is used by persons.

THE CHRISTIAN IN A SECULAR ENTERPRISE

Management tools can be used by Christians in the "secular world" in distinctively Christian ways. This is the first implication of the fact that organizations and enterprises are "amoral."

A second implication, to be explored later, is that enterprise tools can be used by Christians to accomplish Christian task objectives. We'll examine the second implication later. For now let's see how a Christian uses enterprise tools in a "secular vocation."

As a Christian businessman, Clyde struggled for years with his desire to obey God and his desire to implement biblical teachings in his everyday life as the manager of an enterprise. As he struggled and studied, invariably his commitment found expression in the way in which he treated people in the process of managing his enterprise. Every teaching in the Bible related to interpersonal relationships should continue to guide him in enterprise. Furthermore he has discovered that obedience to these principles greatly enhances his effectiveness as a business leader. To this day he has not discovered any conflict between his efficiency and effectiveness in management, and the teaching of the Bible. To put it another way, he has never had to compromise the goals of good organization (the most efficient relationship between people, money, materials, and facilities for the accomplishment of an objective) while complying with biblical standards of Christian behavior and lifestyle.

Who are the people with whom the Christian manager must concern himself? First, there are the people who have invested in the enterprise. These are the persons who own it or who have bought stock. In the case of a nonprofit corporation, where there is no stock or investors, this group would be the contributors, who provide the money necessary to operate. Second, there are those who work in the enterprise carrying out the various functions necessary to achieve the task objective. The third group is composed of the people being served by the products or services provided by the enterprise. The fourth group is composed of people who live in the community in which the enterprise operates. The Christian manager must seek the highest good of the people in all four groups in compliance with Jesus' commandment that we "love one another." As we study Jesus' concept of love, we realize that love is not simply a feeling toward people. Instead, it is a manner in which we behave toward people, the way we treat them. We are to treat others so that their needs are met and they are served.

Obviously the Christian manager has a delicate balance to maintain. He must be sensitive to the impact of his actions and decisions on every group. He cannot favor one in a way that would abuse another. For instance, let's say the purpose of a particular organization is to provide transportation for the people of a certain city. Let's say a Christian manager has a person working for him. (To make the case more difficult, let's suggest the person is both a Christian brother and a friend.) If that Christian employee is doing an inept job in the role assigned to him, he would quite possibly be damaging the quality of transportation being provided for those the organization serves. How will the Christian manager handle the problem? He will, of course, provide all the help possible to assist the employee to grow in his ability to do the job assigned. But what if in spite of help the worker remains inept? One temptation is to rationalize, to argue that the employee is a Christian brother and needs the manager's counsel and support and the money the job provides. But wouldn't this be a violation of the Christian responsibility to be a good steward to those served by the enterprise? It is not easy to make such decisions. But recognizing the obligation as a Christian to serve all those whose lives are affected by the enterprise provides a very different motivation for the action finally taken than would the motivation all too often ascribed to those in business: personal profit alone.

The fundamental Christian consideration, then, in viewing organizations and enterprises seems to be this: Do they have Christian people with Christian motives who are treating people in a Christian way in both establishing objectives and selecting means? The basic issue is not whether an organization is "Christian" or "secular." God can call a person to an enterprise that provides evangelistic crusades to serve people and the Lord, or he can call a person to an enterprise that serves the shelter needs of people as a means of serving the Lord. Scripture makes it clear that God calls people to a variety of tasks. In no way is God's calling to an enterprise less "Christian" than a calling to a full-time ministry in missions or church leadership.

In summary, then, organizational systems and management systems are amoral tools. It is the use of them that is Christian or non-Christian. In the hands of saints, the use should be good. In the hands of non-Christians it may sometimes be bad. Obviously the same could be said about cars, hotel rooms, or radios.

ENTERPRISE AS A MINISTRY TOOL

At this point we have established enterprise and management as neutral tools that can be used in good or bad ways, depending on the motivation and commitments of the managers. We must now raise a more difficult issue. If an enterprise is not morally *wrong*, why have we so adamantly insisted that it not be confused with an organism? Why have we insisted that the church not be ordered as an organization?

In other words, if enterprise and management systems are effective ways to achieve objectives, why shouldn't the church use them as tools to accomplish those goals the Bible says Christ seeks to accomplish in our world?

For an answer, let's review some basic concepts and then suggest specifically how enterprise fits into the area of mission.

The church gathered

When Christians come together to be the body of Christ, they are in reality members of an organism. The principles of order and leadership in a living organism are different from, and stand in contrast to, the principles of order and leadership in a traditional organization.

The key differences that we have explored in this section between an organism and an organization are found (1) in their priorities and (2) in their natures. The first priority of an organism must always be the nurture, growth, and maturity of itself and its members. The first priority of an enterprise must always be the successful achievement of its task objectives. As we saw in chapters 13 and 14, there is always a tension in these between people and task priorities, a conflict that management theorists have not been able to resolve, although they have made many attempts to do so.

One proposed solution has been to model organizations on the pattern of biological organisms. This has proved impossible to accomplish in practice and it has been criticized theoretically on the basis of compelling observation. The members of an organization are separate individuals, each with personal will and purposes, but the members of an organism are not. By nature, then, organisms and organizations are essentially different at this critical point. So the analogy between social organizations and living organisms is invalid. The *types of order* within the two systems are not and cannot be the same.

The thing that sets the church of Christ apart and makes it unique is that, because each Christian as he or she matures is able to bring his or her will into submission to the will of Christ, *only the church has the potential of functioning as an organism!* When the Bible teaches that we *are* a living organism, the body of Christ, we are being taught that a completely different kind of functioning (and thus leadership) is to be characteristic of the church, one that can never be applied to any other association of human beings.

When the church gathers to be the church, then, and when believers are functioning as body members, the principles governing our lives together will be body principles, not enterprise principles. We cannot use enterprise systems with their different order and priorities to function or grow as the body. We must, because we operate with different priorities and on a different order, search the Scriptures to discover those principles of leadership and relationship that are uniquely appropriate for our life as an organism.

Much of the failure of the church in the world can be traced to the attempt of its leaders to import enterprise systems and tools into the body. The body must "make increase of itself in love" in God's own organismic way. The ways of an enterprise will not work within the church.

The Christian in mission

It is a common thing to make a distinction between the "church gathered" and the "church scattered," or "the church in mission."

This is, however, a very dangerous way of conceptualizing. Earlier in this chapter we argued that it is an error to speak of a "Christian organization," because it is the people in an organization who behave in a Christian or non-Christian, a moral or immoral way. The "organization" cannot be personalized as if it were an entity, and personal characteristics should not be ascribed to it. We want to suggest that the same fallacy is repeated when someone speaks of "the church in mission." It is not "the church" that is involved in a mission. It is Christians, who are members of the church. *The church is the body.* Individual Christians, and groups of Christians, may—and should—set out to accomplish those tasks to which God calls them. And when setting out to accomplish a task, these Christians can and should utilize good enterprise management tools. But the local body should never be shaped as an organization, nor as the local body set out to accomplish tasks. The local body must seek always and only to be the body of Christ and to live as an organism, building itself and all its parts to maturity. As an organism, the local body is not to take on tasks or the enterprise form. Instead, we can be free to encourage individuals and groups of Christians to hear God's call to mission and in answering that call to organize themselves as an enterprise (and use all the tools of effective management) to reach the objectives to which God calls them.

How can the church protect its identity as a body, and still encourage a godly use of enterprise principles by individuals and groups of Christians called by God to mission? The details will be explored thoroughly in the fourth section of this book. The general principles, however, can be stated here. Put simply, the church's identity and function as a body is protected when its leaders

1. accept as their responsibility the fostering of those relationships that make for a healthy and responsive organism
2. reject the ownership of systems designed to accomplish tasks
3. encourage others to accept responsibility for ministry tasks to which they are called by God

For instance, let's suppose that a congregation faces a situation in which there is a need for a strong peer fellowship group for adolescents. Several members of the body, all of whom have children who are young teen-agers, express that concern. One or two even consider leaving the body to find a local congregation that is organized to provide that "youth group" service.

In the traditional approach, which is organization and enterprise oriented, the leaders of the congregation learn of the need for a youth program, prepare a job description, consider an addition to the staff and funds from the church budget, assign search committees, and interview candidates. In this pattern the leaders of the congregation see themselves (and the church) as responsible to achieve the objective of meeting the peer-group needs of their adolescents. To reach that objective the church adopts an enterprise approach. This is how the church has characteristically handled such problems, and, in doing so, has lost God's unique, organismic way of meeting needs. The church has become an institution rather than a living body, and the leaders of the church have become controllers of an enterprise rather than ministers who lift up Jesus Christ as head.

What is the alternative? First, the leaders of the congregation must refuse to accept as their responsibility the ownership or control of any system (such as a "youth group") that is called into being to meet a task objective. At the same time, the leaders must recognize the validity of the objective and the need for the task to be accomplished; so they should support and encourage those God has called or will call to reach that objective!

Second, the leaders should approach the need in a body way. They should share the need with the members of the congregation, explain the problem, and ask the whole group to pray that Christ the head will meet the need. The expectation is that Jesus the head will make His will known through members of the body and act through members of the body. Prayer and sharing the need should result in individuals' sensing the burden and call of God for this task. The leaders should help *them* plan and pray about how to achieve the objective. Perhaps three couples will be called to develop a "Young Life" or "Campus Life" type of ministry to the youth of the congregation and community. Church leaders can encourage, support with their prayers and advice, and in other ways help the mission team provide a successful ministry to youth.

But who *owns* the youth ministry? The church? No, the team God has called to that ministry owns it. Is it a church program? No, it is a ministry of certain members of the church but it is not a church program. The ministry team is responsible to God for the conduct of its mission. The leaders of the church are responsible to provide a body context in which these ministry team members can grow and mature in Christ and become even more responsive and obedient to the Lord.

Now it should be clear from what we have seen in this section that the ministry team may well want to use (in a Christian way) enterprise management principles in carrying out its mission. After all, there are people, materials, money, and facilities to be related to one another in such a way that the product or service can be the most successfully provided. Enterprise management principles are simply tools to utilize in accomplishing tasks. In fact, in any mission or ministry that Christians undertake they should be free to use enterprise management principles as tools in a distinctively Christian way.

But the church itself is *not* called by God to accomplish such tasks. The church is an organism and as such it must build itself up in love by promoting individual and corporate maturity. For this priority to be successfully accomplished, church leaders must function in a body way and never be drawn into the conduct or control of systems (organizations) designed to achieve task objectives.

By clearly separating the ownership and control of all missions of Christians from the church leadership and freeing the church leadership to function in a body rather than an enterprise way, the church is enabled to function as an organism.

God calls Christians to mission. He does *not* call "the church" to mission.

Minimum maintenance functions

We have noted that churches are typically networks of enterprise systems, with their "spiritual leaders" functioning as a board that controls multiplied missions or ministries. This characteristic of congregations is reflected all too clearly in the organizational charts we see in texts on church administration and in those charts included in the constitutions of too many congregations.

Many would argue immediately (and correctly) that to remove *all* enterprise systems (task and objective focused systems) would in fact make it impossible for the church to function as an organism. For instance, most local congregations meet in a building that they own or rent. One necessary task is to raise a budget to make the required payments so that the place will be available. Since this is clearly a task or objective, enterprise principles will need to be used. Someone will need to be there to pass the plate or have envelopes printed, to count the money given, to bank it, and to write checks.

The point is valid. Some things need to be organized along enterprise lines to make it possible for the body to function as a body in the real world. And logically the leaders of the church will ultimately be responsible for seeing that these functions are successfully carried out. Such things, and such things only, are minimum maintenance functions, that is, *tasks absolutely necessary for the body to gather as an organism.*

But the question we are raising is this: Does the fact that spiritual leaders will ultimately own or control *some* enterprise kinds of functions invalidate our distinction between organism and organization? If some, why not all? Wouldn't the fact of such maintenance systems suggests that enterprise management approaches are justified *throughout* the church?

The answer to this kind of question is, we believe, obvious. Ownership or control by the spiritual leaders is required *only* when a system is necessary to enable the church to meet and function as the body. Most of the things Christians do, do not require such control. Even such activities as the distribution of the resources of the church are seen in Acts as an enterprise system. When the Greek-speaking widows did not receive their fair share of food and support, the apostles refused to accept the responsibility, but led the congregation to set up a team of deacons who would be responsible for this program.

This left the apostles free to "devote [them]selves to prayer and to the ministry of the Word" (Acts 6:4).

The *priority,* as we have seen in this chapter, is the key. Is the objective of a group of people to deliver some goods or a service to others? If so, it is immediately placed in a task framework, and the utilization of enterprise principles is valid. In such a case, the spiritual leaders of the church will realize that their calling is *not* to control that ministry but to provide a body context in which those who are responsible for the ministry can grow in Christ and thus be enabled to conduct their enterprise in a more godly and responsive way.

What minimum maintenance functions should be under the control of the spiritual leaders of the congregation? Only those, we repeat, that are essential for the congregation to function as a body. Let's look at one or two illustrations of what are *not* minimum maintenance functions.

One we have already given: the formation of a "youth group" so as to build a Christian peer group for teens. If this is a need in a particular congregation, then Christ can be expected to work through the members of His body to achieve the objective. The spiritual leaders of the church can encourage the members of the body to pray about possible involvement and see if Christ may be calling them to that ministry. When He has called out a ministry team, that team will then be responsible to Christ to achieve the objective. The spiritual leadership will not control the project; those ministering will be responsible for it.

Is the Sunday school such an integral part of the program of the church, one of those "minimum maintenance functions"? We do not believe so. The Sunday school is an enterprise. Its objective is to deliver Bible teaching to learners of all ages. Members of a local body may and should be called to be part of that ministry. But those who are called to that ministry should also be responsible for conducting it.

What is disturbing about this point of view is, of course, that we are all afraid of what might go wrong if we abandon control. In human organizations this is a very valid fear. We cannot, in any social organization composed of individuals with independent wills, simply turn people loose! *And unless there is a supernatural dimension to the church of Jesus Christ, we cannot afford to "turn people loose" in our churches either!*

But this is the whole point. The church *is* supernatural. No human being is the head of the church, whether he is a pastor, a board member, or a bishop. Jesus Christ is the living head of His body the church and He is able to express His will in and through us as we surrender ourselves—and our control—to Him.

In essence, by using enterprise principles to let church leaders control others in the church, we place chains on Jesus. We are struggling to retain what He asks us to surrender—control. For it is Jesus who is Lord.

Think of it for a moment.

Jesus is Lord.

We speak it in our confessions.

Jesus is Lord.

We sing it in our services.

He is Lord.

We print it boldly in our doctrinal statements.

Jesus is Lord!

Why, then, do we fear to surrender control, which Christ never intended us to have, to the One who we say is Lord? Why can't we trust Him to work in us and in other people?

We *can* trust Jesus to be Lord of our lives and the Lord of our brothers and sisters. We can trust Jesus to be "head over everything for the church, which is His body." In the next section of this text we will explore ways to practice the lordship of Christ in the spiritual leadership of His church.

PROBE

▶ *case histories*
▶ *discussion questions*
▶ *thought provokers*
▶ *resources*

1. Make a list of all the "programs" in your local church. Include all agencies and activities in which there is a responsibility (or "authority") relationship that might be shown on the congregation's organizational chart.

   Which of the ministries are really "maintenance functions" (necessary for the congregation to gather and function as the body of Christ)? Which could be so structured as to be "owned" by those responsible for the conduct of the ministry and not controlled by "the church"?

2. The chart on page 202 indicates that most churches will function somewhere on a continuum from *organism* to *organization*. Even churches functioning almost entirely as organisms will have "pockets of organization" carrying out the minimum maintenance functions discussed in this chapter. At the same time, most churches functioning in an organization mode will have pockets of organism.

201

FIGURE 30
ORGANISM-ORGANIZATION CONTINUUM

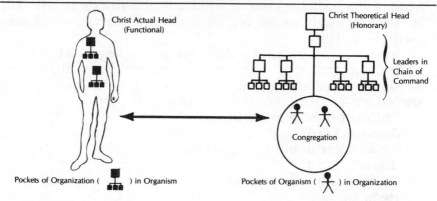

Christ Actual Head (Functional)

Christ Theoretical Head (Honorary)

Leaders in Chain of Command

Congregation

Pockets of Organization ( ) in Organism

Pockets of Organism ( ) in Organization

It's important for us to be aware of where our own local church is along this continuum, and to be aware of the key characteristics of each system.

The organism system is one in which task activities are carried out by believers in an atmosphere of (1) maximum freedom, (2) a high sense of ownership by those conducting the ministry, and (3) a minimum of control by elders or other official church leaders.

When do we move from one system to the other? We cannot define movement strictly in terms of the agencies that a church has or does not have. Instead we must define the movement in terms of the *perceptions of the body members.* If the members or the leaders of the church conceive of the church as a well-run institution under a pastor or leaders, then the body will function as an institution not an organism. If on the other hand the members perceive the church as a fellowship, in which each is to be actively involved in ministering under the leadership of Jesus, then the body will function as an organism and not an organization.

With the tools this continuum concept provides,

a. Develop a questionnaire to determine what perception of the body the leaders or members of your church have.

b. Administer the questionnaire to a number of members.

c. Try to determine how and/or why these people see their church as they do.

d. Determine what strategies (if any) the results of the questionnaire might suggest for use in developing a strong organism perception.

3. Make a telephone survey of at least half the members of your congregation. Ask each of them what he or she is presently doing to express his faith or to serve others. Make a list of these ministries and their objectives. Also note any impact of the ministries that those you call can report.

What impressions do you have of the objectives Jesus is currently reaching through people in your congregation?

4. The following is a brief list of the *key concepts* found in this section of the text. Write a paragraph on each concept, telling what it implies for leadership in an enterprise and/or in the church. If you are unable to define clearly in your own mind the issues raised by a key concept, review this section of the text.

KEY CONCEPTS

a. In any enterprise there is an essential conflict between task accomplishment and the needs of the people who serve in the enterprise.

b. There is *order* in both ogranizations and organisms, but the order is of an essentially different character.

c. An enterprise can never be an organism, even though managers may express Christian concern for its members.

d. The tools or disciplines of an enterprise can be used by Christians both in "secular" work and in Christian missions.

e. Spiritual leaders need to encourage members of Christ's body to accept responsibility for the achievement of those tasks Jesus wants to accomplish in our world through His body.

f. Spiritual leaders in the church should not accept responsibility for, or take control of, task-focused ministries or missions, as though these could be "church programs."

g. Spiritual leaders in the church must recognize that they are body leaders and that the "church" cannot be shaped to accomplish any task/product/service objective.

h. There is no such thing as a "Christian organization" or "the church in mission." Such concepts are myths based on a very serious misunderstanding of reality.

5. For many years some in Christian circles have criticized "parachurch" organizations. They have argued that if the church were doing its job, there would be no need for such organizations as Young Life or Campus Life (Youth for Christ).

Suppose that you are speaking with a person who comes out with strong criticism of a parachurch organization, questioning whether it should ever have been begun and whether it should be supported. This individual argues that the organization should *not* be supported by Christians but that it should be disbanded and the same ministry undertaken "by the church," since "the church is the only institution besides marriage ever established by God."

How would you react to his assumptions in the light of what

has been said in this chapter? Write out a detailed, thorough response to him.

6. At this point in our study, do you personally feel it would be *easier* to function as an enterprise leader or as a body leader in the local church? Why? (Specify clearly the factors you considered in determining what "easier" and "harder" mean to you.)

7. Do you now personally feel it would be more scriptural to attempt to function as an organism or as an organization in your local church? Why? (Clearly specify the factors you considered in your determination of "more scriptural" and "less scriptural.")

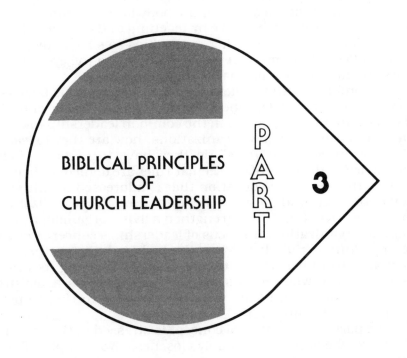

BIBLICAL PRINCIPLES
OF
CHURCH LEADERSHIP

PART

3

Our view of the body of Christ as an organism, in contrast to an organization or institution, has led to a radical rejection of many traditional church-leadership concepts. In particular, those ideas that lead to the management or direction of the life of the local church are suspect, for they seem to intrude on the role Jesus Himself is called on to play as head of the church. This view is supported not only by a biblical understanding of the church as a living organism, but also by a biblical description of leadership. Human leaders, given authority by God to build up and equip members of the body for their ministering works, are servants who serve by teaching and example. They are not "dictators," but rather, as Phillips so succinctly paraphrases Peter, "examples of Christian living in the eyes of the flock committed to your charge" (1 Peter 5:3).

The problem with the view developed so far in this book is, however, a very practical one. If spiritual leaders in the church of Christ are not to function in the common leadership roles of human institutions and organizations, how are they to lead? What resources and "tools" do they have to perform their ministries, if the tools of the secular ruler are denied to them?

It is this very basic question that is addressed in this section of the text. And the answer comes through the realization that if we are to build and strengthen a living organism rather than an organization, the focus of leadership's concerns must be on *relationships.* It is when the body is knit together, as Paul says in Ephesians, with each part performing its function, that the whole grows and matures and, as a mature expression of Jesus in the world, is available to Him to perform His continuing work.

One particular relational concept is stressed in the coming chapters: allegiance. Not simply closeness. Not simply fellowship. But commitment to loyal service. The body of Christ grows into working maturity when there is a growing allegiance of its members to each other and to God Himself. Out of the kind of commitment to persons that allegiance expresses, a healthy and responsive body grows.

In this section, then, our first concern is allegiance; then we will consider how God has provided leaders with resources that enable them to build up the body of Christ by building allegiance among its members.

PART 3

BIBLICAL PRINCIPLES
OF CHURCH LEADERSHIP

A Description of Allegiance

Building Allegiance: Relational Presuppositions
Allegiance to One Another: Shared Life
Allegiance to the Father: Prayer and Worship
Allegiance to the Spirit: Giftedness
Allegiance to the Son: Personal Responsibility

How Leaders Build Allegiance

Body Organization
Ownership, Consensus, and Freedom
Confidence and Support
Communication

The Random House Dictionary of the English Language *defines "allegiance" as "1. the loyalty of a citizen to his government or of a subject to his sovereign. 2. loyalty or devotion to some person, group, cause, or the like."*

BUILDING ALLEGIANCE: RELATIONAL PRESUPPOSITIONS

This definition brings a very basic issue into focus. The keys to a healthy life in the church as an organism are relational, not institutional. At heart we are a people called to give total loyalty to Jesus Christ, our head, and to be devoted to our brothers and sisters in God's family.

We can catch a glimpse of the importance of allegiance if we skim the first Corinthian letter. How blunt Paul is with these believers! How forcefully he labels their actions as unspiritual and worldly! "For since there is jealousy and quarreling among you, are you not worldly? Are you not acting like mere men?" (1 Cor. 3:3).

Glancing at the letter's major divisions, we see many different causes for the disputes within the body, many different areas where something other than *allegiance* is controlling the behavior and shaping the lifestyle of this congregation. Somehow the loyalty owed to Jesus Christ and the devotion owed to brothers and sisters has been lost sight of. Other issues, other loyalties, have replaced them! The focus of the members of the body has shifted from deepening personal relationships with God and one another to issues that, though real, must not be allowed to become a cause for subdivision.

Glancing over the issues that Paul deals with in 1 Corinthians, we can see how contemporary many of them are:

CHAPTER 15

Focus on human leaders (1 Cor. 1–4). Various groups within the church identified themselves as followers of different human leaders. "I follow Paul," some proclaimed, while others announced for Peter or Apollos or "Jesus only!" Paul points out that all human leaders are at best "servants of Christ." Loyalty is owed to Him, the Master.

Allegiance to human leaders cannot be substituted for allegiance to Jesus, the head of the church.

Focus on "harmony" (1 Cor. 5). Christ, the Lord of the church, has clearly identified sins that the body is decisively to reject. In fact anyone who chooses a sinful lifestyle is to be confronted and, if unwilling to repent, to be isolated from the fellowship. This kind of confrontation was too painful for the Corinthians; they were willing to sacrifice holiness for a superficial harmony.

Allegiance to Christ had been sacrificed for "peace."

Focus on personal "rights" (1 Cor. 6). Business disputes developed between members of the body. Each eagerly defended his rights in the matter, and cases were even taken to pagan law courts. Paul urged that such disputes be settled in the family. Surely someone with enough wisdom to make a fair judgment could be found!

Allegiance to one another had been sacrificed for gain.

Focus on Christian liberty (1 Cor. 8–10). A dispute arose

over eating meat offered to idols. Some argued that the gods of the pagans have no real existence; therefore no harm could come from eating such meat. Others felt deeply that association with anything pagan was an affront to Jesus. In the argument each appealed to "knowledge," and both forgot "love" (8:1–3).

Allegiance to one another had been sacrificed for disputes about freedom and propriety.

Focus on women's rights (1 Cor. 11). Paul's preaching of the gospel has lifted women to full personhood, full participation in the body (cf. Gal. 3:26). In Corinth women demanded such symbols of equality as the right to remove the veil at worship. The demands were based on the assumption that to be truly equal, women must be the same as men.

Allegiance to other members of the body had been sacrificed for a cause.

Focus on hierarchy (1 Cor. 12–14). In the church at Corinth, the more spectacular spiritual gifts had been given greater honor. Individuals were evaluated by the gifts they exercised; spirituality and importance were confused with function.

Allegiance to each member of the body as worthy of love and honor had been set aside in favor of a ranking system that bases honor on performance or role.

Each of these issues—real issues that deserved to be confronted and worked through—created problems for the church in Corinth *because the members of that body made the issues the focus of their allegiance.* They failed to realize that allegiance is personal: first to the person of the Lord, second to the persons who are the Lord's. *When we make conformity to our own personal system of belief or behavior the test of fellowship, we attack the very basis of what the church is as an organism.* The church of Jesus Christ is not an association formed to promote this issue or that belief or a certain practice. The church of Jesus Christ is a living entity composed of member cells whom God Himself has made part of the body by His gift of new life in Jesus. Because we *are* one, we are called to maintain the unity of the Spirit in the bond of peace (Eph. 4:3). Because we *are* one, the focus of body life is to be on our allegiance to Jesus Christ as head and to each other as part of His family. See the chart on page 211.

ALLEGIANCE AS THE CONTEXT FOR GROWTH

As we have looked at the New Testament concept of the church, we have already recognized the importance of per-

FIGURE 31

	FIRST-CORINTHIANS ISSUES THAT DIVIDE THE CHURCH AND THREATEN ALLEGIANCE	
Chapter(s)	Issue Defined	Modern Expressions
1–4	Focus on human leaders	"I am Calvinist (Lutheran, etc.)." "I follow Bill Gothard (Bob Schuller, etc.)."
5	Focus on harmony	Homosexual ordination, e.g.
6	Focus on rights	Lawsuits over church property, between Christians, etc.
8–10	Focus on doctrine	Armenian/Calvinist Charismatic/noncharismatic Renewal/traditionalist Baptist/Presbyterian Church splits Nature of inspiration (inerrancy/final authority in faith and practice, etc.)
11	Focus on issues	Ordination of women E.R.A. "Youth man" or "C.E. Director"?
12–14	Focus on measures of spirituality	Pastor/laity division Works hierarchy in churches (Sunday school teacher, board member, etc.)

sonal relationships. But let's examine a few more passages that illustrate the fact that relationships *are* given biblical priority.

For instance, in Ephesians 3 Paul speaks of the church as a family and of the need for Christ to dwell in our hearts through faith. Paul immediately moves on to a prayer: "That you, being rooted and established in love [for each other], may have power, together with all the saints, to grasp how wide and long and high and deep is the love of Christ, and to know this love that surpasses knowledge—that you may be filled to the measure of all the fullness of God" (Eph. 3:17–19). Note that our experience of Christ's love is linked to our relationships with other members of the body, for it is "together" that we experience the love of Christ and are filled with Him.

This same emphasis is found in Romans 12–15, which is in fact a theology of sanctifying relationships.

We begin with allegiance to Jesus, offering God our total being for His use (Rom. 12:1–2). Immediately the apostle links us to the body, stressing our oneness with our brothers and sisters and our interdependence with them for growth

211

(12:3-8). This interdependence can be experienced, Paul shows, as we learn to live together in love, harmony, and deep devotion to each other (12:9-21).

As far as the society outside the church is concerned, we are to live in submission to this world's authorities (Rom. 13:1-7). Yet even here we base our behavior on one great debt: to love one another, knowing that love "does no harm to its neighbor." And that love leads to purity as well (13:8-14).

As for relationships within the church, we are to accept each other—even those who are weak in the faith. People can differ in practice—one, for example, can be a vegetarian, another a meat-eater—but these differences are to be ignored. Jesus is the sole judge of His servants. We are to "stop passing judgment on one another" and, instead, must determine to do nothing that could cause a brother harm, for brothers are to be loved and served. Every effort is to be bent to develop a context for peace and mutual edification; differences are to be set aside and replaced by acceptance (Rom. 14:1-23).

Finally Paul urges the strong to bear with and bear up the weak, once again calling for "a spirit of unity among yourselves as you follow Jesus Christ, so that with one heart and mouth you may glorify the God and Father of our Lord Jesus Christ." We are to "accept one another, then, just as Christ accepted [us], in order to bring praise to God" (Rom. 15:5-7).

In both the Ephesians passage and the extended Romans section we see continual stress on the following qualities:

- Love
- Unity and peace
- Acceptance
- A nonjudgmental attitude
- Spiritual growth

It is these values, rooted deeply in a love-motivated loyalty to Jesus Christ and to one another, that are keys to the health of the body. It is into a lifestyle of growing allegiance that spiritual leaders are to guide members of each local congregation, so that each congregation may *be* the body that it *is*.

INSTITUTIONAL ALTERNATIVES

There are alternatives to allegiance. In most cases, these alternatives tend to stress the *differences* that distinguish a particular church or institution from others. We sometimes call believers to make a commitment to our particular group or church because

- We are charismatic (or noncharismatic)
- We are Brethren (or some other denomination)

- We are loyal to Pastor X ("You should hear him preach!")
- We have the best youth program in the valley
- We don't believe in wearing lipstick or in wearing dresses above the knees and we carefully guard the length of men's hair
- We are the only Bible-believing church in our town
- We stress evangelism (or social service)
- We offer a graded choir program for every age group
- We are governed by elders (or congregationally, or by bishops)
- We trace our history back to Peter himself (or Luther or Calvin—or someone else)
- We minister to the upper middle class (or blue-collar workers or some other group)
- We are committed to renewal—we meet in homes, not church buildings
- We have verbal, plenary inspiration in our doctrinal statement, and one who doesn't accept it can't teach Sunday school
- We baptize believers, and only by immersion
- We have closed communion
- We have an invitation at every Sunday service

These, and many other distinctions that may have some validity, are advanced to set a particular congregation apart from other competing congregations in an area. Because such differences tend to define institutional churches, the test of loyalty to Christ and to the organization tends to be increasingly viewed in terms of these differences. We are recognized as "good Christians" and accepted by the particular group we associate with if we are *with them* in their differences. *Conformity, not allegiance, tends to become the socializing goal of the group.* This is seldom by conscious or deliberate choice. But it *is* what happens.

Consider the following cases:

Bill

Bill is a young lawyer. He has an inquiring, challenging mind and has been dissatisfied with some of the formulations of faith he was taught in his childhood. Now he is trying to bring into his church a more open style of dealing with issues. Bill first approached the Christian Education committee to ask for a "discussion" class to break the lecture pattern that had been so well established. The committee rejected the request. So Bill began to gather a small group of young adults who met in his home for prayer and Bible study. This was

213

viewed with great suspicion by the church and the pastor, who felt that a professionally trained man ought to be there to see that the group did not fall into doctrinal error. Bill has spoken out in congregational meetings about the "lack of love" in the congregation, a charge that has been met with a great deal of hostility. Bill likes to keep wine in his home for special meals but doesn't dare let the members of his church know for fear of their reaction. The last time he was nominated for church office he was soundly defeated by those who were suspicious of him and his probable "doctrinal weakness."

Carol

Carol was converted about three years ago. She was thrilled and excited and immediately began to share with her friends what Jesus meant to her. She tried to share her witnessing experiences with members of the church she had begun to attend. The pastor listened to her and seemed excited, but other members would just nod and smile and drift away.

Soon Carol was approached by leaders of several of the church's children's programs. She was recruited to be a leader and was told that as a Christian she would need this role in order to "serve the Lord." Carol knew nothing about the Bible when she was converted. For about two years she was continually excited about the content she learned at the church services and adult Sunday school classes. But when Carol tried to ask questions or share personal experiences, her attempts were pushed aside. Mastery of doctrine was stressed; personal items weren't seen as appropriate for Bible-teaching settings.

When personal problems grew, Carol was afraid to share them. No one else in the church seemed to have problems, and she felt ashamed that she was such a poor Christian. She dropped out of her teaching responsibility and began to skip more and more church services. She quickly became aware of the fact that she was now viewed by the other church members as a "backslider." She could only agree with them that something was desperately wrong in her life.

Bill and Carol are real people. Both are in churches that have developed institutional lifestyles and maintain institutional loyalty by pressing for *conformity* to their pattern of life. In each church the acceptable member (1) is quiet and obedient to the leadership; (2) fits into well-defined institutional roles; (3) is identified by *what* he or she believes; (4) maintains a comfortable, impersonal distance from others;

(5) does not express personal problems; (6) attends a defined number of church functions; and (7) refrains from certain kinds of behavior, such as drinking wine. In each case conformity is enforced through a quiet but all-pervasive social pressure that unofficially expresses disapproval and lack of acceptance.

Allegiance and *conformity* are the two primary forces leaders in the church can rely on to build loyalty and cohesiveness. One is a *relational force,* stressing—as does the New Testament—love, unity, peace, acceptance, and nonjudgmental attitudes. The other is a *social force,* stressing—in contrast to the New Testament—traditions, roles, types of communication, dress, and behavior. Allegiance permits and may even value differences, for the focus in allegiance is on the commitment of persons to one another. Conformity cannot permit deviation, for the focus of conformity is on approved patterns of belief and behavior as the basis for acceptance by the group.

For a church life that is in harmony with what the Bible teaches about the nature of God and the nature of the body, *the forces of conformity must be decisively rejected. The unity of the body must be built solely on allegiance.*

The concept of an organism, whose unity is found in a biblical affirmation of allegiance, will be extremely helpful to us as we seek to understand the role of spiritual leaders in the local church. In order to present Jesus Christ as the head of a healthy body, leaders in the church must focus their efforts on building allegiance.

It *is* the task of leaders in the body to equip it. This is done in a corporate sense by building the bonds of love among the members of the body and between the body (corporately and individually) and our Triune God.

PROBE

▶ *case histories*
▶ *discussion questions*
▶ *thought provokers*
▶ *resources*

1. Think of your own church experience. What are the "conformity" pressures (often unstated, but very real) existing in it? How many people in the fellowship are so committed to *you* as a person that they would continue to love and minister to you if you stepped out of the pattern of "acceptable" behavior?

2. Are there some doctrines or practices that are so integral to what

Christian faith is that they *do* provide a basis for acceptance or rejection? Make a list of those differences that you feel would require you to reject fellowship with another believer.

3. Study Romans 12:1–15:14 *carefully* in view of the list you just developed in answer to number two above. What insights does Scripture provide? What are the implications of the Romans passage for your list?

4. Look at the chart on page 211. By yourself or with others, add more items to the preliminary list of "divisive issues" begun by the author.

5. When the New Testament speaks of leadership, it usually speaks in the plural. Timothy and Titus, for instance, were to recognize (appoint) *elders* in every place—never *an elder*. The conclusion that many have drawn is that our contemporary approach that tends to exalt a single "pastor" to a lonely place atop the organizational chart is without biblical precedent. Instead, the Bible seems to indicate a multiple, local, lay leadership team.

   The concept of allegiance suggests one reason why a team of leaders may be essential. Recall that the resources servant-leaders have for their ministry are their *teaching* and their *example*. If there is only a single "top leader" in a congregation, he might teach allegiance, but how could he model it? Yet a team of leaders can model allegiance in their relationships with each other. Differences can be shown, nonjudgmental behaviors demonstrated, and a deep love and commitment to each other lived out on the leadership team. In this way a team can model allegiance, while an individual leader cannot.

   How many other reasons can you think of that might help explain why the New Testament usually refers to plural rather than singular leadership? Jot down your ideas now; more reasons will be suggested later in the text.

6. Building allegiance within the team of spiritual leaders is a challenging and long-term process. One aid, developed by Dr. Norm Wakefield, is available from Dynamic Church Ministries, P.O. Box 35331, Phoenix, Arizona 85069. It involves a twenty-week, carefully designed process that will help local church leaders better understand their leadership role and in the process build closer relationships. It's called "Becoming a Team."

PART 3

BIBLICAL PRINCIPLES
OF CHURCH LEADERSHIP

A Description of Allegiance

Building Allegiance: Relational Presuppositions
Allegiance to One Another: Shared Life
Allegiance to the Father: Prayer and Worship
Allegiance to the Spirit: Giftedness
Allegiance to the Son: Personal Responsibility

How Leaders Build Allegiance

Body Organization
Ownership, Consensus, and Freedom
Confidence and Support
Communication

"Above all," Peter says, "love each other deeply, because love covers a multitude of sins. Offer hospitality to one another without grumbling. Each one should use whatever spiritual gift he has received to serve others, faithfully administering God's grace in its various forms" (1 Peter 4:8–10). In these few brief words we see again the constant New

ALLEGIANCE TO ONE ANOTHER: SHARED LIFE

Testament vision of the people of God living shared lives— lives marked by love, by hospitality, and by service.

In Paul's terms allegiance to others in the body of Christ can be summed up in one simple thing: "Let no debt remain outstanding, except the continuing debt to love one another" (Rom. 13:8).

On the night of the Last Supper the disciples were confronted by Jesus with what He called His "new commandment." It sounds so simple on first reading. "Love one another. As I have loved you, so you must love one another. All men will know that you are my disciples if you love one another" (John 13:34-35).

How was this a "new" commandment, when the Old Testament speaks so clearly of neighbor love (cf. Deut. 11)? Its newness seems rooted in three things: (1) *A new relationship:* In Jesus' church, neighbor love becomes family love. In the church, which is Christ's body, we are now brothers and sisters, linked together by our organic relationship with Jesus and the Father. That new relationship calls for a greater and deeper love than any other human relationship could. (2) *A new standard.* In the old economy there was a standard for love: "Love your neighbor as yourself." Now Jesus gives Himself as the standard: "Love one another *as I have loved you.*" This love commitment steps far beyond the old and, reaching out to care, offers to sacrifice the lover for the benefit of the one loved. How much deeper a love is called for when Jesus' love for us, not our love for ourselves, is the standard we are to follow. (3) *A new outcome.* Finally, Jesus points out that His kind of love, expressed self-sacrificially within the fellowship of the body, will have a unique outcome. Outsiders will look at the shared life of the church, be stunned at the love expressed, and "know that [we] are [Jesus'] disciples if [we] love one another." The witness of the body of Christ to the presence of Jesus is a witness given to the world in the form of visible love within its fellowship.

Nearly every New Testament letter reflects this central "new commandment" given by Jesus. Romans 12–15 describes the love lifestyle in terms of mutual acceptance and a nonjudgmental attitude, insisting that we must "be devoted to one another in brotherly love" (Rom. 12:10).

First Corinthians 12 and 13 describe shared life, stressing our need for each other and the necessity that there be "no division in the body." Because of this necessity, love is God's "more excellent way" to spiritual maturity, far different from the exaltation of spiritual gifts.

In 2 Corinthians 3 Paul describes an open, sharing lifestyle in which the masks behind which we hide are stripped away. Throughout this Letter Paul advocates this kind of openness.

Galatians 5–6 describes life lived in the Spirit and gives

the first sign of His control as "love" (cf. Gal. 5:22). Paul urges that our freedom in Christ be used to "serve one another in love" (5:13).

Ephesians devotes chapters 4 and 5 to the believer's new life and again roots the teaching in the fact that "as [God's] dearly loved children" we are to "live a life of love, just as Christ loved us and gave himself up for us" (5:1-2).

Philippians 2 describes the concern members of the body are to have for each other as "looking not only to [their] own interests, but also to the interest of others" (Phil. 2:4). It reveals the attitude of Christ in His "taking the very nature of a servant" as the model for our attitude and love.

Colossians 3 and 4 is devoted to describing the Christian life. We are told: "As God's chosen people, holy and dearly loved, clothe yourselves with compassion, kindness, humility, gentleness, and patience. Bear with one another and forgive whatever grievances you may have against one another. Forgive as the Lord forgave you. And over all these virtues put on love, which binds them all together in perfect unity" (Col. 3:12-14).

First Thessalonians 2 describes Paul's love relationship with those to whom he ministers. First Timothy reminds us that the goal of the command to teach sound doctrine is "love, which comes from a pure heart and a good conscience and a sincere faith" (1:5), and 2 Timothy portrays the gospel as a pattern of sound teaching accompanying faith and love (1:13).

Over and over again—in John, in Peter, in James, in the Book of Hebrews—the stress on love within the body of Christ is repeated. Hebrews even makes it clear that when we come together as Christ's body we are to interact with each other, encouraging each other and considering "how we may spur one another on toward love and good deeds" (10:24-25).

Allegiance to one another in the body of Christ is based on love, expressed as love, and experienced through love. *We cannot live as the church unless we are growing in our personal relationships with each other, and deepening in our devotion to each other.*

PATTERNS FOR SHARED LIFE

Our acceptance of love as a biblical imperative and our study of the New Testament descriptions of love in action give us insights into patterns that we want to build into contemporary church structure. It is not necessary that every church become a "small group" or a "house church." But it is necessary that a context be provided for coming to know each other well and for the expression of love. This is the responsibility of the leaders, who serve individuals but are also to shape the lifestyle of the congregation.

What can leaders do to build deeper personal relationships? An awareness of the impact on relationships of three common communication settings in the church provides helpful clues:

Type one: *one-way communication.* In this very common communication setting, one person typically speaks, the rest of the congregation listen. The seating pattern reflects this expectation. The speaker is on a platform in front of rows of pews or chairs provided for the listeners.

This type of setting is potentially effective for dealing with ideas or concepts. It should especially be used when the communications goal is to share a body of information in a clear, logical, and brief way.

FIGURE 32
COMMUNICATION SETTING

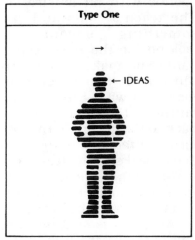

However, this type of setting does *not* encourage members of a body to know one another. No interaction is expected: preaching is not a "one another" kind of thing, but a "one to many" experience.

In most churches the Sunday morning service has this form. In some congregations nearly *every* gathering takes this form, with chairs arranged in rows and the person in charge standing before the rest to speak. In a church where all gatherings fit the one-way format, there is likely to be little shared life. The communication pattern that dominates the experience of believers when they gather loudly proclaims that interaction and coming to know one another as persons is not highly valued.

Type two: *two-way communication.* This is also a common communication setting. We see it in classes and at times in more formal board and committee meetings. The seating in such a meeting may be a "row" type seating or a less-formal half-circle. But several distinctive aspects of the communication pattern identify it clearly.

We can see that pattern in a typical adult Sunday school

221

class. The teacher has finished a lecture covering a portion of Scripture. Now he or she asks the group a question: "How do you think a person might put this truth into practice today? Jack, what do you think?" Jack responds with an illustration. The teacher nods and says something encouraging, looking for the next respondant. Sue makes her contribution. The teacher comments on what Sue says and bounces the responsibility back to the group. In this pattern *the teacher is typically involved in every interaction:* Jack speaks to the teacher, the teacher responds, Sue speaks to the teacher, the teacher responds, and so on. Watch such a class or a board meeting and you'll notice that seldom if ever do members of the group speak directly to each other.

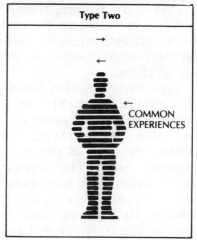

FIGURE 33
COMMUNICATION SETTING
Type Two

COMMON EXPERIENCES

Another fascinating thing can be observed about the *content* of the interaction in this type of setting. There may be a shift from talk of concepts only to illustration and application. But almost never does a class member use the personal pronoun *I*. Instead, illustrations are given in terms of: "Well, a person might . . .," or "Someone could. . . ."

This kind of sharing in the body of Christ *is* important. We need to talk together and help each other see the broad implications in the Bible truths we study. So a discussion that leads us to think together about a general application of Bible truths does have value.

But again this pattern of interaction does little to help us come to know each other as persons. It does not open us up to one another for the sharing of our lives. The lack of "I" communication tells us that the persons involved still feel a need to remain masked, that the deeper feelings or personal experiences that help us truly know one another are withheld.

Type three: *complex communication.* A third communication pattern involves a face-to-face setting and a free flow of interaction.

Here we need to picture a smaller group of people in a living room or in church, with chairs pulled together in a tight circle. There is no obvious "leader" here; each person seems to speak up spontaneously to address the group as a whole and/or individuals in it.

People in this communication setting find it easier to share more significantly and personally. The warmth and intimacy of the smaller group, the freedom to react spontaneously, the informality— all make this a more natural setting for talking about inner experiences and feelings.

What is striking, then, when we look at communication settings in the church

FIGURE 34
COMMUNICATION SETTING

Type Three

← INNER EXPERIENCES

and see the types of interaction they involve is the fact that the *type of interaction* in essence limits the *content of interaction*. In a type-one setting, where interaction is one-way, content will be primarily ideas or concepts. In a type-two setting, where communication is focused through a teacher or leader, the content of interaction may move into descriptions of common experiences, but it will seldom move into personal sharing of inner experiences. In a type-three setting, however, we can expect the greatest freedom to move to the kind of sharing that involves inner experiences. And it is this sharing of inner experiences that enables us to truly know, and truly love, our Christian brothers and sisters.

There is a place in the life of every congregation for each type of interaction. But where a church has developed a meeting pattern that completely omits type-three settings, we can expect little development of a New Testament kind of love in the fellowship.

An analysis tool

Our observation of the impact of communication patterns on the encouragement or discouragement of love relationships in the body provides us with useful tools. The first potential use is in the analysis of the patterns of life in our own congregation.

For instance, we might immediately ask two questions. First, how many of the meetings of our gathered congregation are primarily type one, type two, and type three? We may look over our programming and find that the Sunday morning service is clearly type one, that a "School of Christian Living" held Sunday evenings is type two, and that several small groups that meet various week nights are designed to be type three. It may appear that there is a well-balanced program in such a case.

But we need to ask a second question. What percentage of the congregation is involved in each setting? We may discover that 80 percent participate regularly on Sunday mornings, 18 percent on Sunday evenings, and only 9 percent in the week-day small-group programs. In such a case, we have to conclude that 91 percent of the congregation is probably *not* in settings where Scripture's imperative love-relationship is being nurtured, developed, and expressed.

Doing such an analysis can help leaders of a local church locate needs and see the direction in which the congregation needs to move. As a rule of thumb, many churches operate on the assumption that at least 70 percent of the congregation need to be involved in some type-three relationships. Movement toward this goal is a primary responsibility of the leaders.

So it may be good for you to stop and do a rough analysis of your own patterns of local church life.

FIGURE 35
INITIAL ANALYSIS OF PATTERN OF CHURCH LIFE

Interaction type	One	Two	Three
Interaction pattern	$\rightarrow$	$\rightarrow$ $\leftarrow$	𝄪→
Percentage of meetings in our church in this pattern	___%	___%	___%
Percentage of people in our congregation involved in this type experience ___%			

DETAILED ANALYSIS

It is also helpful to do a detailed analysis of all meetings the members of the church attend. What happens in these meetings? What pattern of interaction dominates? Is there more than one type of interaction that takes place?

In doing the more detailed analysis (using the chart on page 225), you will find that there *are* many meetings believers attend in which the group involved is small. But it may very well be that a significant sharing of life does not take

FIGURE 36
DETAILED ANALYSIS OF PATTERN OF CHURCH LIFE

Typical "Meeting" Occasions	Number of Persons Involved	Dominant Type of Interaction	Secondary Type of Interaction
Worship service(s)			
Sunday school class			
Worship committee			
Evangelism committee			
Christian Education committee			
Deacons or elders board			
Trustees or deacons board			
Visitation committee			
Prayer meeting			
Cottage prayer groups			
Elective classes			
Membership classes			
Sharing groups			
Home Bible study groups			
Visitation teams			
Choir			
Pioneer Girl's staff			
Women's Missionary Society			
Building committee			
Missions committee			
Children's church staff			
Camp committee			
Sunday school cabinet			
Youth cabinet			
Evangelistic Bible studies			
Sunday school workers' meetings			
Retreats			
Pastoral staff			
Other groups			

place in those meetings. For instance, the church board is a "small group." But too many church boards function as policy setters and decision makers—as managers, rather than ministers. And too many church board meetings are conducted in formal ways that limit personal sharing and that make ministering to one another seem out of place. Simply because a group is small does not mean there is much opportunity for a significant sharing of life experiences, even in a type-three setting!

Developing type-three interaction

We just noted that the meeting of a few Christians in a small group does not guarantee that their interaction will move from a formal "ideas" level of sharing to the personal "inner experiences" level the New Testament describes as integral to loving one another.

How do we help develop a climate of love and openness where impersonal institutional patterns may have long been established? Some suggest that the institutional church must be abandoned and a new form adopted. Others opt for starting new congregations, where they feel there will be no need to "fight" established patterns. It's true that it is difficult to work toward a change of patterns that are deeply ingrained. But since the church is the body of Christ, and Jesus is Lord of the church, He is powerful and able to work within His people. We would be wrong to quickly or lightly abandon brothers and sisters because we are discouraged about the unbiblical patterns that have become established in the congregation. Instead we need, without criticism or antagonism for what the body now is, to work toward the reality described in Scripture as the heritage of a church that is family and that is body.

Here are some practical approaches that can be taken by the leadership of local congregations to work toward the climate of love and openness that is one mark of Christian community.

Modeling by leaders

When a congregation begins to move toward an allegiance pattern of life, the pastor will probably be the one to initiate the change. Few congregations at the start will have well-developed teams of leaders, or elders (deacons), who are familiar with the ministry of oversight of the body.

So it will be largely up to the pastor to model the focus on people and the commitment of allegiance to brothers and sisters that provide the relational perspective I have been advocating. How can the pastor provide a model? In many simple ways: By using personal illustrations in sermons that reveal him to be a human being. By inviting groups of people into his home to come to know him and his family—and each other. By interviewing a member during each service, giving him a chance to share what God is doing in his life. By placing "appreciation cards" in the pews and encouraging people to use them to jot notes of thanks to anyone in the congregation who has served or helped them. By gathering different groups of members to help him plan his sermons, encouraging them to share areas in their own lives where the Scripture passage to be expounded in the sermon speaks to them.

Most importantly, the pastor will need to encourage and possibly initiate a regular gathering of elders or other spiritual leaders, not to "do business," but to come to know and love each other. There is no more important first step than this: to begin to build into the experience of the leaders those relationships that Scripture says are to mark the congregation as a whole.

As the elder team becomes more and more an intimate fellowship of believers who love one another, the model they present to the congregation can be a powerful force for growth and change.

Introduction of non–setting-structured experiences

Patterns of church meetings develop over a period of time and actually fix the expectations of people as to what is and what is not appropriate behavior.

As a child, I used to bring the cows in from the pasture on my grandfather's farm. They all headed placidly into the barn, each seeking her own stall. But what a commotion there would be if one cow went into the wrong stall!

This is a good example of "setting structure." The cows had learned just what they and others should do when entering the barn. Any change in the routine was extremely upsetting. The setting had structured, or determined, their expectations.

We have the same thing in the church. If someone sits in the Browns' pew, the Browns are disturbed. If we sing one verse of a hymn instead of the regular two, someone is sure to comment. If we are so radical as to suggest dramatic changes—such as opening up the service to the sharing of personal needs and joys from the congregation—charges of theological deviation are likely!

One way to work toward growth in the understanding of

the meaningfulness of personal relationships is to introduce such experiences to members in some setting that is *not* already structured. That is, place believers in new settings where no pattern of expectations has been established.

For instance, Pastor Henry Dick in California set up "fellowship training groups" of from ten to twelve persons for short eight-week courses, held after the regular week-night service. When these courses had been taken by a number of different members of the congregation, many spontaneously established small Bible-study and prayer groups. Other church leaders have used retreats or camp experiences as opportunities to lead persons into significant sharing experiences. Getting members of the congregation into a "game" weekend, and using such communication games as the Ungame, is another strategy. One Lutheran pastor in Minneapolis took two hundred members of his congregation to the Leamington Hotel for a weekend retreat designed by a guest leader to build interpersonal relationships among the membership.

Moving people out of normal structures and into new settings for an introduction to interpersonal experiences of a type-three nature is one way to help the body take the first steps toward allegiance to one another.

Gradual change of setting-structured experiences

This strategy looks at existing structures in the church and asks how they may be gradually changed to include greater sharing and allegiance.

Take a church board meeting. Often the board meeting follows formal *Robert's Rules of Order* procedures. Reports are read, issues are discussed, votes are taken. The board functions as a decision-making or management team, not as servants whose calling is to minister through lifestyle and teaching among the body members. How can we change a board meeting, with its historically established procedures, to a type-two interaction setting—for at least part of the time the board is together?

One strategy involves bringing members of the leadership team together outside of the regular place of meeting at a time *just before* the time of meeting. At that time personal sharing and prayer for each other is encouraged. An atmosphere of allegiance is developed, in the expectation that it will carry over into, and shape, the time of the regular meeting.

Other groups have attended leadership-training seminars, such as the one held at Wheaton College's Honey Rock Camp each year, cosponsored by the college and Dynamic Church Ministries, of Phoenix, Arizona. In a week-long setting, with at least 50 percent of the leadership team present, much can be done to train and build relationships among the leaders.

It is difficult to change established patterns. Yet it *can* be done.

Introduction of new setting-structured experiences

This strategy involves beginning new programs or activities that, in time, become new "traditions." These established programs define the expectations of participants as to what is valid and expected behavior. If these new experiences are carefully designed, they will support the sharing lifestyle that builds allegiance to other members of the body.

Examples of new setting structures are the "Body Life" meetings held at Peninsula Bible Church in Palo Alto, California, and described in Ray Stedman's book, *Body Life*.

Another example comes from Indiana, where a local church began a "sheep and shepherds" ministry. Each member of the congregation is invited to identify himself or herself as a "sheep" or a "shepherd." Each sheep is paired with a shepherd. the two are to meet weekly and share what each has discovered in a common passage of Scripture, to pray for each other, and to keep in touch. In the ministry, deepening relationships soon began to develop and have spilled over into the other meetings of the body.

There are many approaches that can be developed in local congregations to build a sharing lifestyle. Through coming to know one another, allegiance (or commitment to each other as brothers and sisters) is developed. What is important for the leaders of the church is

1. to be aware of the need for the kind of interaction that builds interpersonal relationships and love
2. to analyze the patterns of gatherings of Christians in their own congregation
3. to take wise steps toward building into the experience of all members of the local congregation opportunities to grow to know and love each other.

These are the first steps toward building allegiance within the body.

PROBE

▶ case histories
▶ discussion questions
▶ thought provokers
▶ resources

1. An excellent book that shares ways one leadership team has worked to build allegiance on the interpersonal level is Don Bubna's *Building People Through a Caring Sharing Fellowship* (Wheaton, Illinois: Tyndale, 1978).

2. A six-session videotape/interaction series on allegiance relationships for use with leadership teams and/or whole congregations is available from Dynamic Church Ministries, P.O. Box 35331, Phoenix, Arizona 85069.

3. Playing together is an important part of building allegiance. Plan for a local congregation a "fun day" that would have as a clear side benefit growing to feel and be close to each other.

4. Here's the enthusiastic report of one young pastor who is working toward building a leadership team that will function in a biblical way:

> *I was pastor of our church for about seven months before any type of elders meeting was held—and that first meeting was called just to see if our group still existed! In reality their ministry to the "spiritual" needs of the people was almost nonexistent. The total of what was done for the year 1977 by the elders was to pray for several sick people in the congregation. While not minimizing this service, I would have to conclude that if that is all the "spiritual ministry" our congregation required during the year, then we are either dead or institutionalized to the hilt!*
>
> *Where do the elders fit in? I would say that they had abdicated their spiritual ministry and had left it to others. I place much of the blame for the confusion on our structure. We are now at the point where we have to elect a certain number of men each year to fill the positions, and there is not any consideration of spiritual qualifications. And the elders are still pretty much elected on the basis of "the nice, older men who have stood by the work."*
>
> *Do the elders serve the flock? A little, at best. They serve by praying for the sick. Increasingly now they have become more visible through such things as leading the communion service, teaching in a service, and having regular meetings (at least people know they meet and probably think that in some way they are doing something!). There is not, however, any*

servant model presented by this group. Most of the men think they are elected only to "make decisions."

Are they elected on the basis of their spiritual qualifications? Well, here is an area that we pay lip service to. We have the attitude that an elder should be a "good Christian man." We don't go much beyond that. And I doubt if many folks could even locate the scriptural passages dealing with spiritual qualifications. It so happens, however, that we would likely discover that each man meets the standards—if we were to study through them together.

So what's "with" our elders? Not much, really! They are pretty sharp men on the whole. They love God and enjoy a life of spiritual growth. I pin the fault on (1) a structure that does not in any way address the biblical criteria and (2) former pastors who have not "equipped the elders" for their work. I am now convinced that about two-thirds of the problem can (and will) be corrected through some personal attention to these men. Already we are putting together an exciting ministry.

Generally I will capitalize on strengths that are now present. First, the church constitution calls for the work of the elders in the church. It's already written down. I'll make the most of that!

Second, the group of men who are now elders are godly men whom I really look up to and respect. These are men who sincerely love God and are open to His Word. They may not ever have exercised their full potential in the body because of ignorance, but with some encouragement, patience, and instruction they are open to anything that can be demonstrated from Scripture. This is crucial. It is probably our greatest strength and will be jumped on and exploited to the hilt!

Third, the constitution also requires that the elders "assist the pastor in the spiritual ministries of the church." If that isn't a wide-open statement, I don't know what is! What isn't spiritual? Already this has been appealed to, and the response from both the executive board and elders has been good.

Finally, I will capitalize on a personal strength—an increasingly open willingness to let God have full reign in the things He wants to accomplish. I am moving further and further away from preprogramed ideas of what I think should be. And I am now increasingly enjoying a new freedom to let God do His own thing in our lives and in His body!

That summarizes where we are generally. Now I would like to conclude the project with a bit of what we have done to address our situation specifically, what we are doing, and the kinds of things we hope to see as God allows. I find this part very exciting! And while the earlier evaluation of our present situation may seem unduly negative, I am genuinely excited about what's happening in our body with the elders.

I began a little over a year ago to pray for a significant ministry by our elders to our congregation at some future time. Soon thereafter I read a bit of Gene Getz's work in Dallas and focused my prayer on a similar type of thing for our people if the legitimate need was there and if the men came together for ministry. Some important steps were taken.

I began to have lunch with a different elder each week just to get to know the elders a bit better and become their friend. Soon thereafter we decided to hold monthly meetings but we still weren't entirely sure what we would do during the meetings. I presented to the executive board an idea that they agreed to—to try to keep the "business type" decisions limited to the board, while other matters, such as the church calendar, guest ministries, etc., would go to the elders. Any inquiry by someone to present their work to our congregation (e.g., missionary candidates) was considered by the elders instead of the pastor alone. After about a year they have a real handle on what will be happening in the coming weeks.

A major step was then taken. We assigned an elder to pray for each group of people in the congregation at least each week. This was an idea they quickly owned and took to! We have continued to expand this as new Christians have been added to the fellowship.

At our meetings I began presenting to them for their counsel any matters that had come to the pastor's attention. This was to shift away from the old pattern that the "pastor is the head of the church and makes all the decisions." It was a small but significant step for us. I have consciously played down my role here. I began by forcing their attention on necessary matters and now it's slowly developed into their thinking that I do not call the shots. By "forcing their attention," I mean presenting ideas for them to consider that previously would have been made automatically by the pastor. From time to time there was a puzzled I-never-thought-of-it expression, but now the elders really see we are taking their leadership seriously in this area.

But we've been talking about "business type" things again. What about the spiritual ministry? I tried to model what I thought Scripture suggested. I frequently invited their prayer informally before or after a service. Our meetings began to

232

focus on church needs—spiritual ones, too, and not just the hospital cases. The elders are approached on any discipline question. And we have progressed to the point where we can honestly sit down to evaluate a particular function for its ministry value. This is something they had probably never done before.

The group has now developed a real identity again. After one year, that is a solid step. We know we exist and have at least a vague idea why. In the last two months this past fall we began talking to our congregation about a maintenance ministry. Starting with our weekly prayer lists that cover the entire congregation, we have seen a need and are including visits to the homes of our people. Interaction on this idea first came over lunches together. Now we are talking specifics at our meetings each month and have set up January 1 as our target date for implementation.

What's involved? We are not completely sure just yet, but are already putting together some thoughts that include (1) each elder's assuming responsibility for a portion of the congregation (we are in the process of deciding how to divide the people), (2) establishing some form of regular contact (e.g., at least a visit in each home every two months), and (3) interaction about, and prayer for, church needs from the visitation at the monthly elders' meeting. Final details will be worked out at our meeting in December.

One of the things I will share at our next meeting is the servant-leader concept. Our elders are ready to learn about a support ministry to the people and to shift our perspective from a control group to a support group. This concept will need real attention so that we will not begin to "lord it over" our people.

In the new year our meetings will gradually minimize the "business type" decisions we have grown so accustomed to. I have tentatively thought of the following pattern for our meeting:

Reading from The Measure of a Man (or a similar book)	15 minutes
Interaction on The Measure of a Man	20 minutes
Maintenance Ministry Interaction/Prayer (to provide an opportunity for the elders to share some of their work with our people— joys, needs, advice, etc.)	45 minutes
Church Calendar (guest ministries, topics for sermons, evaluations, etc.)	10 minutes

It looks binding, but it isn't. It is a suggestion and guide, *nothing more. I do want interaction time on any content presented and for our ministry to the people so that it stays a ministry and doesn't degenerate into another institutionalized program.*

Another thing I will continue is the regular informal lunches with individual elders. This has probably helped me as much as anything to become friends with the men and to develop their trust and confidence in each other. They respond to a model!

What will happen after that? Who knows? The elders have already suggested we consider a training program for some younger men. That sounds super! There will be lots of kinks to eliminate concerning the servant-leadership principle, I am sure. That will take time, perhaps months or even years. I believe we can realistically expect in the next five years to see elders chosen because of their spiritual qualifications. And who knows—maybe we will have the courage to address the whole dilemma of the elder–executive board–deacon relationship.

Looking back now over the past year at all the energy I have invested in reading with, and praying for, the elders at the church; the work involved in actually writing down my thoughts in this project; and the interaction, I would say I have learned a two-step formula that is putting us on course. It is not a "pat" answer, but still it has worked remarkably well for us. The answer has been (1) to discover what the Bible says and (2) to model it! Sounds simple, I know. But it works. And this is the direction in which we are continuing to head.

PART 3

BIBLICAL PRINCIPLES
OF CHURCH LEADERSHIP

A Description of Allegiance

Building Allegiance: Relational Presuppositions
Allegiance to One Another: Shared Life
Allegiance to the Father: Prayer and Worship
Allegiance to the Spirit: Giftedness
Allegiance to the Son: Personal Responsibility

How Leaders Build Allegiance

Body Organization
Ownership, Consensus, and Freedom
Confidence and Support
Communication

Paul's Ephesian letter contains this statement: "I kneel before the Father, from whom the whole family . . . derives its name" (3:14-15). Our identity as a family is rooted in God's nature and character as Father.

This is an important concept. Our total life and our iden-

ALLEGIANCE TO THE FATHER: PRAYER AND WORSHIP

tity as believers are ultimately rooted in God. Coming to know God the Father better is to come to understand ourselves and our life in the world better.

But even more important, coming to know the Father in a deeper way is the root of our allegiance to Him.

The atmosphere was charged; you could feel the anger of the leaders beating against Peter and John who stood bound before them. These two apostles had aroused excitement among the people by healing a lame man in the name of Jesus and had been called before the Sanhedrin. After the bitter shouts and accusations had quieted, the leaders of the people of Israel, frustrated in their efforts to win the approval of the crowd, could do nothing more than demand: "Stop speaking to anyone in this name!"

Released, the two disciples went back to "their own people." The church gathered and the two told the body what had happened. And the Scripture says,

> When they heard this, they raised their voices together in prayer to God. "Sovereign Lord," they said, "you made the heaven and the earth and the sea, and everything in them. You spoke by the Holy Spirit through the mouth of your servant, our father David:
> 'Why do the nations rage,
>   and the people plot in vain?
> The kings of the earth take their stand,
>   and the rulers gather together
>   against the Lord
>   and against his Anointed One.'
> Indeed Herod and Pontius Pilate met together with the Gentiles and the people of Israel in this city to conspire against your holy servant Jesus, whom you anointed. They did what your power and will had decided beforehand should happen. Now, Lord, consider their threats and enable your servants to speak your word with great boldness. Stretch out your hand to heal and to perform miraculous signs and wonders through the name of your holy servant Jesus" (Acts 4:24-30).

CHAPTER 17

This incident in the life of the early church shows us another dimension of allegiance: building interaction in the body of Christ. But here our interaction is not a horizontal, one-another kind of experience. Here interaction is with God the Father Himself.

Looking at the incident closely, we can see several elements of the interaction situation that are extremely important for local bodies to experience today. Let's look at these elements more closely:

1. *The reality of our lives.* The Acts 4 interaction with God came out of the life experience of His people. The disciples and the early community confronted the opposition of the Jewish leaders. They claimed an authority to prohibit speaking in Jesus' name and theoretically had the power to enforce their demand. Confronted with this problem and deeply feeling their need of divine help, the men and women of the early church turned to God.

2. *The corporate experience.* While the problem faced might initially seem to be that of only two men, there was an immediate move to report the experience to the gathered body. The need of the two disciples soon became the burden of all: what affected one part of the body had an impact on all.

This need to interact with the reality of the life of fellow members was and is a corporate need: life in the body is for sharing, as is the Godward response to need!

3. *God's self-revelation.* Immediately the church began to focus on God together. The body recalled central revelations from Scripture concerning who God is by nature, and together they focused on Him. God's sovereignty was known from Creation. It was known by His prophetic revelation of the future. It was known in their immediate history, in Jesus' death according to God's plan. What God had revealed about Himself was now recalled by the church and related to the specific need they faced!

4. *Affirmation of God in worship.* In their first words, the gathered church rehearsed who God is. But this rehearsal was not addressed to the body. It was addressed to the Father. It is an example of pure worship: addressing God with praise for who He is by nature, affirming Him in the glory of His essential nature.

Note that the affirmation is directly related to the life need of the body. The two disciples had been attacked by those who claimed the sovereign right to demand silence from the church about Jesus and now the church appealed to God as the one who is truly sovereign. In the light of who God is as sovereign Lord, the claims of mere men to power receded to insignificance. In the vision of God as sovereign Lord, the church found the strength to obey Him and to confront the powers of this world.

5. *Prayer to God.* Like worship, prayer grew out of the interplay between the situational need and God's self-revelation. Counting on God as sovereign, the body requested boldness to speak the good words about Jesus and requested that God would demonstrate His sovereign power in unmistakable ways. Convinced by their vision of the Father that He could and would act for them, the body addressed prayer to Him in complete confidence.

6. *The result.* The outcome of this interaction with God is reported in Acts: "They were all filled with the Holy Spirit and spoke the word of God boldly" (4:31).

God, clearly perceived by the church and affirmed and appealed to in His essential nature, acted on behalf of the body.

It is important that we recognize each of these elements as we explore the role of leadership in the building of a deeper relationship with God the Father in the body and in individuals. Worship and prayer in the church today are the primary human interactive responses to God the Father's revelation of Himself in Scripture and history. To strengthen the worship and prayer life of the body, we need to

- guide the corporate experience of the gathered body
  - by relating the reality of our life experiences
    - to the reality of who God is by nature
- and respond to God's revelation of Himself
  - by worship and prayer
    - that is addressed to Him and is responsive to His self-revelation.

GOD'S SELF-REVELATION

As we think of our interaction with God the Father and building allegiance to Him, we must take as our starting point God's first Word to us. Worship and prayer are both *responsive* in nature, not initiative. God Himself has taken the initiative and spoken to us clearly about who He is. G. W. Bromiley comments:

> That human emotions and reactions are involved in worship is, of course, undeniable. Awe, fear, gratitude, and love may all be experienced in worship. The point is, however, that these are not the controlling factors. They do not constitute the true essence. In the Bible the beginning lies in the object of worship rather than the subject. Nor is this an indefinite object. It is not the mystery behind the universe. It is not the universe itself. It is not an unknown factor. It is not man's own potentiality. The object of worship, at once its starting-point and controlling factor, is not a projection of man. It is God.
>
> God is self-declared in the Bible as the living God who is from eternity to eternity, who made the world, who created man in His image, and who set Himself in relation to man.[1]

Because the biblical Word is so clear, we can know God well in His relation to man. God is sovereign, loving, holy, forgiving, fatherlike, gracious, all-present, all-powerful, judging, delivering, saving, creative, tender, and so on and on.

This revelation of who God is by nature meets the deepest needs of our hearts and lives. We live in a world where there is much that is evil. Aware of that, we need to see God in His nature as sovereign Lord, working His good even through our difficulties. We are often frustrated by our inadequacies. We need to see God as adequate, able to work even through such

---

[1]G. W. Bromiley, "Worship," *Zondervan Pictorial Encyclopedia of the Bible*, ed. Merrill C. Tenney, 5 vols. (Grand Rapids: Zondervan, 1975), 5:975.

weak beings as ourselves. We are troubled by our sins and failures. We need a vision of God as holy, with a dynamic holiness that works forgiveness in Jesus and goes beyond the initial work to reshape us progressively toward a holiness like His own. We experience grief. We need to know and experience God as the "God of all comfort, who comforts us . . ." (2 Cor. 1:3-4). We long for joy, and we see Him as the giver of "every good and perfect gift" (James 1:17). We confront enemies, and we need the vision of a God who loves His enemies, and gives His children the charge to be like Him (Matt. 5:43-44). We panic when our finances are low. We need to catch a vision of God as the one who is even concerned with the sparrow's fall and who places far greater importance on our lives than on the sparrow's life (Matt. 10:29). We agonize over a decision. We need to see God as wise, who gives wisdom to all who ask him (James 1:5). *In every situation, in every need, there is a revelation of God's nature that invites us to find our total resource in Him!*

This revelation of God, an unveiling of who He is by nature, is given to us so that at every turn our lives may be linked to our Lord. He is, and is to be, the center of our lives. He speaks and shows Himself to us. Now, as the body, we respond to that self-revelation with worship and prayer.

A CORPORATE EXPERIENCE

The pattern given in Acts 4 and in many other passages of Scripture reveals believers responding to God's self-revelation in worship and prayer. What we have is a picture of *interaction*. And it is interaction that is always involved when any persons seek a deeper personal relationship, especially one that will lead to allegiance. Coming to know God the Father, like coming to know a neighbor, involves a process in which we speak and listen *to each other*. The Father speaks to us about Himself; we respond and together speak to Him. As we come to see and know Him better and respond to Him appropriately, we find a unique stability and security. We become aware that we are living, not just in this world, but encapsuled by the supernatural. In short, we become aware of "the hope to which he has called [us] . . . , and his incomparably great power for us who believe" (Eph. 1:18-19).

While there is to be in each of our lives space for private worship and prayer as our individual response to the Father, there is at the same time a definite priority given to worship and prayer offered by us together as the body of Christ.

We catch sight of this priority in many little ways. The Lord's Prayer instructs us to say *"Our* Father . . . . Give *us* this day. . ." (Matt. 6:9, 11). Jesus spoke of two or three agreeing in prayer and of His being "in the midst" of such little gatherings (Matt. 18:20). The Old Testament worship patterns are full of corporate festivals and feasts at which all the people were told to gather.

Why this stress on the corporate? We can suggest a number of reasons. First of all, we *are* "one" in the body. My brother's joys are my joys, his sorrows my burden. The "one mind and one heart" of Philippians are to characterize us as we share our lives and open them to one another for mutual support, encouragement, and commitment. How, then, could we not share this great central experience of the Christian, our most intimate interaction with the Father? How could we not together affirm Him in His nature, bring Him our needs, and rejoice as we see the answers to our prayers?

Second, the body and the relationships nurtured within it are the context in which new believers learn faith's lifestyle. They learn from teaching and from modeling, from example and from shared experiences with others. How, then, could we not worship God together and come to Him in prayer together, and in this way teach each other how to worship and pray? The corporate experience is still, as it was in ancient Israel, the training ground for private worship and prayer.

Shared worship and prayer also build in the body a common understanding of who God is. As the members of the body lift Him up together, each person receives a vision of Him that is common to the others. After all, it is God who is the center of our life and faith. We need a common understanding of who He is if we are to have a true and deep unity of purpose and heart. Affirming God together and relating our shared life and needs to Him will build a community of believers that has the only stable center—its growing knowledge of God.

A final reason for corporate worship is that God seeks it. When we respond to Him, we draw near to Him for a fellowship He enjoys. Just as we enjoy interaction with our loved ones, so God enjoys these times of sharing that we have with Him.

Interaction with God, involving a clear focus on some quality or characteristic of His and our response in worship and prayer, is basic to the health of the body of Christ. And guarding the health of the body is the task of the elders or spiritual leaders of the church.

PLANNING FOR WORSHIP

Are there principles of interaction with the Father that can help the spiritual leaders of a congregation shape its worship experiences? Surely. But first, let's note that we cannot *program* worship. We can create a context that may lead to worship. But there is nothing we can do to guarantee that true worship or prayer will take place.

This shouldn't trouble us. After all, God *is* sovereign. He is the One who acts in self-revelation, calls for our response, opens our eyes and hearts to Himself, and shapes us all. All we do in ministry must always be done with the deep awareness that we are totally dependent on God's gracious action in the situation for any spiritually significant result. Yet it is also clear that God has revealed principles to guide us and show us the ways He has chosen to work among us. To be aware of these principles and to use them in designing worship times is not to "program" worship, but instead to honor God by giving Him the setting His Word suggests He seeks as the context for His grace to overflow.

What characteristics can we suggest as appropriate in a setting designed for worship? Working from our examination of Acts (and other passages not explored in this brief chapter), we can suggest the following:

1. As much as possible, worship times should reflect the present experience of the congregation or its members.
2. Worship times should begin with a focus on who God is by nature. Seeing Him clearly, as the object of worship, is central to both worship and prayer.
3. Worship and prayer should be addressed *to God* by the congregation. The focus should not be on singing or talking *about* God: this is a time for direct address.

Let's look briefly at each of these three elements and see how they may be reflected in our services.

Reflecting present experience

A death in the congregation. A birth. Christmastime. Easter. A time of gossip and the resulting pain. The joy of a marriage. Four generations of a single family. A family restored through forgiveness. A graduation. Someone long-prayed-for coming to the Lord. A young couple responding to God's call to missions. A community crisis. Pornography. A financial need. Friends and members moving to a new part of the country. Fear. An epidemic of sickness. Sin. Thanksgiving.

These are just a few of the many experiences that flow in and through the life of all congregations. They are times to turn for a fresh glimpse of God.

A division occurs in the church over "tongues." Or over attitudes toward the new youth worker. Someone is hurt because he didn't receive the recognition he felt was due him. Several members of the body hear a radio preacher proclaim that God wants all His "kids" to be rich—and they wonder why they are not rich.

A woman is bitter because God hasn't healed her sickness. A brother is close to despair because of his son's involvement in drugs.

As we live among the people of our local body, these and many other experiences will be discovered, sensed. All of them are to be and can be the shared experience of the body of Christ. And each of these things is to be and can be related to God and seen in the light of who He is by nature.

This is the experiential root of our worship experience, for it is experiences like these that enable us to truly appreciate the answering quality in God that meets our needs and shows us the total sufficiency to be found in Him. Out of the reality of our shared lives, we come together to *be* the body and to look together in praise, adoration, worship, and prayer to the One who is the source and center of life for us.

Who God is by nature

The object of our worship is the heart of our worship experience. Our subjective experience and the life experience that stimulates our look to Him are not the heart of worship or prayer. *God* is the heart and the proper focus of our devotion.

But see how each of our experiences serves to illumine something special about God as He has revealed Himself to us.

We experience a death?	We worship God as everlasting Life.
There is a birth?	We see Him as the giver of life to His people.
Christmastime?	We see Him as Love incarnate.
Easter?	We see Christ's self-sacrifice. We see Him as the ultimate Servant.
Gossip?	We worship God as Truth.
Marriage?	We see God as our Husband and the body as the bride of Christ.
Four generations of one family?	We see God as the Father who does not change.
A family restored?	We see God as the healer, the worker of miracles.
A graduation?	We see God as our Hope, the holder of the future.

For each of our experiences God has a revelation of Himself, and through our experiences His perfection is seen with greater brightness and clarity. We fasten then on who He is. We see Him, and in that revelation we, as a believing community, find the sacred center for our life together.

Sometimes attributes of God, like those listed above, are associated not so much with experiences in the congregation as with the sermon theme. If we preach on 1 Corinthians 13, it is appropriate in worship to focus on God as love. If we speak from Matthew on God's supply, we might worship Him as faithful, or as the giver of every good and perfect gift.

In such cases the design of the worship time is to lead the body of believers to focus on God, to hear this freshly repeated revelation of who He is, and to respond in worship and prayer.

Addressed to God

Worship and prayer can take many different forms in our services. There can be liturgies, readings, testimonies, music. There can be confession, petition, intercession, thanksgiving, praise. The possibilities are endless.

But it's important to remember that what we seek to do in worship in Christ's body is lead each and every person to interact with God. We enter into a divine-human dialogue. We are not talking to each other *about* God. Talking to each other about God is not interaction with God and, surprisingly, it does not help us know *Him* in a deep and personal way. Rather, in worship we are together talking directly with and *to* God.

This is one of the weakest elements of the life of many churches. We sing, but our songs are often addressed to each other, speaking of our subjective experience. Songs like "I've Got Joy," "Blessed Assurance," and "I'm So Happy" may be a satisfactory expression of faith. But they are not worship, are not addressed to God, and do not specifically direct our thoughts to Him. Other songs do speak about God, but not to Him: "God Is So Good," "The Old Rugged Cross," "This Is My Father's World." Here God is the subject. But still we're not interacting with Him. We are addressing each other about Him. And then there are the true worship songs. "Great Is Thy Faithfulness"; "Father, Again to Thy Dear Name We Raise . . ."; "My Jesus, I Love Thee." Here a new and vital dimension is added. Here we lift our eyes and hearts, gaze directly at God, and speak *to* Him.

Now we are interacting with God.

Now we are in worship and prayer.

Now we will grow to know Him, not just about Him.

Dr. Robert Webber, in an excellent study on the early church, makes the following observation about worship:

> The principal purpose of worship is not to teach but to worship God (although a person alert to the structure of worship will find it a constant means of learning the faith through rehearsal). God is praised as Creator, Redeemer, and Judge. The worshiper praises, magnifies, and glorifies Him not only for who He is, but also for what He has done in providing life, redemption, sustenance, hope, and many other blessings. In this way worship becomes an experience of God. The worshiper is carried through an experience in which the opportunity is given to make a fresh commitment to Jesus Christ as Lord and Savior. This model of early Christian worship is an excellent example of the combination of evangelical spirit and historic substance and should be given serious consideration in evangelical circles as a model for worship renewal.[2]

Whether it is called renewal or not, to build a healthy and responsive body, leaders must be deeply concerned about guiding the corporate experience of the church into true and meaningful interaction with God the Father through worship and prayer.

INTERWEAVING WORSHIP

Recently Larry taught a course in the Wheaton College Graduate School. He flew from his home in Phoenix every Monday, taught for six hours, and flew back Tuesday mornings.

On the last night eighteen of the fellows from the class joined Larry at 10 P.M. for basketball. They played in Alumni Gym till after midnight. Then, there on the court, some of the guys brought out orange soda pop and a couple of rolls, and they shared communion. They worshiped God together, remembered Christ's death, and praised Him for the joy He had had in sharing their game with them.

It was a time of worship.

In Colorado, Clyde had friends from the body in for supper. As they shared, a need was expressed. Immediately Clyde responded, everyone at the table paused to join hands and bring the need to the Father, who was able to meet the need.

It was a time of prayer and worship.

The point of these two illustrations is a simple one. Worship and prayer—our focus on who God is by nature and our interaction with Him through these two forms of response—are the privilege of God's people everywhere and at all times.

---

[2]Robert E. Webber, *Common Roots: A Call to Evangelical Maturity* (Grand Rapids: Zondervan, 1978), p. 103.

We live in His presence. He is always with us. We can lift our eyes and our hearts to Him at any time. And we need to learn to practice His presence.

Of course we need to learn to practice His presence in our church services as well. We need to *redesign*—often—the service for true worship. For instance, the pattern used in one church (figure 37) reflects the principles discussed in this chapter.

This outline may look too "liturgical" for many. It's not meant to be a pattern for everyone. But it is meant to *show* a pattern. There's an awakening of an awareness of God's presence. There's a listening as God speaks to us of Himself. There's a response to God, a hearing of His Word to us, and a response to that Word. In the whole experience the focus is Godward, not manward. It's the *focus,* not the form, that's important. But it *is* important that our forms increasingly have this focus.

It may be simply five minutes set aside initially as a worship "insert" that contains these elements. It may be a redesign of the total service. Or it may be that as a leader each elder, in visiting or sharing or being in a small group, becomes sensitive to the opportunities that arise out of shared experience to turn thoughts to God and guide the members into meaningful worship and prayer.

But whatever ways are chosen, interaction with the Father is important. It is important that we know *Him.* It is important that we see prayer and worship for what they truly are and that we become a praying, worshiping people with a deep and true allegiance to our wonderful Father-God.

PROBE

▶ *case histories*
▶ *discussion questions*
▶ *thought provokers*
▶ *resources*

1. Look over half a dozen bulletins from your church services. Does the pattern of the service reveal an adequate worship and prayer emphasis? Analyze the music sung. Does it address God? Is it about Him? Does a central theme reflecting who God is by nature run through the entire service?

2. Undertake one or more of the following projects with one or more members of the leadership team of your local body:
   a. Discover all the music addressed *to* God that you can and classify it by the attributes it speaks of or implies.

FIGURE 37
A PATTERN OF WORSHIP

We Enter God's Presence

Choral Call to Worship

Congregational Prayer of Confession

Pastoral Prayer of Praise for Forgiveness

We Hear God Speak of Himself

Praise to God for His Faithfulness

Responsive Reading: Psalm

Choral Reading: Gospel

We Respond to God's Self-Revelation

Congregational Hymn: "Great Is Thy Faithfulness"

Praise for Your Faithfulness: Becky and Jan Jones

Silent Praises

The Gloria

Offering

We Hear God Speak to Us

Sermon: The Test of Faithfulness

We Respond to God's Word

Prayer of Commitment

Benediction

b. Look through your hymn book. In how many hymns can you make minor wording changes to have them speak *to* God?

c. Make a list of experiences or needs in your church right now. Then go from that list to note a corresponding or answering attribute of God (see page 243 for examples).

d. How many forms of prayer are there? Look up words for prayer in a concordance or other resource book.

e. Do a study of prayers recorded in the Bible. How many would be good for your congregation to learn to pray?

f. Plan a "worship workshop" for the congregation, perhaps on a retreat.

g. Work together to plan worship fitting around the themes of the next four sermons given in your church.

h. Begin making a file on worship forms and services and ideas.

i. Read several books on worship. Recommended are:
James D. Shaughnessy, ed., *The Roots of Ritual* (Grand Rapids: Eerdmans, 1973).
Ralph D. Martin, *Worship in the Early Church* (Grand Rapids: Eerdmans, 1975).
The Draft Proposed Book of Common Prayer and Other Rites and Ceremonies of the Church (New York: Seabury, 1976).

j. Plan a variety of settings in which you can informally introduce worship—in your home, your gatherings with others, etc.

3. The excellent "Working Paper on Worship" quoted below was prepared by members of Chicago's LaSalle Street Church.

WORKING PAPER ON WORSHIP

In the narrowest sense, worship is the response of the total person (intellectual, emotional, and volitional or commitment-making part) to God in the ascription of praise to Him for who He is (characteristics or attributes) and what He has done (words, attitudes, and deeds). It is an emotional and committing response to an intellectual evaluation of God. As heroes call forth our admiration, praise, and enthusiasm in spontaneous response, so much more does God. The word used for worship means to crouch, to kiss, to do homage, to prostrate oneself, to reverence. Further, true worship always reaffirms previous commitments and makes new commitments based on the new understanding achieved in the service. These are the "gifts" of the Spirit to which Jesus referred when He said, "God is spirit, and those who worship him must worship in spirit and truth" (John 4:24, RSV).

In its broader sense, worship is the offering of any gift to God in love—a gift of the Spirit mentioned above, a material gift, or the gift of a deed, a relationship, or even a vocation if they are "in His name." This makes worship a life-style and transforms all the secular into the sacred.

In either case, the primary posture of the worshiper is giving. Worship essentially is *giving* rather than *getting*.

1. Worship is a direct dialogue between God and the congregation so the worship service should be structured on this basis rather than the congregation and the minister talking to each other about the third person—God. This means the hymns used primarily should be those addressed to God as prayers (praise, thanksgiving, confession, consecration, petition, and intercession) rather than those addressed to our fellows (testimony and exhortation). Time also should be allotted for listening to God speak to us through Scripture, the sermon, the sharing of a fellow believer, and the quietness of meditation. Since true dialogue is two-way communication, time also must be allotted for our response to God in both structured and free prayer times.

Example: Litany: UNITY IN DIVERSITY

Leader: Our Father, here we are, having come from our private little worlds, feeling fragmented and alone.

People: Thank You for bringing us together anyway.

Leader: Our Father, some of us didn't feel like coming today because we thought no one really cared.

People: But You care. Thank You for caring.

Leader: Sometimes we've found it difficult to see anything of each other except our different shades of clothes and skins.

People: We're grateful Your vision isn't so superficial.

Leader: Lord, we've felt at times others haven't given us the respect we were entitled to because of our education or position.

People: Thank You for making us feel important by coming among us as an ordinary worker, a carpenter.

Leader: At times this past week we've scorned the failure of the weak and envied the success of the strong.

People: Remind us of the new understanding of failure and success brought us through the cross and the empty tomb.

Leader: As men, we fear our women want to take away our manhood; as women, we feel our men treat us as servants.

People: Lord God, You who have been a mother and a father to us, help us recognize each other's dignity as persons without denying each other's gifts as men and women.

Leader: Some of us feel we're left out because we're young and wear long hair, and others of us, because we're old and obsolete.

People: Eternal Christ, help us build bridges across the years that separate us.

Leader: Young and old, men and women, black and white—in all our multitudinous variety we have come together today to worship You.

People: Our Father, we thank You for all the richness of our colors and cultures. Help us to use our differences to enrich each other's lives. Help us to build Your kingdom out of our diversities.

Leader: And so, as we pray the prayer Jesus taught His disciples, help us to recognize in it our common needs, our common resource, our common goal.

All: (The Lord's Prayer)

2. The worship service should be a model for one's private devotions so anyone who attends even a few times can develop a viable quiet time of his own, unaided. The crisis of personal devotions comes in most cases as the result of never learning how to worship. One should get in the habit of listening to God and responding with the six various types of prayer.

a. Worship and Praise—either use a hymn or single out a characteristic of God cited in Scripture.

b. Thanksgiving—thanks for something God has done in your life, in the Christian community, or in the world.

c. Confession—should include a general confession that over against the Creator you are a "creature," as well as specific shortcomings of both commission and omission.

d. Intercession—standing before God shouldering the needs and concerns of others and presenting them to him.

e. Petition—telling God about your own needs.

f. Commitment or Consecration—the giving of oneself to God both generally and in specific commitments.

Example: Prayer of Confession (In Unison)

Father God, we confess that we are not what we should be or could be as Your people. We are not happy about this. When we pause in Your presence, we know we need Your Spirit's work in us. Why? Because the closed mind, the stubborn attitude, and the unforgiving spirit make us too hard. Our recklessness, carelessness, and scurry after the less important have us working against You. At times we are too sensitive—at other times not sensitive enough. We sulk; we complain; we don't reach out to anyone else; we submerge in self-pity; we sit there. We don't listen; we don't speak up; we don't involve ourselves—and so we contribute to this world's troubles, and to the breakdowns between us. We know it—and we need your prompting Spirit! Hear our continuing prayer . . . .

3. Worship should be the discovery of Christ with the congregation and not for them. The staff should not do all the worshiping for the congregation. Ample time should be allotted for lay participation and for spontaneous response. Further, since God dwells in each believer, He can speak through each Christian to the staff as well as through the staff.

Example: Consumerism Point and Counterpoint

Man ever finds his life in tension. Can we consume without becoming consumer-oriented? In our church life (the gathered Christians) will we merely receive and not give?

We will contrast some thoughts from Scripture with how society might react.

In the Area of Security

Scripture says: (SOUTH SIDE of congregation reading)
Matthew 8:20 (RSV)—Foxes have holes, and birds of the air have nests; but the Son of man has nowhere to lay his head.

Society says: (MINISTER reading)
If you've got it, flaunt it; which is to say—if you haven't got it or aren't getting it, then you just aren't with it. Security is the name of the game, and security is money or power.

Scripture says: (NORTH SIDE)
II Timothy 2:11, 12—If we have died with him, we shall also live with him; if we endure, we shall also reign with him; if we deny him, he also will deny us.

Society says: (MINISTER)
Eat, drink, and be merry and ignore death. You only get what you take.

Scripture says: (SOUTH SIDE)
Isaiah 12:2—Behold, God is my salvation; I will trust, and will not be afraid; for the Lord God is my strength and my song.

Society says: (MINISTER)
Don't trust anyone. Live as a practical atheist. Security is only found in what you control.

In the Area of Convenience

Scripture says: (NORTH SIDE)
Matthew 7:13, 14—Enter by the narrow gate; for the gate is wide and the way is easy, that leads to destruction, and those who enter

by it are many. For the gate is narrow and the way is hard, that leads to life and those who find it are few.

Society says: (MINISTER)
Don't buck the tide unless it pays in money or power. You're only young once, so do your thing. Take the easy way.

In the Area of Labor

Scripture says: (SOUTH SIDE)
Ephesians 4:28—Let the thief no longer steal, but rather let him labor, doing honest work.

Society says: (MINISTER)
You're not a thief unless you get caught. Everybody has an angle—whether it is outright theft or just deception in use of time or resources.

4. Since our worship service is attended by people of various spiritual, social, cultural, and intellectual backgrounds, there must be special appeal for each until we go to multiple services. Each should hear his own musical sound every Sunday, if possible. Thus each service should contain classical, folk, country, soul, and Gospel song musical forms blended together in tasteful fashion. Special programs featuring one of these forms should be a regular part of our church program. Similarly, the Scripture and the sermon must contain applications relevant to these various groups. Again, individuals from each of these diverse groups should be asked to participate formally in the service. Let the church glory in the diversity of the Body of Christ as well as its unity.

Example: Spirituals from the black church, country music, selections from classics such as Handel's *Messiah,* anthems, chants from ancient liturgies, etc.

5. We should keep the basic elements of worship from service to service in order to give security and freedom to the worshiper. However, the way each is done may vary from Sunday to Sunday in order to avoid triteness and "ritualism."

Example: The Scripture reading may be read by one or more persons, dramatized by a group, sung by the choir, read with guitar or instrumental accompaniment, presented through choral speaking, read responsively between pastor and congregation or pastor and choir, accompanied by a mime, or recited antiphonally by one side of the congregation speaking to the other.[3]

---

[3]James Hefley and Marty Hefley, *The Church That Takes on Trouble* (Elgin, Ill.: David C. Cook, 1976), pp. 227-32.

PART 3

BIBLICAL PRINCIPLES
OF CHURCH LEADERSHIP

A Description of Allegiance

Building Allegiance: Relational Presuppositions
Allegiance to One Another: Shared Life
Allegiance to the Father: Prayer and Worship
Allegiance to the Spirit: Giftedness
Allegiance to the Son: Personal Responsibility

How Leaders Build Allegiance

Body Organization
Ownership, Consensus, and Freedom
Confidence and Support
Communication

The Spirit is the quiet member of the Trinity. Jesus said, "He will testify about me" (John 15:26). We do not pray to the Spirit, nor in the name of the Spirit, yet He is with us in our prayers, entering in, guiding, interpreting (Rom. 8:26-27).

In the same way the Spirit is with us in ministry. He gives gifts. He enables. He is the Minister in our ministry. In a very

ALLEGIANCE TO THE SPIRIT: GIFTEDNESS

basic way you and I are simply expressions of God's Spirit. He is the One who reaches out through us to touch and heal.

Building allegiance to the Spirit involves freeing each believer to live confidently as an expression of the Spirit. It means helping each believer trust the Spirit's presence enough to serve.

Many Christians begin their quest for personal significance by turning to the Bible's teaching on spiritual gifts. They turn to Scripture, study the words in the lists— outline possible meanings—wait and wonder—seek out a role in the church organization that they hope will fit them. In focusing on the "gift" and wondering about "it," they lose sight of the heart of giftedness.

Why? Because we are again facing a relational issue: the issue of our relationship with God the Holy Spirit, the third person of the Trinity. The way to approach giftedness and to discover our individual significance within the body is to begin with *interaction*. We need to learn how to interact in our daily lives with the Spirit and in the process come to know His presence. Growing in that relationship, we discover that He is in fact expressing Himself by ministering through us in special, individual ways.

THE THEOLOGICAL BASE

CHAPTER **18**

Our interaction with each of the persons each other, has a theological basis. The basis for our life with the Spirit is clearly taught in Scripture.

The first reality is that God the Holy Spirit comes to live within our personalities. At conversion He joins us to Christ and He Himself is both the bond and the testimony of our union (1 Cor. 12:12; Eph. 1:13-14). This new relationship with God the Spirit is an exciting one: He who was once *with* the disciples is now *in* each of us.

The Spirit's presence is the source of our ability to minister and to serve. He is the giver of spiritual gifts; He is the source of the power that activates the gift and enables it to function. He is also the One who *leads* us, speaking in us the directions of Christ our head. Romans puts it this way: "You, however, are controlled not by your sinful nature but by the Spirit, if the Spirit of God lives in you. . . . Those who are led by the Spirit of God are sons of God" (Rom. 8:9, 14). References to quenching and grieving the Spirit in the New Testament relate to this fact. The Spirit is the voice of God within us. He speaks to lead and to direct. We are to be responsive to His voice.

Hebrews points out the significance of an obedient response to the daily voice of God. It was, Hebrews says:

As the Holy Spirit says:
Today, if you hear his voice,
do not harden your hearts
as you did in the rebellion . . .
(Heb. 3:7-8)

The writer then speaks of the "todayness" of God's voice giving guidance to His people. And again comes the warning: "Today, if you hear his voice, do not harden your hearts as you did in the rebellion" (3:15). The historical reference is to the generation whom God called to enter the Promised Land but who drew back. They disobeyed, and Scripture defines that disobedience as "their unbelief" (3:19). As the discussion continues into Hebrews 4, we realize that each generation, each individual, is given a "today" guidance. And each of us has the privilege of entering into what is called God's "rest" by responding obediently whenever we hear His voice in our today.

And what is the "rest"? It is, says the writer to the Hebrews, "resting from [our] own work" (4:10). It is freedom to minister to and to serve others in God's strength, realizing that He who has designed the universe is even now implementing that grand design through us.

As we respond, we find the fruit of obedience ripening in us. We find that obedience brings blessing to us and to others. We find that we *can* minister, that our lives can touch others for good. We find that God the Holy Spirit does express Himself through us, that we do have a gift capacity and a truly significant role to play in Christ's body and in the world.

So the search for significance in the body—and this is what we are each looking for when we focus on biblical teaching about gifts—begins not with gifts but with relationship. The search ends successfully as we become increasingly aware of our relationship with the Spirit, as we learn to listen for His voice and respond with obedience as we are led.

Relationship deepens into allegiance to the Spirit as we live a life of responsive obedience and find Him leading us to live a truly significant life.

PURPOSES OF THE FATHER

A second approach to understanding giftedness and the allegiance pattern of life in our relationship with the Holy Spirit is to recall the purposes that God has chosen to accomplish through the body of Christ. We looked at some of the purposes in chapter 4 of this text. There I suggested that God's purposes are complex and many-faceted. Through the body of Christ, God is continuing His work in our world—a work of ministry too encompassing to be summed up under the typical headings of "evangelism" or "nurture."

The complexity of the task given to the church is an argument against human attempts at the management of Christ's body. Only Christ, intimately knowing the gifts He has given each believer and the needs in each local setting, is able to function as head of the church and to guide individuals and groups into the fulfillment of His mission.

But interaction with the Spirit involves God's taking the initiative through leading. Our response is obedience. Giftedness and leading then must be intimately related to God's purposes. See the following chart for a partial listing.

FIGURE 38
THE COMPLEX PURPOSES OF GOD IN THE BODY

In fact, we can suggest that a more appropriate way to guide the members of the body into an allegiance to the Spirit than direct teaching about His gifts is (1) to teach the reality of the believers' relationship with the Spirit and encourage their responsiveness to His leading, and (2) to teach the body about the many purposes God is eager to enable them to accomplish as Christ's body, sensitizing them to the many ways we can serve and minister to others.

Gib Martin, pastor of Seattle's Trinity Church for some thirteen years, gives the following illustration of this approach. He emphasizes helping members of the body listen for God's voice.

> I try to help our believers understand that each one is a priest. So if God has burdened you about a particular need in a person's life and you are able to meet that need and minister to that person in a situation in which you find yourself, then proceed prayerfully and thoughtfully. If you need assistance in terms of ideas or prayer, then it is a good idea to contact a leader.
>
> Bill, a pilot with a major airline here, came to me. He had been in the church most of his life but had never felt free to minister. He went through our School of Christian Living, which dealt with giftedness and the nature of the church, and now is excited about working with boys. He has two sons who are grown and now has a ministry with boys that is beginning to develop in new and refreshing ways. But always before, Bill had to operate in an over-under position. He always had to be sure that he had permission to do whatever he did. Well, working with me was frustrating at first. He would ask for permission and I would say, "You already have permission." He'd say, "What do you mean by that?" And I would say, "The Lord has called you to be a servant. If I can be an encouragement to you, I will be glad to, but the Lord has called you already. Now, I don't want to have you serve unless the Lord is telling you to do that."
>
> I made Bill begin to listen to what the Spirit of God was telling him to do, because he would start doing a dozen different things and then complain that he was overinvolved. I'd say, "Bill, did the Lord tell you to do that?"
>
> He first took on the assignment of managing our Center. It was an ambitious project. Now all of us were glad he was going to do it, because he's a capable guy and very earnest. But before long you could see it was wearing him out, and he was beginning to resent people who didn't fall in line. They weren't responding to his ministry. Later he confessed that much of what he did was done out of habit and former concepts of ministry. He suddenly came to a point where the spiritual-giftedness concepts were so stunning he realized he could resign everything. He decided to back off from everything and take only the assignment the Holy Spirit would give him.
>
> I can say I'm excited to be a ministry partner with Bill in a wholly new way. Now there's freedom—where the Spirit of the Lord is, there is freedom. Now Bill is functioning under the lordship of Christ as a ministry partner, not in the "chain of command" structure he used to want. And it's beautiful to see the way the Lord is using Him.

NOT CHAIN-OF-COMMAND

This last observation brings me to one other vital concept in this examination of giftedness. In many churches an attempt is made to *institutionalize* giftedness. That is, the lists of gifts in Romans and 1 Corinthians are studied and an effort is made to correlate the gifts with organizational roles. Gift of teaching? Of course. You fit in Sunday school. Gift of helps? How about on the building committee? Or folding bulletins on Saturday night? Showing mercy? Join the Women's Missionary Circle and roll bandages for Bangladesh. In this way "gifts" can be brought under an organizational chain-of-command control.

Attempts at institutionalizing gifts are well meant. But they miss a vital and central reality. Gifts are not primarily related to institutional maintenance. Gifts are related to *building persons.* Gifts are exercised in direct, person-to-person contact. This is why Hebrews stresses meeting together. It is in interaction that our gifts function and we spur one another to love and good works by encouragement (Heb. 10:24-25).

This is not to say that Bill's management of the Trinity Center was not a contribution to the life of the body. It was much like the contribution of the deacons in Acts 6 who took on a service task (distributing food to the widows) as a help to the community, to free the apostles for prayer and the ministry of the Word. There are maintenance services that can be offered to the body and be a contribution. *But the primary context for the exercise of spiritual gifts is relational and interactive.*

Look at the representative list of gifts given in 1 Corinthians 12. Each gift operates in an interpersonal context in which members of the body are interacting with each other.

> Now to each man the manifestation of the Spirit is given for the common good. To one there is given through the Spirit the ability to speak with wisdom, to another the ability to speak with knowledge by means of the same Spirit, to another faith by the same Spirit, to another gifts of healing by that one Spirit, to another miraculous powers, to another prophecy, to another the ability to distinguish between spirits, to another the ability to speak in different kinds of tongues, and to still another the interpretation of tongues. All these are the work of one and the same Spirit, and he gives them to each man, just as he determines (1 Cor. 12:7-11).

However we may understand these gifts and their contemporary function, it's clear that not one of them is exercised outside of a relational context. The ministries mentioned are *to* and *by* individuals or groups of individuals or in the gathered body.

Again, recall the fact that in every gift and body context in the New Testament detailed instructions on how to live a "one another" kind of life are given. Additional evidence is given to show that gifts are to be exercised in the interaction that takes place between persons. One pastor put it into perspective when he said, "If God has burdened you about a particular need in a person's life and you are able to meet that need and minister to that person in a situation that you find yourself, then proceed prayerfully and thoughtfully." In other words, don't try to identify gifts with organizational roles. Discover those gifts in people by recognizing that we are called to *serve* our brothers and sisters. In coming to know our brothers and sisters we recognize and are burdened by a need in someone's life. Then, moved by love, we reach out to try to meet that need. *In the ministry, our spiritual gift emerges as God the Spirit touches our brother or sister through us.*

ENCOURAGING THE EXERCISE OF GIFTEDNESS

So far in this chapter, several key ideas have been suggested, each of which deserves further study and will be developed more extensively in a forthcoming Zondervan book, *A Theology of Personal Ministries: Giftedness in the Local Church.* These are the key ideas:

1. An awareness of the living presence of the Holy Spirit and our relationship to Him is the basic *understanding* the body needs to move toward the exercise of its giftedness.
2. Learning to sense the Spirit's leading and to respond obediently to His voice is the basic *training* the body needs to move toward the exercise of its giftedness.
3. Catching a vision of the many purposes God intends to accomplish through the living church is the basic *orientation to ministry* that the body needs to move toward the exercise of its giftedness.
4. Realizing that God the Spirit ministers to others through us as we come to know them and sense a call to serve them is the basic *relational commitment* that the body needs to move toward the exercise of its giftedness.

As these four ideas become a growing part of the experience of the members of Christ's body, those members will increasingly seek to serve others personally, and we will all learn that filling roles in institutional programs is *not* what ministry or giftedness is all about.

These four insights can help leaders in the local church to encourage believers to let the Spirit guide them into those personal ministries from which their gifts will emerge. The leaders need to teach. They need to model. They need to encourage and instruct as Gib Martin encouraged and instructed Bill in the above story. As members of the body realize that they are able to serve others significantly and then begin to minister, their gifts will emerge and be recognized by the body.

This is actually the only way giftedness can be *known.* A person may want a particular gift. A person may try to serve others in a way that expresses that giftedness. If, in fact, when a person is gifted in serving in a particular way God the Spirit touches and enriches his life, his good work will be recognized. The ministering person and the body will both realize that this special gift is his contribution to the body.

Larry has a lovely secretary named Lawana. She came to Phoenix from Newport Beach, California, to work with him. As a church secretary in California, she had a large group of friends, all of whom found they could share their needs and problems with her and sense God's healing touch. Though she has been in Phoenix only a few months, Lawana already has half a dozen friends who come to her for this same kind of ministry. And the members of the church she was a part of in Newport Beach still call her long distance and sometimes fly her "home" for a weekend so they can share her friendship and receive her ministry. This gift of counseling or encouragement, or whatever name you might want to give it, *is recognized and known by the members of the body.* In the close and loving relationship Lawana develops with people, the Holy Spirit expresses Himself in a beautiful way, and people who know His healing touch through her recognize the gift at work.

Lawana might have spent years studying the "gift" lists in Scripture and years in prayer that God would show her her gift. And she might never have discovered it. Instead, Lawana has become involved in the lives of her friends. As she has served them, her gift has emerged. *It is in the functioning of the gift in the context of close and loving relationships that a gift is recognized and that others affirm the presence of a particular gift in us.*

So a leader's role is to help the members of the body realize the Spirit's presence in them and, following His leading, actively step out to serve others. As they serve, the giftedness will emerge, whether previously recognized or not. As they serve, our brothers and sisters will find the fulfillment of each one's yearning for significance. Each one will be a partner in a ministry with God.

PROBE

► case histories
► discussion questions
► thought provokers
► resources

1. The following song ("Expressions" by Donna Crenshaw) sums up some of the teaching on giftedness a congregation needs to know. Learn it and teach it to members of your congregation.

EXPRESSIONS

Donna Crenshaw, 1978

Arm in arm, hand in hand, we'll learn to walk up-on this land, 1. ex - pres - sions of God's Spir - it, our 2. dis - co - ver - ing with each o - ther His

hands His hand of love in sim - ple acts of
gift in ev - ery one

ser - vice, Lord, We do be - cause we care — 1. The 2. Our

Spir - it brings the heal - ing That makes the bro - thers
Lord's e - ter - nal pur - pose Will find ex - pres - sion

whole.
there.

© Copyright 1979, Dynamic Church Ministries.
Used by permission.

2. The Dynamic Church Ministries video seminars (which focus on interaction in the body, giftedness, and prayer and worship) contain the following exercise to help participants understand their gifts and get involved in personal ministries that will help them discover their own areas of giftedness. You might want to use the exercise on a retreat or obtain the video seminars themselves. (Write to: Dynamic Church Ministries, P.O. Box 35331, Phoenix, Arizona 85069 for retreat or other information.)

a. List below the names of people or groups whom your life touches.

1. _____ 7. _____
2. _____ 8. _____
3. _____ 9. _____
4. _____ 10. _____
5. _____ 11. _____
6. _____ 12. _____

b. Write down any of the needs of those persons or groups that you are aware of.

1. _____ 7. _____
2. _____ 8. _____
3. _____ 9. _____
4. _____ 10. _____
5. _____ 11. _____
6. _____ 12. _____

c. Go over the first list and circle the numbers of two persons or groups you feel *most concerned* about.

d. In groups of four, talk together. Each person should share with the others the two persons or groups he is most concerned about. Together talk about how you can best serve that person or group.

e. Plan ways to serve them this week.

This activity can also be related to the "purposes" chart on page 257. How do the needs you isolated relate to the purposes God has revealed for Christ's body? How might your service help fulfill these purposes? Pray that God the Spirit will touch lives through your contact this week.

3. It's encouraging to see resources being developed for use in the body that are not institutional but personal in orientation. One such resource for boys has been developed by the "Sky Clubs" under the leadership of Gary Jenkins, a United Airlines pilot, once an elder at Trinity Church in Seattle, now living in the Chicago area.

These clubs, by the way, are designed to function best in homes and with neighborhood groups. Anyone interested in building a personal ministry with Sky Club resources may call Gary Jenkins or Jack Bryant at 1-312-358-2236, or write them at Sky Club of America, 2155 W. Frost Road, Schaumberg, Illinois 60195.

One of my Wheaton College graduate students, Dann Spader, interviewed the Sky Club leadership and developed the following description. Read it to get a feel for the differences between the "institutional" ministry of a local church and a "personal" minis-try of members of Christ's body—something this chapter has stressed as vital to the understanding and building of a people that exercise their giftedness in allegiance to the Spirit.

Gary and Jack mentioned three major principles at work in the Sky Clubs. First, there is a conceptual style of learning with accountability. The goal of all teaching and learning is to have the boys learn concepts from practical experiences. Each club member learns memory verses, listens to the chaplain, and does an assignment—all focused on a single theme. Through the week, each boy is given an assignment based on what he has just learned. The goal is getting the boys to "do" rather than just "hear" the Word of God.

The second major principle at work in the Sky Clubs is that of attempting to turn the hearts of fathers toward their children and the hearts of the children toward their fathers (Mal. 4:5–6; Luke 1:17). The leaders attempt to bring families together (Deut. 6; 11; Ps. 78:5). A major goal of the Sky Club is involving the father with his child in a nonthreatening way to help him with the basics of living in general and specifically in living the Christian life. In Jack's words, "People seem to have lost the ability to take an event and use it for teaching purposes." The Sky Clubs are creating an event to teach a truth in a very real, pertinent, and effective context. In other words, the Sky Clubs attempt to create a learning experience for boys and their fathers.

Third, the Sky Clubs teach parents to teach their own children. They do not want to usurp parental authority in the training of children, but to aid parents in teaching their children. Gary explains that this principle is not expressed verbally because it would frighten parents away—but it is in the background.

Feeling strongly opposed to competition as an incentive, Gary and Jack use six major incentives: (1) The long-range incentive. With a group of no more than five boys, a leader can relate in a close, loving way with the boys. This motivates most boys. (2) The approval incentive. The boys try to please their "cloud captain" and parent as they work to achieve their ranks. (3) Peer pressure. Boys are awarded for their achievements, so a common desire to excel is created. (4) The craft incentive. As the boys progress in the club, they also progress in their craft program. (5) A point system. Competition is not against other boys but against their own previous record. They strive to improve over their previous week's scores. (6) Accountability. Each week the boys receive assignments. The leader checks to make sure they become doers of the Word rather than just hearers.

I am excited about the potential I see in the Sky Clubs. Perhaps of greatest merit are the boy-leader and boy-parent relationships. Based on the right incentives, they can be extremely constructive in building or restoring the discipling process in a boy's life. Since the relationships are not based on competition or performance, they support and train the boy. As the leader relates to the boys in love, he becomes a model to them. As a parent becomes actively involved with his son in completing an activity, they both benefit. Creating an event to facilitate teaching and learning between a father and his son is immensely worthwhile.

The Sky Clubs' conceptual thematic approach to learning is a good one. Using Scripture memorization, lesson study, and message time to convey a single truth is a very effective method of teaching concepts. Accountability is an added incentive.

Perhaps the greatest merit of the Sky Club approach is its boy-leader relationships. Providing an event for the father to teach his child and for the leader to be a servant and model to the boy, and developing an incentive program based on love rather than competitive achievement or performance, constitute an exciting and fresh approach.

If the Sky Clubs can bring boys and their fathers together, create a simple but effective craft and achievement program, and provide a few home or church models, the sky can be the limit as to how effective they can be.

4. Gib Martin and one of the other leaders at Trinity in Seattle made up a list of 120 of the 400 members of the congregation, showing some of their personal ministries. What is significant about this list is that these are "spontaneous" ministries; the Holy Spirit has led these people into these various kinds of ministry and service *without* the direct involvement of the local church leaders. Instead, each person was encouraged to reach out and serve (see below).

A LOOK AT A MINISTERING PRIESTHOOD

The following is a sampling of those in the body at the Trinity Church who are significantly involved in priestly functions *on a daily basis*.

1. Tim (engineer): elder, finance council chairman, youth outreach, hospitality, marriage counseling
2. Chet (computer science): Sunday school teaching, Christian education, counseling, ministry of service (electrical and mechanical skills)
3. Edna (housewife): discipleship ministry to women, secretarial skill, hospitality
4. Jerrie (Christian pre-school): encouragement-and-mercy ministry, child evangelism, ministry of service, college-career ministry
5. Larry (engineer, construction): elder, marriage counseling, administrative skills, encouragement, ministry of service (e.g., building, facilities maintenance)

6. Lorann (homemaker): leadership with women's service ministries, nursery administration, child-care, ministry of encouragement to mothers, marriage counseling, hospitality
7. Dan (pastor, English teacher): outreach to foreign students, hospitality, home-ministry center, worship council, home Bible study
8. Terry (secretary): ministry through music, encouragement, discipleship to women
9. Ron (commercial painting, pastor): ministry of mercy, hospitality
10. Bob (car salesman): head of tape ministry, ministry of giving, hospitality
11. Kathy (secretary): missions, prayer support
12. Florence (homemaker): hospitality, women's fellowship, Bible school, Sunday school, ministry to children, child-care, ministry of giving
13. Jeff (camp program director): youth outreach, follow-up, youth evangelism, men's discipleship group, teaching
14. Jean (church administrator): ministry to women, women's discipleship, counseling, secretarial skills, ministry of service and administration
15. Ken (computer, business): prayer support, missionary prayer support, men's discipleship, church finance council
16. Maria (computer, business): ministries to women, hospitality
17. Rich (insurance broker): youth team, teaching, worship council
18. Jim (engineer, business): campus evangelism and discipleship, college-career Bible studies and ministries, counseling
19. Peggy (CPA): Sunday school administration, teaching, discipling of young girls, bookkeeping skills for church and Grapevine Shelter ministries
20. Roberta (teacher): missionary to Africa, discipleship with women, ministry of service and administration, hospitality
21. Jerry (auto body professional): ministry of mercy, counseling, Grapevine Council, hospitality and encouragement
22. Pat (dental technician): ministry of mercy, communications skills, ministry of service, hospitality
23. Mike (intern): home-ministry center, hospitality, teaching, discipleship, worship council, ministry of music
24. Becky (secretary, homemaker): hospitality, home Bible study, home-ministry center, discipleship, ministry of music
25. Grace (professional telephone services): witnessing, prayer support, encouragement, hospitality, ministry of service
26. Elizabeth (widow): prayer-chain coordinator, prayer support, hospitality
27. Dick (banker): Grapevine Shelter ministries, ministry of mercy,

elder, counseling, teaching, ministry to children, ministry of encouragement

28. Sue (homemaker): ministries with children (VBS, children's church), resource teacher, ministries to women
29. Don (engineer): elder, marriage counseling, home Bible study, hospitality
30. Myrna (homemaker): ministry of encouragement, women's discipleship, hospitality
31. Virginia (saleswoman, homemaker): hospitality, youth outreach, ministries to women
32. Tom (computer science, business): financial advisor
33. Marybeth (teacher): ministries to women, discipleship, teaching, service
34. Steve (engineer, business): elder, teaching, ministry to university students
35. Sue (homemaker): ministries to women, ministry of music, service
36. Phil (real estate): men's prayer team, men's discipleship, preaching-teaching, hospitality
37. Sherry (homemaker): women's discipleship, hospitality, ministry to children, VBS
38. Ron (commercial painting): counseling, ministry of mercy, arts and crafts development
39. Esther (widow): service, encouragement, prayer support, office helper
40. Steve (builder): home-ministry center, hospitality, discipleship, teaching
41. Melody (secretary, homemaker): development of ministry in the arts, ministry of encouragement
42. Tom (contractor, retired pilot): elder, hospitality, ministry to widows
43. Margaret (artist, homemaker): ministry of service, hospitality, ministry to widows
44. Al (driving teacher): missionary, prayer support, discipleship, teacher, hospitality, counseling, ministry of mercy, service
45. Nancy (homemaker): ministry to women, leader of women's fellowship, ministry to small children, hospitality, counseling
46. Clarice (homemaker): prayer support, home-ministry center, ministry of service, youth interest
47. Mits (business): elder, evangelism with Gideons, missionary support, ministry of music, initiator
48. Mary Lou: ministry of encouragement, giving, prayer support
49. Mary: ministry to youth, Campus Life staff, hospitality, counseling
50. Dorothy (homemaker): head of country store, rummage sales,

prayer support, book reviews, ministry of mercy and counseling, Grapevine Shelter ministries, service ministries

51. Marlene (church secretary, homemaker): counseling, encouragement, organization and secretarial skills, ministry to children and youth, Sunday school, community involvement
52. Bill (engineer): ministry to alcoholics, hospitality, encouragement
53. Sigrid (nurse): ministry of encouragement, hospitality
54. Buzz (builder): men's discipleship, home Bible study, hospitality, ministry of discipling young men
55. Gary (pilot): Sky Club, ministry to young boys, hospitality, counseling, prayer support
56. Lloyd (chaplain, pastor): missionary, hospital ministries, teaching, preaching, ministry of mercy
57. Tom (mechanic): prayer ministry, men's discipleship, youth leadership, teaching, mercy, giving, service, encouragement
58. Sue (homemaker): ministry of service, prayer support
59. Arvilla (homemaker): Grapevine Shelter ministries, counseling, secretary, bookkeeper, service
60. Marc (teacher): missionary work, teaching, evangelism, ministry to children
61. Penny (homemaker): mission work, evangelism, hospitality, service
62. Forrest (retired): Sunday school, counseling, hospitality, ministry to foreign students, teaching, ministries to young parents
63. Marcee (business): ministries to children, Sunday school, teaching, service, discipleship with women, college-career support, prayer support
64. Willa (nurse): missionary to Africa, ministry to youth, discipleship with young girls, teaching
65. Doris (teacher): evangelism, witnessing, outreach
66. Phil (CPA): ministry of music, leadership with music, financial advisor, hospitality, home Bible study
67. Cheryl (nurse): ministries to women, home Bible study, ministry of music
68. LaDonna (Grapevine staff): ministry of mercy, encouragement, service, counseling
69. Pam (homemaker): ministries to young girls, Pioneer Girls, arts and crafts, ministries to children, service, hospitality (open home)
70. Duane (businessman, custodian): youth activities, recreation coordination, family ministry, prayer-discipleship group with men
71. Lloydine (homemaker): ministries to young girls, Pioneer Girls, ministry to teens, counseling, foster-home care

72. Ivan (car salesman): ministry to delinquents and alcoholics, counseling, ministries of mercy
73. John (school counselor): ministry to strangers (travelers), foster-home care, hospitality, facilities upkeep, administration of facilities care
74. Marilynn (teacher): hospitality, foster-home care, ministry to women, mercy
75. Linda (homemaker): mercy, service, Bible Study Fellowship, evangelism
76. Dan (pastor): missions, World Concern staff, teaching, administration of work with missions
77. Linda (homemaker, secretary, wife of pastor): hospitality, counseling, mercy
78. Paul and Julie (retired): campground ministry
79. Maynard and Chris: evangelism, church encouragement, church planting, traveling to the unchurched
80. Scott and Pam: full-time ministry in dramatics, encouragement to churches, evangelism, ministry of music, hospitality
81. Steve (business): ministry to alcoholics
82. Jane: missions, discipleship overseas
83. John (engineer, business): ministry of music, worship council, organ and piano playing, small-group music, individual teacher of music
84. Candy (homemaker): service, ministry of music, discipleship with women, hospitality, small-group music
85. Gail (secretary): ministry to children, ministry to alcoholics
86. Emy Lou (widow): prayer support, hospitality, writing and illustrating children's books, teaching children
87. Sue (homemaker): ministries of mercy, open home, foster-child care, ministry to young children, nursery, counseling, service
88. Mark (staff of church): service, prayer support, elder, encouragement, counseling
89. Barney (retired businessman): restaurant ministry, giving
90. Bill (Campus Life staff): youth leadership, youth resource person, teaching, preaching
91. Dwight (teacher): now serving in Sweden, Bible school, evangelism
92. Jane (homemaker): teacher, VBS, missions support, secretarial work
93. Matt (student): evangelism, ministry of mercy (shelter), music
94. Mel (businessman): now serving full time with Mission Aviation Fellowship in Irian Jaya
95. Lucy (homemaker [Mel's wife]): hospitality to other missionaries, teaching
96. Margaret (librarian, homemaker): library ministry, counseling

97. Doris (medical attendant): ministry to several nursing homes, ministry to children
98. Mike (educational psychologist): teaching, counseling, Bible study, encouragement
99. Marie (widow): office assistant, group leading
100. Rob (businessman): giving
101. Wadad (professor): choir directing, ministry of music, counseling, teaching
102. Chris (counselor): teaching, counseling, ministry of mercy
103. Ed (counselor): counseling, Sunday school teaching, small-group Bible study
104. Dave (student): practical helps (e.g., mechanical and electrical repair), service
105. Verne (insurance broker): evangelism, hospitality, giving
106. Sol (psychiatrist): counseling, extending mercy
107. Don (teacher): ministry to high-school students
108. Florence (widow): Bible-study teaching, office assistant
109. Ken (independent): teaching, counseling, writing, pastoral ministry
110. Robin (homemaker): hospitality, discipleship, counseling, ministry to women
111. Kathy (secretary): ministry of music, ministry to the elderly, prayer-support team
112. David (doctor): educational ministry to larger community
113. Susan (doctor): educational ministry, ministry of music, ministry to children
114. Lou (pilot): evangelism
115. Betty (homemaker): teaching, ministry to children
116. Jackie (homemaker): ministry to children, ministry of art, food co-op ministry, prayer support
117. Doug (teacher): elder, marriage counseling, ministry to youth, printing
118. Darlene (homemaker): ministry to youth, practical helps and mercy, counseling, hospitality
119. Duke (chimney sweep et al.): practical helps (e.g., planning gardens, lending equipment), men's discipleship
120. Elizabeth (homemaker): practical helps (e.g., teaching food canning and bread making, food co-op ministry
121. Bill (retired engineer): ministry of mercy, practical helps, maintenance of facilities, prayer support

PART 3

BIBLICAL PRINCIPLES
OF CHURCH LEADERSHIP

A Description of Allegiance

Building Allegiance: Relational Presuppositions
Allegiance to One Another: Shared Life
Allegiance to the Father: Prayer and Worship
Allegiance to the Spirit: Giftedness
Allegiance to the Son: Personal Responsibility

How Leaders Build Allegiance

Body Organization
Ownership, Consensus, and Freedom
Confidence and Support
Communication

We've stressed it over and over again: Christ is the head of the church—the functional *head of the body.*

What does this mean in terms of allegiance? For one thing, it means leadership standing aside and letting Him be head. For the body as a whole, it means learning to look to Jesus, not to human leaders, for direction. For each of us,

ALLEGIANCE TO THE SON: PERSONAL RESPONSIBILITY

it means accepting personal responsibility for the ministries into which Jesus calls us.

We'll learn more about how this can be built into the life of a local congregation in later chapters. For now, we need only to affirm that allegiance to the Son means learning to interact with Him as head of the body, and head of every individual.

Interaction is again our starting point as we think of the way allegiance to Christ is developed. We begin by describing the nature of the interactive relationship God's people are to have with the Son.

We have seen that Jesus' role as head of the church is one of responsibility for the life, support, growth, and transformation of the body (see chapter 1). Ephesians 5:21 is particularly critical here. Ephesians portrays Jesus' headship as expressed in His being Savior of the church (5:23). He "gave himself up for her, to make her holy" (5:25-26). Christ's sacrifice on Calvary is the great action He took to win His bride, and in that one act He has laid the basis for the total purifying work that He accomplishes in the present and future. Every relationship that we have with Jesus and every work of His in our lives are fulfillments of what was completed in His cross. We never see or meet Him without the print of the nails in His hands and the scar of the wound made by the soldier's spear in His side. His every touch rehearses the depth of His self-sacrificial love.

19

Our response to Him is always on this same basis. He comes to us, and when we hear our Savior speak, our hearts are stirred. The importance of this heart response (bending willingly to the desires of the lover) is seen in Christ's teaching in John. "If any one loves me," Jesus explained, "he will obey my teaching" (14:23). This theme is repeated, and stated in the reverse as well. "He who does not love me will not obey my teaching" (14:24). And again in a fresh way, "If you obey my commands you will remain in my love" (15:10).

The significance of these statements is tremendous. Only love will free us to obey. *One who does not respond with love to Jesus' presentation of Himself as sacrificial love will not obey!* He who finds love translated into acts of obedience will live in constant awareness of the love of the Son of God. The interaction we have with Jesus is an interaction of love extended and love given in response.

How then do we deal with the fact that as head of the church, Jesus is the one we look to for direction and guidance? Why isn't it *His* voice that we hear, and why isn't obedience our direct response to Him? These functions of guidance and obedience/response are associated with the Spirit! The answer is in something Jesus said about the Spirit. "When he, the Spirit of truth, comes, he will guide you into all truth. *He will not speak on his own; he will speak only what he*

273

hears . . . He will bring glory to me by taking from what is mine and making it known to you" (John 16:13-14).

The Spirit is the guide and the voice. But the words are Jesus' words! And what the body recognizes is Jesus Himself, speaking through the Spirit.

"My sheep listen to my voice; I know them, and they follow me," Jesus once explained (John 10:27). When the Spirit speaks, the voice that is heard is recognized as that of Jesus. And the love that Jesus awakens in His people is translated by love into obedience to the voice. *Only love* can move a person to true obedience. *Only obedience* is the visible evidence of the love.

Our interaction with the Father, Son, and Spirit are related to our total personality, our total capacity as persons. Our minds, our hearts, and our wills are all touched by God. A response on *every level* must be nurtured in the people of God if the Lord is to have the healthy, responsive body He yearns to head.

BUILDING ALLEGIANCE TO THE SON

Our interaction with the Son is both on a heart level, in terms of love, and on an action level, in terms of an obedient response to the voice of the Spirit, which we recognize as Jesus' own. To build allegiance to the Son, we must help the body not only recognize Jesus as the living, loving Savior but also learn to bring all things to Him as head.

Not long ago in Larry's local congregation in Scottsdale, Arizona, we used a hypothetical story to help the body explore how to deal with problems in view of Jesus' active headship over our body. The congregation was asked to suggest how it either fit or failed to fit with the Bible's presentation of Jesus as sole head of the body. Here is the history:

> Bob and Carla are concerned about their thirteen-year-old and the other young teens of the church. Nothing seems to be planned for them. So one day they go to the pastor and insist, "Pastor, the church has just got to start a program for young teens."

After discussing this in teams, the congregation made these observations about Bob and Carla:

1. *They approached the pastor as head.* They seemed to assume that the pastor was responsible for the church and its ministries. They went to him as though he were the functioning head of the church and demanded that he take action.

2. *They had the problem solved.* They did not come with a problem but with a solution. They jumped over the whole

process of defining the problem and insisted that the church implement what they saw as the solution.

3. *They had the traditional solution.* They went to history for the solution to the problem. They went back to what the church has always done (in recent history) when a youth problem arose.

4. *They had a poor attitude.* The whole tone of the word *insist* seems out of place. Are they in control of the leaders and the body?

5. *They passed off their responsibility.* They apparently did not consider that *they* might be responsible for the solution to the problem they felt in regard to their daughter and others of her age. They did not sense a personal responsibility but they felt it was the responsibility of the "church" (i.e., the institution) to do something.

The main points of the congregation's analysis were valid. All too often we treat the pastor and/or other leaders as though they are really the head of the church. We do not look for new options but to the past for solutions or programs to guide us. We are insistent and demanding and quick to try to make others responsible. Of course, this is easy to understand when the church takes the form of an institution and there are committees and boards and church employees whose job descriptions say that they *are* responsible!

After a lengthy discussion on the negatives, Larry asked the congregation to suggest an alternative. How might a couple like Bob and Carla, who have an honest concern, handle that concern *in full recognition of Jesus' headship?* Here were their suggestions, and their reasoning, with which he finds himself in general agreement.

1. *Bring the problem to the real head of the church.* We don't *know* that Bob and Carla haven't prayed about the problem they sense. But surely when any problems or needs do emerge in the church, bringing that need to Jesus in prayer is the first step to take in view of His headship over "all things."

2. *Share the concern with the rest of the body.* Others in the body may sense the same need. If so, they should be consulted, and their perceptions shared. Also, corporate prayer is one significant way we can "carry each other's burdens, and in this way . . . fulfill the law of Christ" (Gal. 6:2). The body does need to be informed so that the need can be shared within it and so that all can come together to seek the direction of the head for the resolution of the problem.

3. *Talk with others who feel a similar burden.* Meeting

with others and exploring the problem together can be important steps toward solution. God may have an answer already in the wisdom or insight of someone so gifted in the body. Listening to each other for Jesus' voice is an important part of the process.

4. *Look to people, not program, for God's answer.* Because we see the body as people in relationship with each other, because we recognize that God has gifted each member of the body for the common good, and because the purposes of God are accomplished by Christ through the body on earth, we expect the solution to be found in people, not in programs. Setting up a program simply because "that's what churches do" is a tragic violation of headship. No, the concerned ones should pray that God will burden those through whom He intends to meet the need and they should begin to wait for the people who are His solution.

From the data given, we can't even tell what the real problem is. It may be a family problem. Perhaps Bob and Carla's child is rebelling, or perhaps she is sensing too much peer pressure. Perhaps no one else in the church has the same sense of frustration or need that she has. Possibly the answer will come in a word of wisdom from an older couple who are led to go to the house and share their experiences with their own family. Possibly the answer will be in a family that opens its home to the younger teens of the church on Sunday afternoons or week nights. It may be that a traditional "youth program" will be Christ's solution, and He will have prepared believers to conduct it. Or possibly the solution will have to wait, and God will later lead His choice person into the congregation. *The very fact that we do not and cannot know which of these possibilities is the best resolution should alert us to the fact that we need Jesus to be head.* We need to help the men and women in our congregations learn that Jesus accepts personal responsibility for resolving problems! Individually and together these should be brought to Him, not to the pastor or a responsible committee. When we let Him exercise His responsibility, *we also accept personal responsibility for responding to His guidance.* If we look to Him for guidance, each of us must also be ready and willing to hear what He says to us, and respond.

MATURE RESPONSE

Leaders in the congregation help develop allegiance to Christ, then, by building into the life of the congregation a supernatural rather than an organizational approach to problems and needs. The congregation is trained to look to Jesus for solutions. This process involves openly sharing existing needs, praying together about needs, and listening expectantly, each person aware that God may speak to him or her and call him or her to be the solution.

This takes the sense of servanthood that Gib Martin spoke of (see chapter 18) and a deep awareness in each person that the Holy Spirit is able to use *me* in the lives of people. It takes willingness to accept personal responsibility for hearing God's voice and living in obedience to it. It takes a totally different mindset than that developed for institutional rather than supernatural solutions to the problems that arise in every congregation.

But one more thing is vital. And that is that as spiritual leaders we never appeal to any motive other than *love* as the wellspring for a brother and sister's involvement.

It's all too easy to appeal to other motives. We can create guilt or shame. We can appeal to friendship. Or to pride. We can try to make people feel a sense of moral obligation. We can even use fear to move Christians to action. But Jesus said that true obedience to His voice is linked with love and that only love can produce obedience.

And so we return again to interaction. As I come to know my brothers and sisters, I learn to love them. As I see their needs, Christ's love in my heart makes me want to reach out to them, to touch and to heal. Love opens my heart to the voice of God; love moves me to be obedient to His voice. As I obey, I grow in my capacity to love and be loved as well as to serve.

Through this process I grow to a maturity that is totally necessary if I am to be a part of a healthy and responsive body, freed from bonds and sickness to joyfully do our Lord's good will.

REVIEW

What have we said so far in this section? First, that it is leadership's task to be *sensitive to the processes that are going on within the local body* and to work with those processes so that Christ is presented a healthy body.

Second, we have said that the dynamic processes that affect the health of the body are *relational* in character. The relationship among believers must be monitored and guided. The relationship between the body and the Father must be strengthened. The relationship between the body and the Spirit must be encouraged. The relationship between the body and the Son must be nurtured.

Third, each of these relationships is built through *interaction*. The interaction has a specific quality or expression in each case. Interaction among members of the body is to be open and honest, with growing love for one another a result of coming to know one another well. Interaction between the body and the Father involves both His initiating self-revelation and the corporate response of His people in prayer and worship. Interaction between the body and the Spirit focuses on hearing the guiding voice of God leading us into relationships in which we can serve and minister to others. Interaction between the body and the Son involves sensing in the voice of the Spirit the loving tone and self-sacrifice of the Son, with our response of love to Him stimulating us to obey the voice of God.

Understanding these general principles, we then move on as leaders to make sure that a healthy growth is taking place—through interaction toward relationship becoming allegiance.

The whole concept of relationship as the central issue in the health of the body led us to introduce the concept of allegiance. The church does not need more patterns into which to force believers. It does not need new molds into which to squeeze itself. Sameness of belief, of values, and of behavior is not really to be an issue in our Christian communities. Instead of finding our shared identity in conformity to the patterns of a cultural church, we are to find our identity in commitment to persons—in loyalty and love to our brothers and sisters and in loyalty, expressed appropriately, to each person of our Triune God.

Whenever we are successful in helping people take their eyes off meaningless forms and rituals and "acceptable" actions and fix their hearts on the One and the ones to whom they feel deep commitment and loyalty, we will be successful in building a healthy body.

And a healthy body of Christ *will perform* Jesus' ministries successfully in man's world.

A LOOK AHEAD

In the next section we're going to look together at *how* church leaders build allegiance. We want to look at very specific actions and systems that will encourage the growth of allegiance. We'll examine a different concept of organization of the body. We'll think about the implications of individual believers "owning" so-called church ministries. We'll see the role of consensus, how leaders equip, the importance of communicating confidence, and why providing freedom is a key to individual spiritual growth.

It is our hope that we will all find the freedom to let go and stop treating the church of Jesus as though it were *ours*.

He is Head.

He is responsible.

Following His pathway of building allegiance and not conformity will lead to His total transformation of the church.

PROBE

▶ case *histories*
▶ *discussion questions*
▶ *thought provokers*
▶ *resources*

1. One congregation analyzed the Bob-and-Carla situation. Here's another situation. Analyze it the same way: What fits or does not fit with the fact of Jesus' headship? And how might this issue be treated in full recognition of His headship?

   The denominational leadership is sponsoring a Management Seminar and wants the pastor and board members of each local congregation to attend. The letter of invitation says, "Research has proven that when we organize people to reach objectives, objectives are reached. We're convinced that your church can double in size if you'll plan for growth, using our new MBO (Management by Objectives) approach."

2. Having worked through eighteen chapters of this book, try now, *without referring back*, to write a fifteen-page paper that captures the key ideas presented. Use the contents page as a guide. Be careful to select the ideas or concepts that seem to you *central* to the authors' thesis.

3. Write a critique (either supporting or rejecting) the view summarized in your fifteen-page paper.

PART 3

BIBLICAL PRINCIPLES
OF CHURCH LEADERSHIP

A Description of Allegiance

Building Allegiance: Relational Presuppositions
Allegiance to One Another: Shared Life
Allegiance to the Father: Prayer and Worship
Allegiance to the Spirit: Giftedness
Allegiance to the Son: Personal Responsibility

How Leaders Build Allegiance

Body Organization
Ownership, Consensus, and Freedom
Confidence and Support
Communication

The primary purpose of good leadership is to prepare the saints to minister in Christ's name. As overseers, the elders should build allegiance, being sensitive to, and guiding, interactions among members of Christ's body, between members and leaders, and between members and God. It is these relationships that build a dynamic, healthy church.

In this chapter—and in the next three chapters—we will

BODY ORGANIZATION

---

look at specific practices that will help build allegiance to Christ and thus improve both individuals and the corporate group spiritually.

We will begin with two very basic questions: How can the congregation be organized to be Christ's body? And how can an organization avoid the pitfalls into which all institutions are prone to fall?

In the early church, organization was not a problem. McGavran and Arn have summarized New Testament principles of growth and described the earliest form of church organization. In McGavran's words:

> The church grew because laymen told others about the good news. (Remember, the church entered Antioch on the feet of laymen) . . . . The church of Rome was started by laymen. When Paul got there he found four functioning congregations started by laymen. Laymen would preach the Gospel. Laymen would baptize new believers. That's the second principle: much lay leadership.
>
> There was also great sensitivity to the Holy Spirit. Again and again, throughout the New Testament, the part played by the Holy Spirit is emphasized.
>
> We must see the New Testament church as an assemblage of house churches. This didn't mean that if there were 20 or 30 house churches in Corinth, the church was fractured. Paul always speaks about it as one church, the church in Corinth. It was one church even though it met in many different places. As archeologists dig back into those early cities, they find no church foundations before A.D. 160. That means for the first 120 years Christians met exclusively in houses, and this was a great advantage to the church. It met in many different circumstances. It wasn't burdened with the need to build churches. It gave a large number of people an opportunity to lead. "A church" was not a congregation of 5000, 2000, or even 200. A church was an assemblage of 15 or 20 people or, at the most, 30 people. Everybody knew everybody else; they cared for everybody else. It was a household of God.
>
> There are many other principles, but I would like to stress these as we look back to New Testament days.[1]

CHAPTER **20**

This picture of the first 120 years of the church explains why we have so little about "organization" in the New Testament. The church gathered and lived together as family. There were no agencies to staff. There was no building program to support or mortgage to pay. There were no seminaries training men or women for ordination. The church in those early days was not an institution; organization was therefore not an issue. Maintenance was simple and easily assigned to teams of men or women. The appointment of the deacons in Acts 6, for example, was made to carry out a specific task, and the team apparently had full responsibility for its ministry. They were not technically "under the supervision of" the apostles, nor a "department" or "agency" of the organized church. The organizational and administrative issues we face today never existed.

Unfortunately the church changed from a simple household into a complex institution with typical institutional pressures. These pressures have drastically affected our under-

---

[1]Donald A. McGavran, Jr., and Winfield C. Arn, *How to Grow a Church* (Glendale: Regal, 1973), pp. 34-35.

standing of the nature of the church and the role of church leadership. Out of this historic process has come a situation in which the functions of spiritual leadership have been distorted by the need for managers of the organization simply to maintain the institution. Many contemporary theories of organizations and their administration attempt to combine spiritual and institutional roles. But most totally miss the fact that the church is a body, a living organism, and not basically an institution or organization at all. Few have reached the conclusion of this text: that the church cannot be both.

An interesting Roman Catholic author puts the true organizational task of spiritual leaders in the correct perspective:

> A Christian leader has to be able to draw people to Christ and to help them grow in their relationship with Christ; he has to be able to help people come together to form community based on Christ; he has to be able to organize the community in such a way that people get all the help they need to be good Christians—in that order of importance. In order to be a good community dynamically developing, a leader has to do these three things.[2]

Whatever organizational form the contemporary church may take, Clark perceptively insists that it must be designed to support Christian community "in such a way that people get all the help they need to be good Christians." Organizational form must support the life of Christ's body, not simply help to maintain an institution.

In words that reflect the viewpoint that has been developed in this text, Clark goes on to describe the Christian community as a "social grouping which can meet all the basic needs a person has in order to be able to live as a Christian." That community, he suggests, has the following characteristics:

1. It must be Christian. Christianity must be accepted in an open way by those in the grouping and it must be the openly accepted basis for everything that is done in it.
2. It must be an environment. There must be interaction between the people in the social grouping that is personal, that is, relationship oriented and not just task oriented.
3. It must be organized. In order for the grouping to meet the needs of its members, it must have enough organization for the members to be able to work together in service.

---

[2]Steven B. Clark, *Building Christian Communities* (Notre Dame: Ave Maria, 1972), p. 135.

4. It must be large enough. It must be larger than a small group, mostly because there are not enough resources in a small group.
5. It must be local. The members have to be close enough to one another to be in regular contact, so that the grouping can meet their regular needs to live as Christians.
6. It must be complete. It cannot be a specialized community, but it must be concerned with all of what is involved in being a Christian.
7. It must have a unity. The basis for the life of the community must be adequate to hold everyone together. The basis must be Jesus Christ if the community is going to be a Christian community.[3]

ORGANIZATIONAL OPTIONS

Any time the church grows beyond the boundaries of McGavran's "house church," organization becomes an issue. But organization shifts from issue to problem if we ever lose sight of the fact that we organize, not to create a smoothly running institution, but to form a community. The failure to organize specifically for community—for the formation of a living organism—had inevitably led to our current organizational problems.

Let's look at three suggested organizational models for the church. The first two will give us insight into the central elements of the third or "body" organization.

Typical structure

Wofford and Kilinski contrast two kinds of organization.[4] One they call "authority centered" and the other "team centered." The authority-centered approach involves the typical organization chart that, as we noted in earlier chapters, is essential a control system (see figure on page 286).

The authors' critique of the authority-centered approach contains some salient points. Members do not make decisions and goals; decisions and goals are made for them. Leaders spend their time attempting to motivate people to accomplish the tasks they set for them. This need to motivate people often induces leaders to adopt authoritarian forms of leadership that run counter to the biblical teaching concerning servant leadership.

---

[3]Ibid., pp. 70-71.
[4]Jerry Wofford and Kenneth Kilinski, *Organization and Leadership in the Local Church* (Grand Rapids: Zondervan, 1973), p. 162.

FIGURE 39
SUNDAY SCHOOL, TYPICAL STRUCTURE

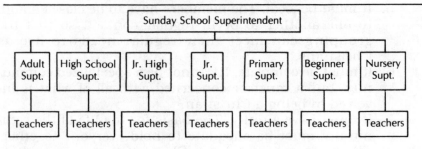

Whatever benefits this type of organization may have in terms of institutional effectiveness, such structures do little to build Christian community. In fact, they often work against community and the development of the allegiance to Christ and other Christians that is central to a healthy body life.

Team structure

Wofford and Kilinski recommend the team-centered organizational approch shown on page 287 and suggest that it has the following advantages:

1. It is an organization in which the basic unit of communication is the group rather than the individual.
2. There is a large amount of mutual influence within each group.
3. Group members manifest their love for, and acceptance of, one another; the group leader is especially warm and accepting.
4. The group possesses a high degree of responsibility for decisions and actions within its area of responsibility.
5. Because many individuals belong to more than one group, coordinated efforts are possible as information is conveyed from one group to another.
6. The membership of the official board of the church is made up of the leaders of all major groups; each group, therefore, has a communication link with the board.
7. The organization has a minimum number of organizational layers.
8. Members participate actively in their areas of responsibility.[5]

---

[5]Ibid., p. 160.

Body Organization

In the team-centered approach, as shown below, the organization structure is in contrast to the reporting relationships indicated in the typical structure. In the former organization the Sunday school superintendent is a member of the official board. He is not an isolated person, but a member of a group at the broadest church decision-making level. In meetings of the board, he interacts on problems that are of significance to the Sunday school, coordinates schedules and plans, and, perhaps most importantly, is influenced, encouraged, and given warm support by others. In this way, he receives stimulation and motivation.

FIGURE 40
SUNDAY SCHOOL, TEAM-CENTERED APPROACH

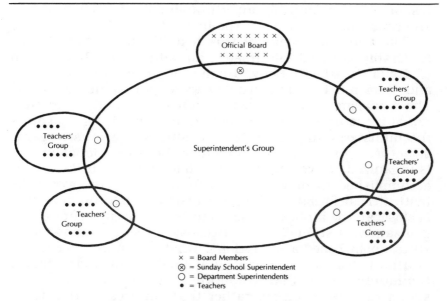

× = Board Members
⊗ = Sunday School Superintendent
○ = Department Superintendents
● = Teachers

This concept of organization is a tremendous advance over the authority-centered pattern. It helps to remove communications barriers and to involve more and more members in significant decision making and goal setting. But a few statements from Wofford and Kilinski's discussion of this approach point up its basic weakness:

> The board may give the music committee authority to make final decisions involving financial expenditures which are within their overall budget limitations. . . .
> You should also form new groups for responsibilities that may not have been handled in the current organization. For example, you may need to appoint a personnel committee if you do not already have one. . . .

287

Regular meetings should be planned for each operating and work group. As the focal point for carrying out the leadership functions, these meetings, in addition to an evaluation of previous activities, should include decision making, problem solving, the establishment of goals, and planning for action.[6]

These statements indicate that though the team approach creates a more effective organization, *we are still dealing with an essentially institutional view of the church.* Groups within the church are formed around tasks. Leaders function to help accomplish group tasks. Relationships involving ultimate allegiance and community issues at the heart of body life are not considered in the organizational design. Board members are not perceived as overseeing in the New Testament sense but are in fact leaders of management groups that are responsible for carrying out, through agencies, committees, and programs, the tasks of the institution.

The main argument of this text has been that church leadership is called to minister, not administer. The church of Jesus Christ is a body, a living organism, and its shape and form must be in harmony with its organic character. The management roles given church leaders and the institutional structures of the contemporary church fight against the ministerial functions of leadership and against organic structures. As to the tasks for which the institutional church is organized, we've begun to see that these are in fact to be accomplished in different ways from those presupposed by institutional forms. Although a team-centered organization is closer to the biblical model than the authority-centered organization, it still falls short because it also presupposes institutionally based assumptions. What the church needs is a noninstitutional organizational model, one that creates community rather than committees and agencies, one that shows how an organism rather than an organization functions.

Body-centered organization

A body-centered organizational approach assumes that the primary purpose of organization is the creation of a community. It does not focus on the accomplishment of tasks but on the relationships of leaders to the body, and of body members to one another. It encourages relationships and the creation of allegiance.

---

[6]Ibid.

288

DESIGN FOR "BODY ORGANIZATION"

The community of those who believe

Organizational charts, whether authority-centered or team-centered, typically make no attempt to represent the entire community. Both assume that organization relates to tasks; therefore only workers, committee members, etc., are represented. The Bible, however, encompasses the entire community, and stresses *relational factors,* not tasks.

To reflect a biblical emphasis, an organizational chart must therefore begin with a simple large circle that encompasses everyone associated with the local body (see figure below). The term "associated with" is purposely used here in place of "members." Since we are organizing according to the pattern of a "body" rather than on an institutional basis, we have to consider all Christians who associate themselves with us to be part of the local ministry. Theologically, if Christ has accepted a person, that person has by faith become part of the family of God. It follows that he or she *is* part of the local family as well. We can hardly reject or classify as less than a full brother or sister one who *is* a brother or sister. If we consider the church to be primarily an institution, we might set up rules for membership and distinguish between those who are "full participants" and those who simply "attend." We might even set up a class system for Christians, accepting fully only those who come through our form of baptism or accept our interpretation of the Second Coming or share our convictions on smoking. This might be justified if the church were merely an institution.

FIGURE 41
THE LOCAL BODY OF BELIEVERS

An inclusive representation of the relationship among all professing Christians who associate themselves with a local Christian body-community.

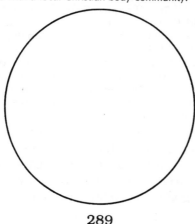

289

But once we view the church theologically as an organism, we must accept all those who are part of the body of Christ as part of our local body. How can we ever justify rejecting those whom God has accepted? How can we ever stand before God and argue that we accept and love only those who agree with our particular viewpoints?

So the overall organizational relationship expressed in the larger circle is inclusive of all who profess Christ and choose to associate themselves with our local body.

This large, inclusive circle represents more than those associated with the local community. It represents the gathering of the community. The gathering in most churches will be a regular Sunday event. Then the body will meet for worship, sharing, and teaching. If we take seriously the notion that interaction builds allegiance, interaction on all four relationship levels may occur in the Sunday setting.

For instance, a "body life" time for members to express needs, share experiences, praise, etc., is a distinct option. This is an option even in a "traditional" church setting. The following report describes the interaction encouraged in an Iowa Presbyterian church after the pastor and one of the elders attended a seminar at which the concepts in this book were taught. The pastor writes:

> Our Sunday worship averages close to three hundred people. For the last several years we have replaced the traditional "pastoral prayer" with what we call a sharing time. It is a time when people can share prayer requests or things that have happened in their lives. Generally this has been a time of asking for prayer for the sick and others in need. After I came back from Wheaton, I suggested that during our sharing time people might tell about something God had taught them from the Word or through experience during the past week. The next week a tenth grader stood up and said, "Last week the pastor said we ought to share some things God has taught us. I was reading in 1 Corinthians, and God showed me. . . ." The look on the faces of the people said, "What was that all about?" Then this past Sunday a man in our congregation stood up and said that this week he had learned something new he wanted to share. He said that he had been studying the word "witness" in Scripture and found that most of the time it was a noun and not a verb. He had always thought of witnessing as something you do, rather than something you are. So maybe little by little the people are beginning to open up at the level of worship and learning that they are members of the body and can and should be able to share and teach what God has shown them rather than leaving the whole job to the pastor.

The community gathering, then, can become a time when interaction involves us in each other's lives and in ministry to one another. As worship is designed to cause members of the gathered body to interact with the Father and as the Word is heard as the loving voice of Jesus, the community as a whole can experience relationships on all four levels of interaction.

It would be a mistake to think of the large circle as representing only the community gathered on Sunday. If we are to build relationships that are appropriate to the body as an organism, we'll find other occasions for gathering. One church plans an annual day of fun for the enjoyment of other Christians in a play setting. Other churches plan regular retreats or caravans to camp sites for weekends. All such events can be designed to build interpersonal relationships and increase the joy of being with other Christians that is so much a part of our being "one body."

Wise leaders will study the times and settings of meetings of the whole community and design these "together times" so as to produce deeper interpersonal ties among all who are a part of Christ's body.

Face-to-face groupings

The emphasis the Bible gives to relationships suggests that Christians should also have more intimate experiences than can be found in the gathering of the whole community. Face-to-face groupings—groups small enough for each member to face, see, hear, and share with others—can provide such an experience.

Different persons will find that the face-to-face groups they feel comfortable enough to participate in fully will be of different sizes. Some need a one-to-one situation, chatting with a friend over coffee or after tennis. Some open up in a group of six, but feel overwhelmed and withdraw in a larger setting. Three couples sharing dinner and the evening, or eight people meeting for prayer, or a family sharing a week's vacation with another Christian family—these situations may provide the best opportunity for a face-to-face experience. Typically, though, a group of ten to twelve, or sometimes as many as twenty or thirty, will constitute a "small group." Such a group is part of the church in that the people in it will be members of the local body. It need not be planned or controlled or organized by church leaders. It may be stimulated, encouraged, and sometimes trained or started by the elders of the body. In many churches that use a face-to-face setting to build allegiance, the goal is the involvement of at least 70 percent of the body members in such settings.

Historically, small groups have been gathered for many different purposes and have had many different agendas. Some, such as the Yokefellow groups, have stressed sharing and interpersonal support. Others have stressed Bible study.

291

Still others have met for prayer. Although each group should feel free to develop a style that meets its particular needs, it is best if as many allegiance-building interactions are present as possible. That is, there should be a significant sharing of experiences with others. There should be an opportunity for ministry to others from Scripture and in other ways. There should be times for prayer and expressions of worship.

Whether gathered as a whole community or in smaller face-to-face groupings, we *are* the church. As the church of Jesus we are His body, an organism, and our life consists of the vital relationships we have with each other and with our Triune God. Our organizational charts and our times together should reflect the reality of what we are and want to become (see figure below).

FIGURE 42
THE BODY IN INTERNAL AND COMMUNITY RELATIONSHIPS

A representation of the members of the body in their face-to-face and extracommunity relationships. Some face-to-face circles will include individuals who do not associate themselves with the congregation itself.

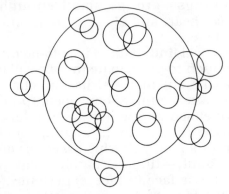

Leadership positioning

The figure on page 293 is the same as the one on this page with one exception: the spiritual leaders (elders) of the congregation have been added. Each leader is shown more than once on the chart: once in face-to-face meeting with the other leaders for ministry to each other and oversight of existing body relationships, and one or more times within the body and participating in face-to-face settings. Note that not all groups have elders in them. Elders should, if needed, be available to support and guide the small groups. And through relationships with the members of those groups, elders will be aware of what is transpiring in them. Yet elders are not "control" members of these groups; instead they contribute by their example and teaching to the body. It is not necessary that each group has a "representative" on the "church board."

From the point of view of institutional organization, this is not an efficient system. But with Jesus Himself acting as head of the church and with the Spirit, His voice, present in every believer, any need for a human institution to provide control does not exist.

This picture of Christ's body and its leaders assumes close contact and much communication among individuals within and across the face-to-face groups and, of course, communication with the whole body in any number of ways.

FIGURE 43

SPIRITUAL LEADERS AMONG OTHER MEMBERS IN THE BODY

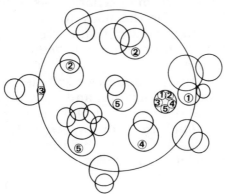

Maintenance functions

Although the body organizes primarily to create relationships, we must still have some way of representing the ways the organism maintains itself. By maintenance we mean the performance of tasks that must be accomplished for the body to function smoothly when it assembles. (We will make a distinction later between "maintenance" and "mission." "Mission" is not shown on the organizational chart.)

In many churches maintenance involves paying bills and caring for church property. In most churches, activities such as teaching children and caring for infants will be seen as essential, in that without providing such services the body may not be able to function smoothly as an organism.

How is maintenance handled in a biblical way? Members of

293

the body whom God leads to do so consent to assume the responsibilities. The figure on page 293 shows a "team structure" with an elder or leader not on the top of the circle. The reason for placing leaders under rather than over those led is that we need a radical revision of our conception of how leaders work with the whole body and ensure its smooth functioning. In the figure on page 295 there are significant differences between the structures. Typically, an elder will make it part of his ministry to *support* those responsible for maintenance and enable them to perform their tasks. His relationship with them will be supportive and enabling rather than directive in nature. At the same time, the relationship of the elder or elder team with maintenance-function workers will be *like* that of organizational leadership in that the elder(s) will, if necessary, step in to be sure that the task is performed.

What is of great practical importance, and will be discussed in greater detail later, is that leaders accurately perceive which tasks are maintenance tasks (e.g., those that must be performed for the body to function as body) and which are not. And in view of that perception, church leadership needs to *limit maintenance functions in the church to the bare minimum.*

In the forthcoming chapters we will discover more of what is implied by body organization and how to make it function effectively. We will develop a set of leadership principles and practices that, though they contrast with the practices of the institutional model, are vital to the functioning of the church as the living body of Jesus Christ.

PROBE

▶ *case histories*
▶ *discussion questions*
▶ *thought provokers*
▶ *resources*

1. Look at your own local congregation. What *minimum maintenance functions,* as defined in this chapter, do you feel must be provided if your congregation is to have a relational lifestyle?

2. A few months ago Clyde Hoeldtke in a seminar on church leadership shared the discovery that is presented below. What do you think of his suggestion? Do leaders in your own congregation function in this pattern?

Body Organization

FIGURE 44

IMPLICATIONS OF ORGANIZATIONAL REPRESENTATION

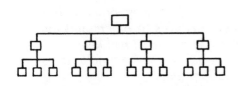

Authority Model	Support/Team Model
1. The leader is conceived of as an authority.	1. The leader is conceived of as a servant.
2. There are multiple layers of organization.	2. There is a single layer of maintenance groups.
3. Commands flow down from the leader.	3. The leader has no command role.
4. There is a tendency for decisions to move *up* to leaders, who are the decision makers.	4. Decision-making functions are made by members of the maintenance team, not the "leaders."
5. There is a tendency for concepts, ideas, and tasks to be the essential data in the system.	5. The unity of the team makes it easier for free and full flow of all types of data, including personal and spiritual.
6. This model has all the drawbacks that have been described.	6. This model has all the added advantages that have been described.

I recently came to an exciting realization as I read some Bible verses I've known all my life. Ephesians 5:21 says, "Submit to one another out of reverence for Christ." Paul shows how wives place themselves under their husbands, husbands under wives, children under parents, fathers under children, slaves under masters, masters under slaves (6:9—"Masters, treat your slaves in the same way").

In Ephesians 4:2 Paul says we are to live, "forbearing one another in love." "Forbearing" seems to include the idea of holding oneself against something. Think of Jesus down on one knee, placing Himself under His disciples, washing their feet, and in a symbolic way pressing Himself against them for the purpose of supporting them (John 13). He was serving the disciples from "under."

Supporting is the normal lifestyle for all Christians, placing ourselves under, pressing ourselves against to give support and

295

love. Pressing against a thing from the side might push it over. Pressing from above will depress it. But from under, we can lift up!

Wow!

Elders and pastors are to do what everybody else is to do. We, especially, can subject ourselves to others and forbear. We have had more time to grow in Christlikeness. We've known God longer, His Spirit has had more time to transform us and lead us to growth and maturity.

This is powerful! I now see that a servant leadership *lifestyle among the people in my church involves me in practicing what the whole group is learning to do! As others in the church begin doing what I'm doing as a servant leader, they will in effect be growing in Christ. They need not try to become an elder; they simply work toward Christlikeness. All I'm trying to do as a leader is be a growing Christian with them!*

To place myself under and to support others is by far our most effective posture. Peter suggests this when he instructs those who are younger in Christ, "Young men, in the same way be submissive to those who are older" (1 Peter 5:5). He is referring back to the leadership posture of the elders, "Be shepherds of God's flock . . . not lording it over those entrusted to you, but being examples" (5:2-3). I suspect that one reason so many people are slow at learning the servant or "under" lifestyle in the church is that the elders aren't modeling it. Unfortunately, men want more power over women, women want power over men, pastors are in power struggles with deacons, kids with parents, and young with old. Too often "the board" or "the pastor" is trying to control everybody, thus establishing a mentality that filters through the whole group. It really gets to be a mess.

Paul's idea is that all, like the elders, are to be subject to one another, not grabbing for power over others.

There are people in my business corporations who can never become Clyde Hoeldtke because Hoeldtke holds the stock and the power over. They don't. But in my church it is entirely different. We as a people are becoming like Jesus Christ, placing ourselves under and supporting, together.

3. The implications of a body structuring of the people of God is far more significant than we may at first realize, particularly in the "little things" that actually shape the lifestyle of the group. The following excerpt from a report by a young woman involved in a unique missions approach in Europe will illustrate some of these implications. Note the *goal* and how this participant felt the achievement of the goal was hindered by the structure.

Body Organization

Basically we were in Europe in hopes of planting a church by modeling the concept of the body of Christ. Many missionaries involved in church-planting ministries have found it very difficult to plant a church all by themselves and are therefore becoming very excited about the rediscovery of the team concept. A team can be very effective in that it has more "manpower," has a diversity of gifts, and can serve as a visual example of how the body works. The team's responsibilities lie in the areas of evangelism and discipleship, but the greatest impact of their presence lies in their corporate witness: how they work, play, study Scripture, pray, laugh, and cry together. That is the most important witness: our life together! How do we relate to each other? How do we handle conflict? How well do we forgive one another? These are the vital elements of our ministry.

One of the very first things that struck me once I got settled into my life on the team, in the apartment, and out on the street, was an undercurrent that I could sense at various times. It seemed something was not quite right, but I couldn't figure out what it was. As the summer wore on, I began to unravel the mystery that had plagued my thoughts for several weeks: there was a grave inconsistency between our words and our actions.

My thoughts kept going back to the fact that we were to be a representative part of the body of Christ that others could follow, and yet something was missing in our relationships. There seemed to be a lack of depth to them, a fear of really opening up and sharing how we really felt. I even caught myself saying things at Bible study that I thought the leader wanted to hear rather than what was really on my mind and heart. Little by little I began to realize that much of the problem stemmed from the structure of the team. We were supposed to be the body and yet we were functioning in many ways like an organization. We had fellowship, studied God's Word together, and had an important ministry. But the thing that bothered me was a definite feeling of hierarchy. The more I thought about it, the more I realized that I felt very much at the bottom of the totem pole as a summer worker. I didn't feel as though I had any real relationship, any real contact, with the "leadership" of the team. I was consciously aware that I was working under certain people and that what they said to do was what everyone did. I was frustrated to see team members who, though they were older and more independent than I, did not have much if any say in most of the decisions that were made. There was no consensus; the team members who had no leadership positions were not included in any of the discus-

sions of how things should be done. As I look back on it, this deficiency was most pronounced in three major areas: (1) communication and relationships, (2) decision making, and (3) working for a leader (there was no awareness of the idea that a leader was a servant).

The last of these three was the key to all the deficiencies. I understand now that by running our team like an organization the leadership was not serving us as Christ did the world. The servant-leader is important in the body for affirming and building up each member, to encourage and challenge the other members to grow, to love, and to accept each member as he or she is.

If this attitude had been present in the leadership of our team, the other two areas (relationships and decision making) would probably not have been problems either. If a leader is a servant, then those he is leading will know him—his good qualities as well as his faults—and will not be afraid to open themselves up to him. They will know that he is not perfect and doesn't claim to be. They will feel free to share their doubts, fears, joys, and successes; to ask for advice; and even to confront leaders when necessary. There will be a give-and-take attitude in all relationships and real freedom to be oneself no matter who is around.

If the leaders had let us in on the decision making, many of the problems that we experienced would never have arisen. There were two aspects of the process that troubled me: (1) As team members we had no part in decisions that were made regarding the team's ministry, finances, or responsibilities; (2) Decisions about such matters as how we were to use our free time or how much time we could spend with members of the opposite sex I do not feel should have been made by the leaders.

I remember several incidents that illustrate the problem perfectly. One day, about the middle of the summer, we decided that since attitudes seemed not the best, relations were tense, and people were tired and frustrated, we would just cancel our appointments and take off for the beach to get away from the whole situation. That turned out to be the best decision we made all summer! We had a wonderful time relaxing and getting to know each other as friends and not just fellow team members. Until that day I had not realized just how special some of those people were! Time went by very fast, and around six o'clock it was time to go, but about half of us wanted to stay and watch the sunset. We thought we could keep one of the vans, and the others could go home in the other two. Well, . . . no! The leaders said no, and that was that! Why? I still don't know! What bothered me most was the way the two-year-termers just gave in and said O.K. When I asked one of my friends about this, he just said, "We have learned that it is useless to disagree once the leaders make up their minds."

Another incident concerned the time the team members could leave on vacation. Vacation officially began on August 1; so many wanted to leave late on July 31 or early on the morning of August 1. But we were told no one was to leave before one o'clock in the afternoon on the first; in the morning we would have a Bible study together and then be assigned a cleaning chore. Following this, we would have a nice leisurely lunch, after which we could do the dishes and then begin our packing and leave. There was no explanation of that decision either!

A third incident stands out in my mind as a clear indication of the importance of the servant's heart in each leader. I remember sitting on my bed in my apartment (which also served as the team dining room) writing letters while the team of three assigned to meal cleanup that day was fulfilling its responsibilities. I was very fascinated by a conversation that was going on between two of the members, a guy and a girl. The guy happened to be the leader of the discipleship squad. The girl was giving him a hard time because it was his turn to wash up, but he had as usual opted to sweep the floor and let her do the dishes. It was a petty thing, but it troubled me that he was never willing to do his share of the work in the kitchen. I prayed a great deal about it and finally got up the courage to confront him. (It took a lot of courage, since I was only nineteen years old and he was one of the leaders.) I asked him straight out why he never offered his help when we needed someone to prepare meals on the maid's day off, why he always got out of washing the dishes, and why he didn't try to lighten the load that always fell on the same people. He said very simply, "I don't feel the kitchen is my place, as a man. Doing dishes and cooking are women's work." (I was just a little bit upset.)

"But," I pointed out, "was it Christ's place to kneel down and wash the disciples' feet?"

That hit home! And by the end of our conversation, God had worked a miracle in his heart! He apologized for his attitude and thanked me for confronting me. That night he came over to the apartment and washed the dishes we had used in preparation for the team picnic the next day. That was all it

299

took: prayer and some honest, tough, loving words. I was scared but it was appreciated!

These incidents helped me to understand the utter importance of having a servant's attitude in the ministry to and with the body of Christ. As I look back on those three months, I can see how many of the problems we faced as a team could have been avoided or solved if we had fully understood the church as it is in the New Testament. Both the leaders and the team members had much to learn from those difficult times.

BIBLICAL PRINCIPLES OF CHURCH LEADERSHIP

A Description of Allegiance

Building Allegiance: Relational Presuppositions
Allegiance to One Another: Shared Life
Allegiance to the Father: Prayer and Worship
Allegiance to the Spirit: Giftedness
Allegiance to the Son: Personal Responsibility

How Leaders Build Allegiance

Body Organization
Ownership, Consensus, and Freedom
Confidence and Support
Communication

To get the proper perspective on organization, we must first visualize relationships within the organism. But there are also tasks that must be performed. How are these handled? And what is the responsibility of leaders for their performance? Can a body approach actually replace the authority system of typical organizational structures and still carry out the mission of the body?

OWNERSHIP, CONSENSUS, AND FREEDOM

Our rather informal structure will function. But there are certain concepts that must first be grasped and applied by the church leadership team. And there are skills that the leaders need to develop.

In this chapter we will look at three basic interrelated concepts. They answer these basic questions: Who owns a ministry? Who makes decisions about the ministry? And can leaders abandon "control" to provide freedom?

MAINTENANCE AND MISSION

In the preceding chapter we noted two different types of "tasks." One is called "maintenance," the other "mission." A "maintenance" function was defined as any task that had to be performed if body relationships were to be nurtured effectively. Providing care for young children and meeting financial obligations for buildings were given as examples of maintenance functions.

A "mission" function is any and every other kind of task. For instance, in Arizona Audrey felt a burden for boys and girls in the church neighborhood who were vandalizing buildings. Rather than being upset, she saw this as God's way of bringing them to the attention of the church body. The "backyard Bible classes" that emerged from Audrey's concern would in many congregations have been plugged into the church's organizational chart as "a ministry of the church." In this local congregation, however, it was not. It was recognized as the ministry of Audrey and her team, their mission and *not a part of the church program.*

When Brad in Colorado saw a need for someone to spend time with the area teenagers, he and his young wife volunteered. Their concern was real and their willingness to become involved with the kids in a significant ministry was appreciated. In most churches Brad and his wife would have been signed on as "youth sponsors," and their activities would have been shown on the church organizational chart. In the local congregation Brad and his wife attended it was not. It was recognized as their ministry, their mission and *not a part of the church program.*

When Gary Jenkins in Seattle caught a vision for what became the Sky Club, he brought the idea to his pastor. They talked much about it, and Gary was encouraged to develop the concept and find a team of men who would share the vision with him. This team was found in the same congregation. In most churches Gary and his Sky Club would have been "authorized" by the official board to be part of the church program and would have been fitted into the organizational chart, with someone assigned to supervise. In this congregation it was not. It was recognized as a ministry of Gary and his team, their mission and *not a part of the church program.*

These three illustrations not only suggest various kinds of mission functions but also demonstrate a key principle: *All*

303

missions undertaken by believers should be the responsibility of those called to them. They should never be made a part of the church's program or organization. The elders or leaders of the church—who are servant-leaders, not managers— should not be responsible. Nor should the church as an institution take on any responsibility for the missions to which body members are called. Even those maintenance functions for which elders must take some responsibility *will not be operated as agencies of the church typically are.*

We can understand the reasons why this principle is so important if we examine the three questions posed in the introduction to this chapter.

OWNERSHIP: WHO IS RESPONSIBLE FOR A MINISTRY AREA?

In the average church there is no doubt about the answer to the question of responsibility. The *church* "owns" its ministries and agencies. The group ultimately responsible for successfully carrying out any given mission is the church board.

The push for job descriptions, for committees and individuals appointed to superintend agencies, and the use of the "authority structure" to chart relationships between workers and leaders in the congregation all reflect this approach. The ultimate responsibility—for planning, for provision of resources, for the supervision and training of personnel, and for the outcome of ministry in any agency—belongs to the church and thus to the "highest authority" in the church, its board. A look at the constitution of most congregations will show that responsibility and authority are both found in the church board, which is in turn responsible to God.

But we have suggested that biblically the church is an organism and that there is one living and active head of the body, Christ. If this scriptural teaching is reality and not theory, then Jesus Himself is the one ultimately responsible. He plans. He makes needed resources available. He calls and leads the members of the body who, being in a living relationship with Him, will carry out His plans. And He is the one who is ultimately responsible for the outcome.

Within the framework of Christ's overall responsibility, there *is* human responsibility. But it is not a mediated or "vicar" type of responsibility. Instead, *the human responsibility is borne by those Jesus has called to a particular ministry to be responsive to Him and His leading in all things.* Leaders in the body are called to serve all members of the body, but they are not called to relieve believers of the responsibility of being open and obedient to Jesus' leading! Elders or spiritual leaders are certainly not called to be Jesus to the other body members, though they must exercise a degree of oversight as responsible leaders (1 Peter 5:1-3).

Our "ownership" question thus has two answers. The first answer is that Jesus Himself, as the responsible leader of each mission or task group, "owns" the mission. It is not owned by the church, and it must not be owned by the church. For the church to insist on the ownership of programs or missions is ultimately to lose its identity as a body and to move toward becoming an institution.

The second answer to the ownership question is that each ministry or mission is also "owned" by those whom the Head has called to man it. Those in a ministry are basically responsible to Jesus for its conduct. Since they bear the responsibility, they must also be allowed to exercise authority to make the requisite decisions under Christ for carrying out their mission.

This is why an organizational chart based on the discussion in the preceding chapter will not show task or mission groups. *The organization of the body represents that for which leaders in the body are responsible.* Leaders in the body are responsible to God for creating relationships that make for bodily growth and maturity. Leaders in the body are *not* responsible for missions, except those to which they themselves may be called and except in the matter of prayer and financial support for the ministry in missions that others are engaged in.

CONSENSUS: WHO MAKES DECISIONS ABOUT MINISTRIES?

I've suggested in the last section that we must guard against the institutional error of giving to the "church" the ownership of those ministries or missions performed by its members. That concept gives us the answer to our second question. If church elders or boards or committees do not "own" a ministry or mission, clearly they are not involved in decision making relating to it; therefore who makes the decisions? *Those who are responsible make the decisions.*

This again gives us a dual level of responsibility. And it is important to distinguish between them. Put simply, Jesus, the head of the church, is responsible for all decisions regarding mission or ministry. Those called to the mission or ministry are responsible to discern God's will.

God's will

How do we know God's will? Christians have long asked this question. Answers have ranged from the mechanical (going through a series of "steps") to the mystical (doing nothing without a "sense of God's leading").

The possibility of knowing God's will rests on a reality that we have already discussed. The Holy Spirit, who is God's voice, is in residence in all believers. Because of His presence, Jesus is, as a living person, well able to communicate with us. Christ's communication may take many forms: Scripture, circumstance, a word of advice from friends, inclination, and so on. But we have received the promise of God's presence, and that means that we will recognize the voice of Jesus when the Spirit speaks (John 10:4).

A fascinating paragraph from the Revised Standard Version of Isaiah suggests added insights. Speaking encouragement to the people of Jerusalem, the Prophet promises:

> Though the Lord give you the bread of adversity and the water of affliction, yet your Teacher will not hide himself any more, but your eyes shall see your Teacher. And your ears shall hear a word behind you saying, "This is the way, walk in it" when you turn to the right or when you turn to the left (Isa. 3:20-21 RSV).

The suggestion here is that leading involves correction and that correction may and often will come after a choice is made. For God's commitment is that if we move down the wrong path He will speak and make the correct way clear.

The implications are exciting. God has not made us automatons but free beings with capacities like His. As we live and grow as Christians and experience His transformation, our values will become more like His values. Our thoughts and understanding will become more like His thoughts and understandings. Our emotions and reactions will become more like His. Our choices and our behavior will become more like His. For our transformation is toward Christlikeness.

Now why does God work in us to remake our perceptions, values, thoughts, emotions, and ways of living? Because we are to express Him in our world, and because *we are expected to use all of these renewed capacities in our daily lives.* We are expected to live life as responsible beings, making choices and decisions and following courses of action that have been responsibly chosen. Responsible decision making is both a practical and a mystical process. It is practical in that we proceed to use all our capacities to make the best decisions we

306

can; it is mystical in that we rely on God to shape our thoughts and understandings and also to speak to correct us if we turn to the left or the right.

Consensus, a safeguard

As we move beyond individual leading to the process in which a team of persons is responsible for discerning the will of God, we find an additional safeguard. This safeguard is illustrated in Acts 15, in which a significant issue was in dispute. Days were spent exploring the issue. Finally the council of leaders reached the consensus expressed by James. In the letter to Gentile believers that came out of this council, these words appear: "It has seemed good to us, having come to one accord. . . ."

This is the heart of consensus. The team of responsible persons, honestly exploring a decision to be made, using all the capacities God has given them, and prayerfully seeking His will, *come to one accord.* When that accord has been achieved, when there is consensus, then the responsible group can move ahead with confidence that the direction in which they go does reflect the will of the Lord.

It's important to understand when a consensus has been reached. In most situations there will be a number of choices that might be made. There may simply be "preferences" involved in the choice of one over another. Yet different members of the responsible team will have different preferences, and sometimes strongly different opinions. In seeking a consensus all the feelings, thoughts, ideas, and concerns of each person need to be expressed and considered. In the discussion there needs to be an honest seeking for God's best way—not a contest to assure the choice of my preference over someone else's. A consensus is reached when all agree that X is probably "the best course, for now." If, however, any one member of the team feels strongly that X is *not* the right course and cannot agree with it, no consensus has been reached.

In seeking God's will in a group situation, it's important to work for and with a consensus process as a safeguard for the ministry and as a way of consciously submitting to the direction of Christ, the Lord and head of the church.

To this point, then, I've suggested that ministry and missions is:

1. *not* part of the church organizational structure or program
2. *owned* first by Christ and second by those responsible to fulfill the mission

307

3. to operate under the headship of Christ, with His will actively sought by those responsible in a consensus-seeking process

What, then, is the role of spiritual leaders in the body in terms of the missions and ministries carried out by body members?

PRESERVING FREEDOM

When Paul writes to the Corinthians to urge them to follow through on their expressed intention of helping brothers and sisters in Jerusalem with financial gifts, he writes with great delicacy. "I am not commanding you," he makes very clear, "but I want to test the sincerity of your love by comparing it with the earnestness of others. . . . Here is my advice about what is best for you in this matter . . ." (2 Cor. 8:8, 10). In the same context he later says, "Each man should give what he has decided in his heart to give, not reluctantly or under compulsion, for God loves a cheerful giver" (9:7).

In making these comments Paul is *preserving the freedom of the believers* to respond, or not respond, as they choose. What is significant to God is the willingness of the response, not the performance alone.

This must also be the constant concern of spiritual leaders today. They seek to help members of the body make their own free and responsible choices *as to the Lord.* Not to the leader. The leader does not command. He advises. And in his advising he makes it plain that each person is free from compulsion or pressure, responsible only to God and not to the leader.

Rod, one of the elders in our local church, was approached by a young divorced woman. Her ex-husband, not a believer, was begging her to remarry him. He promised that if she would, he would become "religious" to please her.

This young woman asked many friends for advice. Each told her something different, and after hearing each one she was swayed to his or her position. Finally, recalling teaching she had heard somewhere that each woman needed a "male covering" to tell her what God wanted her to do, and having no husband or father, she came to an elder of the church. She explained her problem, and Rod spent several hours listening and sharing various Scriptures that might give her insights and guidance. Finally she demanded his judgment. What should she do? Marry, or not marry?

Rod refused to tell her! Instead he advised her to go home and pray about it, and ask Jesus what *He* wanted her to do.

She was furious. He was a spiritual leader. He was supposed to tell her what to do!

Several days later she returned with a different attitude. She had been angry. But finally in desperation she had turned to Christ for direction. And, in ways that were unmistakable to her, she had heard His voice telling her not to remarry her former husband at that time.

Rod's approach illustrates what spiritual leaders must and can do for those responsible to Christ for choices and decisions. First, the spiritual leader must be willing to help the one or ones who have ministry or mission responsibility. Elders are not to make decisions for others in the body: they are to affirm Christ as the head. What elders *can* do is to give insight, suggestions, support, and sometimes advice to help the responsible parties make good decisions.

Audrey's venture into backyard Bible classes illustrates how this works with ministry groups. After sensing that the vandalism around the church building was God's way of drawing the attention of the members of the body to the children in the neighborhood, Audrey approached the leaders of the church with this perception. They affirmed her insight and suggested that since she had been given the concern, God might be leading her to be the solution. The elders asked Audrey to share her idea with the congregation the next Sunday and to ask members of the body to pray about their involvement with her in a ministry to neighborhood children.

After prayer by the church, several women gathered around Audrey to share her concern. This group returned to the elders. What shall we do? The elders and the women talked over a number of options, including Sunday school outreach, released time, etc. After they had shared possibilities, the elders advised the women to pray together and seek a consensus about the direction Jesus wanted them to take. They did, and felt that backyard Bible classes were His answer.

Later they returned. What shall we use for curriculum? How will materials be paid for? A variety of curriculum possibilities were suggested and explained by one elder who had an educational background. Samples were obtained and the women were advised to study them and pray about what to use. As for the funds, again several possibilities were explored. There might be money set aside in the budget. Special offerings could be taken and individual donors sought. The women might choose to pay for the materials themselves. And so on. Again the team of women were asked to study and pray about these issues and seek God's will. They did so. Then they chose a curriculum, deciding to pay for the resource materials themselves.

There were other questions as well. Should we go into the homes of non-Christians? Should we let non-Christian mothers help as coleaders? On these and every other issue that arose, the elders were available to share, to explore possibilities, to support, and to give the women freedom to seek God's will and be responsible for the choices made under His direction.

The cost of freedom? Many will be concerned about extending this kind of freedom. Might not the ministry team members make a mistake? What if they make a choice the elders feel is wrong? Clyde Hoeldtke faced this issue recently in the church he serves as an elder. Here's his report:

> I'm in a support or responsibility relationship, with the twenty people working in our Sunday school ministry. I feel it's my responsibility to help them have a successful experience. One person coordinates the Sunday school team, and I try to be sensitive to his feelings about his ministry.
>
> A thoughtful member of the group came to me and said, "Clyde, I sense our teachers are feeling pretty insecure and not too well equipped for the method we're using." I discussed the problem with the coordinator, and he planned a meeting. He invited me to come and share the philosophy we elders had laid out for the ministry originally, and I was glad to. I used charts and outlines and taught foundational principles from Scripture. I gave a good explanation of how I thought everything ought to work.
>
> I had no sooner sat down than one woman questioned the methodology I was selling. She even had a paper to pass out to all the others showing how *she* thought it should be run. Boy, did I get mad inside. My first thought was, "How am I going to stop this thing before it spreads?" And then another person picked it up and said, "Yes, I think it would be good if we changed that." And then, as I grew more intense and angry inside, the group set up a different system altogether, while I struggled to keep quiet.
>
> Why did I keep quiet? Because I remembered principles of leadership for spiritual leaders. This was *their* ministry: they are responsible to Jesus for it. One beautiful way to demonstrate freedom is to show confidence that God is capable of leading others as He is you and me. They disagreed with my judgment in this case, but I'm not God. My judgment can be wrong. But even if it was their judgment that was wrong, God can still use the situation to lead them into the best way to minister to the children.

Clyde's experience may well be repeated in many ways in many churches. If leaders have their self-esteem tied up in always gaining their point of view and imposing their judgment on others, then this approach to leadership will be painful. *But spiritual leaders are servants.* We are not called to impose our judgment. We are called to help others grow in their ability to be responsive to Jesus and each other. *The allegiance we seek to build is an allegiance that is to Jesus and not to the plans of some human authority.*

In the short term, Clyde's refusal to fight for his point of view might lead to less effective ministry to children on Sunday mornings. It might. But in the long view, if Clyde had fought for that point of view *he would be modeling exactly the opposite of the spiritual leadership principles to which he is committed.* By following the course he did, Clyde gave a vivid demonstration to each person on that ministry team that they *are* responsible to Jesus—not to Clyde—for their choices. And he showed that the leaders of the body have confidence both in Christ and in them and are sure that they will find and respond to God's will.

Unquestionably this approach was right. It was an important step toward building principles of allegiance into the lives of the people in the fellowship he leads.

WHAT DECISIONS DO ELDERS MAKE?

If the freedom and the right to make decisions about ministries and missions that are associated through body members with a local church is surrendered to those members, what do the elders do? What areas of decision making are they responsible for?

The question supplies its own answer. It is always important to first locate the individual or group that is actually responsible to Christ for the conduct of any mission. Thus, for the young woman who wanted guidance about remarrying, the key question was, "Who is responsible for your personal decisions?" The inescapable answer: "You are." Therefore, she had to be guided to make that decision herself, and to seek God's guidance in the process.

Who was responsible for the ministry to neighborhood children initiated by Audrey? Again the answer is clear. Audrey and the other women who with her formed the ministry team were responsible. It's clear, then, that they had to be guided to accept the responsibility and to seek God's will through consensus for the choices that had to be made to have that ministry function.

Even though in the example of Clyde's Sunday school staff the children's ministry is considered a maintenance function, and thus an elder commits himself to be sure it is carried out, still those actually responsible for carrying out the ministry were the teachers. So they had to be given freedom to make the decisions related to the conduct of that ministry, if they were to grow to look to Jesus for guidance and sense their ownership and responsibility.

What about the elders, then? What are they responsible for? The elders are responsible for the quality of life of the congregation and, in particular, they are responsible that the interaction processes described in chapters 15 through 19 are healthy and happening. It is these things that lie in the elders' area of responsibility and are subject to elders' consensus decision making.

For example, the church of which Larry is a member and elder has recently made a radical and drastic decision. They have been led to surrender their buildings and grounds to the denomination and move to house churches. They intend to meet Sunday afternoons in different house-church locations, with a team formed around each elder, who provides leadership. Monthly they'll meet together in a rented facility and, in addition, will plan a number of retreats and camping experiences for the whole congregation.

This decision was made because they felt that for them to fully function as the body, some such pattern was necessary. They do not feel this is required for all churches or that biblical principles permit no other option. But they are convinced this is the direction God is leading *them.*

As this conviction formed and became a consensus, they did *not* ask for a congregational vote. The elders, responsible for the relational processes that take place in the body, accepted the responsibility of making the particular decision. Then they worked carefully to communicate to the congregation what they had decided and why. Again, because the elders are responsible for the equipping relationships and patterns of interaction in the local body, they do make the decisions that relate directly to these issues. But elders do not make decisions in areas where others in the body have been given responsibility. Instead, elders commit themselves to help these individuals and teams make decisions under the guidance of Jesus Christ, who is their living and wise head.

In summary, to make it possible for decisions to be made in a responsible way and to permit Jesus to be the unencumbered head of the body without institutional interference, this chapter has suggested the following:

1. Ministries or missions undertaken by members of the body should be *organizationally separated* from the church. Only the barest minimum of maintenance functions should be seen as related to the organization of the body, and even for them the individuals charged

312

with the responsibility should be encouraged to seek God's will for significant decisions.

2. Missions or ministries called into being and staffed by members of a local body should be seen first of all as "owned" by Jesus Himself. He has the ultimate responsibility, and His leading and guidance must be sought. Second, these missions or ministries should be seen as owned by those responsible for carrying them out. Never must such programs or organizations be considered "church" programs.

3. Individuals and teams responsible for various ministries and missions are to seek Christ's will and utilize a consensus decision-making process as a way to discover that will.

4. The elders or spiritual leaders of the congregation should not be responsible for, and should not take responsibility for, the missions or ministries of members. Instead, they are to be available to help, support, encourage, and sometimes to advise. But they must always provide the freedom necessary for those who are responsible to act responsibly.

5. Elders should accept responsibility for the decisions that affect the lifestyle and relationships of the body, for this *is* their responsibility.

Because Jesus is alive, members of the living body will experience a supernatural coordination in the process. Ownership, consensus, and freedom will help open up the body of Christ to the living touch of a reality long distorted and lost in the crush of man's substitute institutional systems of control.

PROBE

▶ case histories
▶ discussion questions
▶ thought provokers
▶ resources

1. Examine a church constitution (your own or that of another congregation). Revise it to fit the concepts suggested in this chapter.

2. Could this revision of the constitution effectively implement in your church some of the leadership principles suggested? Why, or why not?

3. Many of the principles in this book and in this chapter can be implemented to some extent without changes in church constitu-

tions or formal church organization. Change can come from within the system through changes in the attitudes and procedures of leaders.

Take a typical program of your church, and develop a detailed analysis of how leaders might act to build the biblical principles suggested in this text and chapter into its functioning. Be thorough and complete.

4. Richard Franklin describes how those without "power" work to encourage change. He notes that the effective Community Change Educator (CCE) works in a close personal relationship with the group rather than the individual as the medium of change. The CCE wants to help those in the system learn how and why to make changes rather than make these changes for them. For this "he takes initiative in generating a *learning environment* for change."[1]

There can be many misunderstandings of the CCE and the process involved in it. This approach emphasizes process and climate and rejects control and authoritative answers from outside the group. Here is one possible response to it:

The freedom-urging style of the CCE may at first panic the client group. (If he doesn't know what we ought to do, we're sunk. He's supposed to be the expert, not us.) *His low-control behavior, moreover, may cause the group to test the limits of their relationship—the group's ability to trap the agent into a different style or try his tolerance for rebellion.* (Let's see if he can stand our not doing a thing this session. Maybe he will finally take charge.) *It may take a series of sessions for a working "partnership-in-change" to emerge. How long depends on both the client and the CCE.*

a. How many parallels can you find between the role of the CCE described above and that of the spiritual leader described in the text of this chapter?

b. How do you think people in the local church might react if the leadership style recommended in this text were seriously adopted by the pastor and elders of a specific church? What additional reactions besides the two shown in the above quotation might you project?

c. How might the leaders of a congregation minimize panic or anger from the congregation?

d. If members of a congregation react negatively to a servant-leader style and demand "stronger" leadership, how should the pastor and elders react?

5. The concept of elders taking the responsibility for making deci-

---

[1]Richard Franklin, *Toward the Style of the Community Change Educator.* Pamphlet produced by the National Training Laboratories.

sions that affect the whole body troubles many. They feel this stance is ultimately authoritarian and somehow wrong.

The answer is that this honest concern must take several forms. First, it is the responsibility of the spiritually mature (the elders) to make some decisions under the leadership of Christ that those less mature might be unable to make. Second, this responsibility is not *taken* by the elders; it is *assigned* to them by the head. After all, the "decisions" they make are not to be theirs but His. Third, the way in which directions for the body are communicated to the congregation are very significant. The following case history illustrates an elder-made decision and the process by which that direction for the body was shared with the members. It gives us a good pattern for a servant style of communicating such decisions, in contrast to an autocratic style.

> *If you have an elder structure, your elders make decisions for the whole church. Now that can be a problem. Here's a small group of people making decisions affecting everybody. Don't the people have a role in making decisions? The answer is yes, they do. But it is a communication role, not a decision role. The elders as the ruling group of the church make decisions by consensus. But as elders they never make decisions without communicating with the congregation as full participants.*
>
> *For example, a year or so ago we felt our pastor ought to be given a three-month "leave of absence." So we said, "Bob, go away for three months." There were a couple of reasons for that decision. A lot of people were too dependent on him. He was still "the pastor," and he was being approached as the "head of the church" by too many people. We felt there wasn't a healthy understanding in the body that Christ is the only head. We wanted the people to learn they could live without Bob there. We also felt we should give him to the church at large for a ministry of writing and teaching—he has great gifts in these areas. So we decided to free him from his usual responsibilities. We made the decision. But we involved the congregation in that decision in very important ways.*
>
> *We asked Bob to preach a couple of sermons in which he reviewed some of the basic realities to which we are committed. We are all ministers. Christ gives gifts to the whole body. We depend on Him to work through the body, not just the individual. We then explained the reasons for the decision to release Bob for three months to the church at large. As elders we saw this as a great opportunity to experience something we hadn't experienced and grow in ways we hadn't grown, as well as to make a meaningful gift to our brothers and sisters beyond our own congregation.*

315

Then we divided the congregation up into smaller groups. There was an elder or deacon in each group, and each asked, "How does it make you feel to hear about Bob going away for three months?" Some of the people thought it was great. Wonderful idea! Others said they felt he was deserting them. Some felt Bob didn't love them anymore if he was going to go away like that. The funniest thing was that the ones who felt most deserted had never come to him for counseling. They just felt more secure when he was there. It shows how deeply the distinction between pastor and member had been engrained in a lot of people. Their security was not Jesus, it was Bob.

We found a lot of feelings like these, so we met as leaders and talked about them. We decided to break up into small groups again. Some people suggested that the elders might have an open house on Sunday afternoon once or twice a month to share their ideas with the members. After we had made sure everyone had expressed his ideas, we met to discuss them. First we prayed about them. Then we prepared a report on our responses.

Then Bob went away.

But we continued to function. Each week we had the congregation write down on a piece of paper anything positive or negative that had happened that week as a result of Bob's departure. There were three positive comments to every negative one. We divided them up, three positives and one negative in each pile, and distributed them to our small groups for prayer. The members of each group talked about the negative comment and then prayed about it.

Through that whole process we tried to maintain a spirit of open communication so all our people could express their feelings. The experience was good for us. Some people suffered growing pains. But we learned that people can accept the choices of their leaders, even if they disagree with them, if they are convinced that their leaders have heard and understood their points of view.

That is important. You get rebellion and anxiety when members feel their ideas have not been considered or their concerns have been ignored. So when elders make decisions, it is extremely important that a totally open communication be cultivated. If elders find unexpected antagonism to a decision, they will often rethink it and consider whether the congregation might be God's voice telling them to think again. But in any case, the body must be involved in the process.

PART 3

BIBLICAL PRINCIPLES
OF CHURCH LEADERSHIP

A Description of Allegiance

Building Allegiance: Relational Presuppositions
Allegiance to One Another: Shared Life
Allegiance to the Father: Prayer and Worship
Allegiance to the Spirit: Giftedness
Allegiance to the Son: Personal Responsibility

How Leaders Build Allegiance

Body Organization
Ownership, Consensus, and Freedom
Confidence and Support
Communication

As controls are removed, there is a tendency for people to panic. In general we haven't been trained to be responsible to Jesus. We've been taught by the institutional system to pass our responsibility on to others.

What can we expect from members of the body as a truly responsible lifestyle is encouraged? Misunderstanding. Fears. Anger, as expectations of how leaders ought to behave are violated. Some may leave the congregation. There

CONFIDENCE AND SUPPORT

will be seeming deterioration, as programs that were held together by human effort collapse. And we can expect suffering by leaders, whose motives and responsibility will be questioned.

We can to some extent reduce these reactions. We reduce them by another aspect of a servant leader's ministry within the body. That calling is to communicate confidence and to give support by providing "participatory supervision."

To build confidence in people, freeing them to live responsibly under Christ's headship, we must *have* confidence in them. Often this is difficult. It may even seem impossible. Many Christians simply are not now comfortable or competent in ministry. Many are unaware of the Spirit's presence, or, if they are aware of it, are unwilling to trust Him. Others eagerly accept responsibility, and then consistently fail to follow through. Still others move into a work team, and by their own immaturity, competitiveness, oversensitivity, or simple lack of love, shatter harmonious relationships. No wonder we are hesitant to have confidence in others!

Actually, there's a theological fear behind the fear of many leaders to give freedom and responsibility. It's the fear of sin—the realization that each Christian, like the non-Christian, is contaminated by a sin nature. The control systems developed by churches and the strict control evidenced in Christian homes in relationship to children are at least partly based on the assumption that human beings cannot be trusted. If the worst must be expected, controls must be established to keep others from making the mistakes they are bound to make.

If I see my brother's or sister's identity rooted in his or her sin nature, then I must never trust him or her. I must always guard myself and the work of God against human failure and errors.

CHAPTER 22

This theological question must be faced if I am to function effectively in the body of Christ. We begin by affirming that, yes, we are sinners. But no, our *identity* is not found in our sinfulness.

This can be demonstrated in several ways. First, in the original creation God provides mankind with a distinctive identity. We are beings made in His own image and likeness (Gen. 1:26). Even after the Fall, God's image and likeness, though distorted, are still distinguishable (Gen. 9:6; James 3:9). Second, Psalm 8 and other passages identify man's high destiny. God is not only mindful of man, but crowns him with glory and honor and has shared His own dominion with him. The capacities of a humanity thus honored should never be discounted! Third, and most important, Scripture portrays an eternal future in which we will be freed from every tinge and taint of sin. The work of Christ will come to full completion, and we will be like Him. At that time, with sin removed, we will *still be ourselves*. Sin does not define us. The essense of humanity is not found in our sinfulness, but in our original and eternal likeness to God Himself.

It is an error then to relate to any man, and particularly to our brothers and sisters, as though their defining characteristic were sin. We recognize sin's presence and power and never discount it. But we expect something different and something better for the members of God's family!

Theologically speaking, then, we are not to base our sense of others' identity on the possibility or even the probability of failure.

But what if their behavior *proves* their sinfulness? What if they actually do fall short of what God and we expect? It's probably not so much the theological conviction of man's sinfulness as our experience of other's frailties and failures that leads us to be pessimistic. It is very likely because others have proved over and over that they are *not* responsible that we hesitate to trust them. How can we have confidence in men or women who have failed to earn our confidence by their behavior?

EXPRESSING CONFIDENCE

The apostle Paul faced this issue and provides us with a unique answer. In writing his second letter to the Corinthians, Paul makes these strange statements: "I have great confidence in you; I take great pride in you; I am greatly encouraged; in all our troubles my joy knows no bounds" (7:4). And again, "I am glad I can have complete confidence in you" (7:16). What is so strange about these statements is the persons to whom they are addressed. The Corinthians were the one New Testament church that Paul bluntly called "unspiritual" (1 Cor. 3:13). They are the "problem church" of the New Testament, marked by splits and cliques, by immorality, by doctrinal disputes and lack of love, by division over charismatic issues and battles between the sexes. Looking at this church and its practices and its reaction to Paul, it's clear that there is little or no basis for Paul's expression of confidence. As a matter of fact, evaluated on any realistic criterion, there seems to be good reason for Paul to speak of his *lack* of confidence in these brothers and sisters.

How could Paul, in honesty, express confidence where no basis for confidence existed? The answer to that question is found in 2 Corinthians 4:16–5:21. Let's trace Paul's argument and see the basis that we as church leaders have not only to freely release responsibility to other members of the body but also with total honesty to express confidence in them.

Context

In 2 Corinthians 3, Paul has spoken of the work of the Holy Spirit in the believer's life. That work is one by which we "are being transformed into his [Jesus'] likeness with ever-increasing glory, which comes from the Lord, who is the Spirit" (v. 18). Paul has also noted God's work of writing His Word on our hearts, so that our lives reflect its reality. That Word so written, Paul says, is "known and read by everybody" (3:2). The unique transformation treasure is held in earthen and imperfect vessels: clearly the transcendent power revealed in our lives must belong to God.

It is this great affirmation that is the background for the thoughts Paul now develops.

The principle stated: 2 Corinthians 4:16-18

Recognizing the fact of human imperfection, Paul still says, "We do not lose heart." What is ahead, particularly that eternal weight of glory awaiting us, is beyond comparison with present troubles. Paul's positive attitude comes from the fact that "we fix our eyes not on what is seen, but on what is unseen. For what is seen is temporary, but what is unseen is eternal."

If we observe the behavior of others and consider that behavior the basic reality, we *will* become discouraged. We will soon lose heart and find it impossible to trust them with responsibility. So what we must do is recognize the fact that *whatever we can see can and will change.* What we cannot see is the ultimate reality, and that reality is unchangeable!

The prospect of perfection: 2 Corinthians 5:1-10

In the next two paragraphs Paul looks ahead to perfection. Indeed we *do* groan under our imperfections and look forward to the time when "what is mortal [will] be swallowed up by life" (v. 4). In the meantime we "live by faith, not by sight" (v. 7). We set our hearts on pleasing God, and seek to live as close to the perfected state as possible. Before us, to motivate us, is the judgment seat where rewards will be given out on the basis of what we have done in the body.

A mission of motivation: 2 Corinthians 5:11-15

Accepting this reality, Paul launches enthusiastically on his mission. He is called to persuade men to be responsive and responsible in their Christian walk.

Paul gives an explanation of the motivational principles on which he operates—principles others might think of as insane, but which he believes will cause his brothers and sisters pride. Before explaining, he again draws the basic contrast. Paul is not one of those who pride themselves on a person's position (v. 12). He does not look to the external evidences of accomplishments that men use in assigning status and value to others. Instead, Paul says that he takes pride in "what is in the heart."

This phrase is explained in verse 14: "For the love of Christ controls us" (RSV). Paul's conviction is that the controlling motivation in the believer's life must be love—a love response to Jesus. Not love of money, nor love of power, but love of Christ—my love for Him—controls me. This is, of course, what we saw in looking at allegiance to the Son (chapter 19). Obedience is linked intimately and inextricably by Jesus to love. The one who loves will obey. But here Paul goes beyond that affirmation. He is convinced that love *exists* in the hearts of believers!

Note his theological argument immediately following: "We are convinced that one died for all, and therefore all died. And he died for all, that those who live should no longer live for themselves but for him who died for them and was raised again" (vv. 14-15). The point is clear. The great fact of history is that Jesus *has* died on our behalf. We died in Him. But His death had a purpose. That purpose was that we might also be raised to life! And that the new life we live might no longer be for ourselves but for the one who died and was raised for us!

It is inconceivable to Paul that the purpose of Jesus' death will not be achieved. God is committed. Those who live in Christ *will* come to live for Him, and not for themselves!

A new view: 2 Corinthians 5:16-17

This theological conviction gives Paul, and us, an entirely new perspective on our brothers and sisters. We can no longer "regard them from a human point of view." Mere human ways of evaluation, which must rest on evidence and observed behavior, no longer apply. Why, from a human point of view, Jesus Himself was a classic failure! He came proclaiming a kingdom; He died at the hands of a secular authority. He came to a people He claimed to have created; they rejected Him and demanded His death. He started a popular movement; He was deserted by even His closest followers. No, from a human point of view, Jesus Christ was a failure.

But we no longer regard Him from that point of view! The One who men said was a failure we know as the risen and elevated Son of God. The One whom men hung on a cross we see seated at the right hand of God, waiting a glorious return. The One whom men mocked we honor, and we look forward to a day when every knee shall bow before Him and every tongue confess that Jesus Christ is Lord. Through the eyes of faith we view the dead Jew as the Risen and Ever-living Son of God.

When we turn those same eyes of faith on our brothers and sisters, we see them in a new way as well! "If anyone is in Christ," Paul says emphatically, "he is a new creation." Faith enables us to disregard the evidence of our eyes and to see in the heart of every fellow believer a spark of new life—an ember of love, which it is our mission to fan into a burning flame that *will* bring the promised transformation!

A ministry of reconciliation: 2 Corinthians 5:18-21

This passage is often misapplied as an evangelistic one. It has nothing to do with evangelism. Paul is speaking about the reconciliation of the Corinthian believers (v. 20).

What is reconciliation? Its basic meaning is "to bring into harmony with." We "reconcile" a clock by bringing it into agreement (harmony) with the time announced on the radio. When both tell the same time, speaking as it were with one voice, the two are reconciled.

Our ministry of reconciliation is focused on persons. We as spiritual leaders are called to bring our brothers and sisters into harmony with God and one another. We are to help bring every aspect of each life into full and total harmony with what is real in the heart.

But how? The passage has the answer. Christ's own work on Calvary is the foundation work of reconciliation. Paul says that "God was reconciling the world to himself in Christ, *not counting men's sins against them*" (v. 19)! This is the heart of our own reconciling work in the body.

1. *We are not to count their sins.* Looking at a person's record of failures and sins, we tend to withdraw from him the gift of confidence. We are even likely to try other means than confidence to motivate such a person to respond to Jesus. Rules. Policies. Strict supervision. Control. But certainly never freedom, responsibility, or trust. His failures demonstrate that he cannot be trusted.

   But to evaluate a person on the basis of his performance is to take account of his sins! It is to draw back from the one approach to reconciliation that God took in Jesus. It is to deny the reality of the cross in history and the reality of God in the human heart.

2. *We are not to count their sins against them.* Counting sins will keep us from trusting others with freedom. Counting sins *against* others will give us a critical and negative rather than supportive relationship. We will be disappointed, angered, judgmental. *But these attitudes are not to be our attitudes toward our brothers and sisters!* We support, not judge. Where there are failures, we are needed to restore confidence and to provide support to enable our brother or sister to trust God enough to try again.

When we take this nonjudgmental view of our fellow Christians and when we take the theology of the cross as seriously as the apostle Paul did, then we *will* be able to say to them with honest conviction that Paul had: "I am glad I can have complete confidence in you" (2 Cor. 7:16).

Communicating this kind of confidence, which is based on our total confidence in God, we will be used by God to bring our brothers and sisters to a maturity that, fanned by love in the heart, leads to a productive and holy life.

PARTICIPATORY SUPERVISION

The fact that we have confidence in our brothers and sisters does not mean that we abandon them. As we've seen in earlier chapters, the servant leader comes underneath and provides support to help others achieve their potential.

It is possible that not every person will need this kind of support. But many people in venturing into various relationships or ministries, will need some degree of active support. Audrey and her team of women were given minimum support by the board in the form of advice and encouragement. Others will receive this minimum support and encouragement over a meal or sharing on the telephone. But some will need more support than this.

When Jack and his wife began to take stray people into their home, they began an unusual ministry of hospitality. Often the people who found their way to that home were bent and debilitated by drugs or poverty or alcohol. More than one was unable to function in society. Jack often asked the elders for advice and received it. One day he asked for advice for an especially difficult problem. A new man by the name of Wright had moved in, and Jack didn't know how to handle the situation. Wright was older than Jack and, although he needed someone with authority to deal with him, he was not able to respond to a younger man. Also Wright was very seriously affected by his recent experiences to such an extent that he could hardly put a full sentence together. And he often reacted negatively to Jack's wife.

Jack came to the elders, and two of them found a solution. Jack would be "ordained" to a "ministry of hospitality." While it would be his ministry, his authority would come from the body. Thus, Wright and others would be able to respect that authority without confusing it with parental authority.

The elders explained this to Wright, who agreed to live under Jack's authority. Prayer was made in each room of the apartment consecrating it to the ministry.

However, Jack often found that he had many problems he couldn't resolve. Soon one of the elders invited Jack and his family, with Wright and the others who were at the home, to come to his home one night each week. First they played basketball together and then sat down together to eat and share what was happening. This weekly participation in the life of Jack and Wright was something the elder had to do to give Jack the support and instruction necessary for him to be successful in his ministry.

The ministry was still Jack's. But the elder's participation and supervision (in the sense of giving guidance and advice) was essential support.

There will be many times when a costly commitment to walk through a ministry alongside the person who owns it must be made by a spiritual leader. This in no way robs the owner of his responsibility: the pastor or elder does not make the decisions nor does he command. This participation in no way implies a loss of confidence. In fact, it is a great affirmation of confidence. It's a way for spiritual leaders to say to believers, "I have so much confidence in you that I'm willing to commit significant time to support you!"

As a servant of the church of Christ, a spiritual leader must be willing to make this kind of costly commitment.

These, then, are two simple but important additional principles for making body organization effective. In our relationships with members of the body we are to communicate confidence. And, when necessary, we are to commit ourselves to walk beside them as they grow to competence.

BIBLICAL PRINCIPLES OF CHURCH LEADERSHIP

PROBE

▶ case histories
▶ discussion questions
▶ thought provokers
▶ resources

1. The following cartoons were designed to help spiritual leaders distinguish between confidence and nonconfidence responses. They are part of a leadership-training course developed by Norm Wakefield. (The course itself can be obtained from Dynamic Church Ministries, P.O. Box 35331, Phoenix, Arizona 85069.) Work through the cartoons, following instructions related to completing different types of confidence or nonconfidence statements.

FIGURE 45
CONFIDENCE AND NONCONFIDENCE RESPONSES

TEAM up with a partner. Study the pictures on pages 327 to 331. On the chart below arrange the numbers of the pictures in three rows. One row will lead from birth to the man behind bars. The other will lead from birth to the "successful" businessman. Make your selection according to the positive or negative impact of each event. Some pictures may show neither positive nor negative influence.

Negative	Positive	Neutral
Birth	Birth	
_____	_____	_____
_____	_____	_____
_____	_____	_____
_____	_____	_____
_____	_____	_____
_____	_____	_____
_____	_____	_____
_____	_____	_____
Failure	Success	

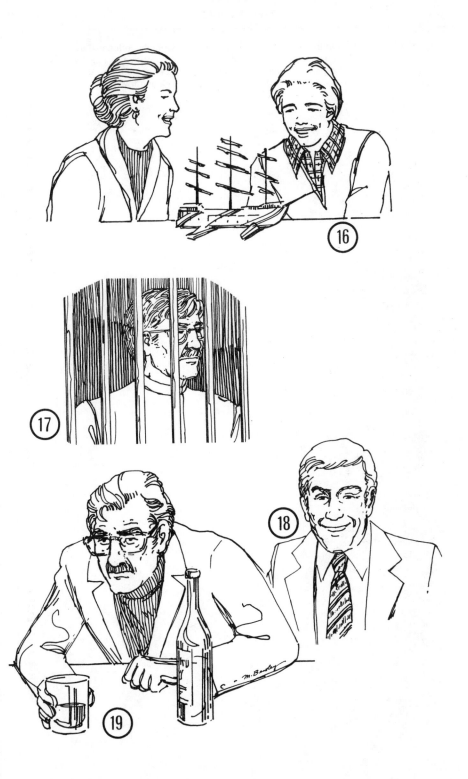

FIGURE 46
LIFE CHART

CHART YOUR LIFE. On the right is a time line. Next to it write the influential events or relationships that have shaped your life. Influences may be positive or negative. Use creative symbols that express the significance of the influences in your life. Also draw a line representing the course of your life according to its high and low points.

13 YEARS OLD TO 21 YEARS OLD

7 YEARS OLD TO 12 YEARS OLD

BIRTH TO 6 YEARS OLD

DISCOVERING "FAMILY" QUALITIES

Listed below are several qualities of the church as a family. These qualities influence Christian growth. Study Romans 14:1– 15:7; Ephesians 4; and Colossians 3 to identify what these passages say about these qualities. Each person in the group should look for one quality.

"Family" Qualities

1. *Family identity:* one body, unity, harmony, etc.
2. *Growth orientation:* growing, maturing, being built, supporting
3. *Rich environment:* variety of gifts and ministries, appreciation of differences, examples from many differing individuals
4. *Love:* supporting, patient, caring individuals; specific expressions of love in action
5. *Constructive feedback:* praise, encouragement, loving rebuke, instruction, correction, building up
6. *Wholesome environment:* shared commitment to good works, loving relationships, rejecting sinful lifestyle, holiness of life, mutual respect, sanctity of relationships

Here are my observations of the above qualities from Scripture:

I. Romans 14:1–15:7

II. Ephesians 4

III. Colossians 3

2. We mentioned in the preceding chapter that the congregation of which Larry is a member has been led to move to multiple house churches. One of the concepts associated with this move is that there will be no "individual" leadership of any house church. Instead, each elder will approach several members of his house church who seem to have leadership potential and invite them to guide its processes with him. This will involve them in keeping in

333

touch with, and praying for, house-church participants and in designing the relational processes for all its gatherings.

- If you were an elder in such a situation, what would you plan to do with your team?
- How might the principles that were presented in this chapter be applied in this situation?
- What dangers in the structure or process above would you want to be on the alert for? When you have defined them, how would you guard against them?

PART 3

BIBLICAL PRINCIPLES
OF CHURCH LEADERSHIP

A Description of Allegiance

Building Allegiance: Relational Presuppositions
Allegiance to One Another: Shared Life
Allegiance to the Father: Prayer and Worship
Allegiance to the Spirit: Giftedness
Allegiance to the Son: Personal Responsibility

How Leaders Build Allegiance

Body Organization
Ownership, Consensus, and Freedom
Confidence and Support
Communication

The organizational model developed in this section of the book outlines an organic rather than an institutional form. In the preceding two chapters a number of practices designed to facilitate the working of body organization were discussed.

1. Missions and ministries are to be owned by those responsible.
2. Decisions are to be made by consensus by those responsible.

COMMUNICATION

3. Freedom from outside command must always be preserved for members of mission or ministry teams.
4. Believers find increasing freedom to minister when leaders communicate confidence.
5. Leaders may have to participate by supervising some believers so they become more competent in their ministry.

To these practices we must add that communication lines must be built and maintained.

Ted Engstrom has this to say about communication:

When lines of communication are open and all people within the organization are cognizant of them, feedback will be automatic. We need resources to test continually the goals and methods employed to bring results. This helps to evaluate attitudes and provide the answer to the question that all employees [note that word!] have: "Why do we do it this way?"

1. Success in communication depends upon gaining acceptance of what is said. Therefore the communicator must carefully plan, not only what to tell, but how to tell it.
2. One of the best ways to gain acceptance is to give meaningful reasons to those being informed.
3. Where persuasion is needed, the oral word can be more effective than the printed word. A face-to-face discussion gives an opportunity to observe reaction and to adapt the presentation to gain the required end.
4. Keep the channels open both ways by inviting employee response. Communications will flow down more easily if a few observations and opinions flowing up are welcomed—even unpleasant ones.
5. In planning to communicate, always seek more than one method. A meeting which is reinforced by a letter sent to the home is more effective than an announcement made only one time.
6. Communication is not completed until the communicator is certain that his message was received and interpreted accurately. The receiver should consider, "What did he mean by that?" The transmitter, therefore, should consider, "What is he likely to think that I mean by this?"[1]

CHAPTER 23

Again the advice Engstrom shares is excellent—for an *institution*. We quote him because it is necessary to see once again some of the critical differences between the institutional and the body forms of organization.

In the institution, communication is focused on tasks. The use of the word *employees* implies that communication is designed to get them to "do it this way." Reference to "gaining acceptance" and "persuasion" and "flowing down" all imply a controlling or authoritative structure of organization. It's clear that once again the concept of leadership is really that of getting other people to do something you have determined you want done.

But all these things have been *abandoned* by servant leaders in the body. We do not pass commands "down" through a structure. We are not, as spiritual leaders, primarily concerned with "getting things done." That responsibility belongs to those who "own" the ministries to which they have been called. Our responsibility is to develop the close and sup-

---

[1]Ted W. Engstrom, *The Making of a Christian Leader* (Grand Rapids: Zondervan, 1976), p. 156.

portive relationships within the body that through meaningful interaction with each other and with God lead to the growth of allegiance.

We want forms of communication that will help people share their lives with each other, encourage the sharing of burdens and prayer, and engage the body in worship and in a mutual ministry centered around the Word of the Lord. In essence, communication within the body is developed not by structuring the kinds of communications channels that Engstrom talks about but by establishing interpersonal networks.

INTERPERSONAL NETWORKS

The key to body communications is building relationships among people rather than setting up structures. Many activities can help. Phone chains for prayer needs are practical. A church newsletter, especially one with columns devoted to God at work in and through members of the body, is an aid. Interviews of members in gatherings of the whole congregation help set a tone. Announcements and reports are also of value. But these tools are secondary to the really critical communications issue, which again focuses on building interpersonal networks.

Our goal of working toward interpersonal networks can be stated simply. We want each member of the body to have at least one and preferably several fellow believers with whom he has significant personal sharing experiences on a regular basis and whom he or she consistently supports with encouragement and prayer. Let's take a brief look at how such interpersonal networks are built.

Face-to-face groupings

The face-to-face grouping discussed earlier is generally the key to strong interpersonal networks. In the early church, in which the body met as house churches of relatively small size, intimacy was assured. Members of the body knew each other well and shared their lives with each other as a normal part of meeting together.

As we trace through great revival movements in history, we find this same kind of structuring. Cottage prayer groups or Wesleyan-type "class" meetings are a nearly universal phenomenon. Especially in the churches of today, where hundreds and at times even thousands are members of a single congregation, the existence of face-to-face groups with which each believer can identify and in which significant personal communication can take place is absolutely vital. Earlier we suggested that a leadership team might set as a goal 70 percent of the body in small group settings. This is a very important goal. The ideal would be 100 percent of the body in such relationships!

The nonformal character of relationships

Actually, we will never achieve 100 percent, and even the 70 percent standard is difficult to obtain. This is particularly so when we realize that we must work to build communications networks in nonformal ways. That is, we cannot simply tell people, "You belong to this 'house church' in your locality; go there on Friday." Such formal assignment may look good on paper but in fact will never be acted on by a significant percent of the body.

It is the nature of relationships to grow gradually, over time, in an informal way. They are generally not programable. What leaders can do is encourage face-to-face relationships and provide opportunities for them to be established.

Our highest expression of togetherness is in our celebration of worship. When we share the Word and the Supper together, as the body of Christ, we are experiencing a unity from which other encounters of fellowship derive a richness and depth of meaning. At the same time, what many members of the body want and need is a close friendship with one or two others. Going to lunch together, chatting on the phone, taking shopping or fishing trips—these are the settings in which many of our most significant relationships are forged. As leaders we should not only encourage such informal friendships—and be involved in many ourselves—but also try to stimulate the content and quality of the relationships that already exist.

Some stimulators can be "programed." For instance, we can ask each member of the body to phone one other person during the week to talk about his or her response to a particular teaching. Or we can ask each person to pray with one other member of the body this week about a particular need. This can stimulate a more personal level of sharing than may be present in some friendship relationships. But there are other, less formal ways to stimulate this sharing too.

Communication events

We've mentioned earlier such things as retreats or camping experiences for the body. We've even mentioned fun times, such as a day for square dancing or other shared experiences. It is helpful if the spiritual leaders, who are responsible for relationships and interaction, carefully design all such events. They should be thought of as events in which relationships and communication can develop.

For example, on a recent retreat with the congregation he serves, our friend Norm Wakefield planned several activities that were specifically designed to stimulate sharing and to build communication.

One of the events was a simulation game. Each member of the body on the retreat (including youth and children) was given a card on which he was instructed how to respond if asked for help. Some were to say, "I'd like to help, but I'm too busy." Or, "Please call again, I can't just now." Others were instructed to call out by name to individuals of their choice, asking them to help with a particular problem. A very few were given cards that instructed them to help whoever requested it.

Leaders then told the group to divide and go to a place in the retreat center where each member would be "alone" but could still hear the others. Some went into closets. Some stood in corners of a room. Some turned chairs away from others and the fireplace. Then those who had the "need help" cards began to call out the names of brothers and sisters asking them to come and help. Time after time the callers were given excuses and reasons why one or another couldn't come to his aid.

Afterward the body gathered and talked about the experience. They shared how they felt about asking and how they felt about not giving help. They talked about the feelings of the few who did come to help and what that help meant. And they talked about the need for friendships in which brothers and sisters could be counted on when they were needed.

On the same retreat Norm structured "Emmaus Walks"— simply a time for two people to take one-hour walks together, with the time divided so that first one person talked about himself for twenty minutes, then the other talked about himself for twenty minutes, and finally they shared the last twenty.

And for fun on the retreat there was the Ungame and other kinds of communication games.

Through these and similar events, a great freedom to share and to have close communication with others in that particular body have gradually grown. There was no formal "programing" of these relationships. But the context, the opportunity, and the guided experiences were planned—and did lead to the building of interpersonal networks along which body communication could flow.

340

Communication

Heterogeneous Groupings

As we explore communication networks for the body, we need to be very careful not to isolate one natural grouping of body members from others. In the institutional church this kind of age or class isolation is pervasive—and destructive.

We see its destructive character in several ways. For instance, in most churches the youth are systematically isolated from the adults by a complete "youth program" that becomes in effect a separate "youth church," with its own times of teaching, fellowship, projects, etc. But one of the basic principles of Christian nurture is that teaching must be associated with modeling. If youth are systematically isolated from mature adults, *where are their models?* Surely a well-meaning college student or recent seminary graduate, himself in his twenties, can't be considered an adequate model of Christian maturity for a group of teens!

We see the same phenomenon for children. And for adults as well, where age-grouped classes squeeze believers into social and learning relationships only with those who are of the same age and interests. Even worse is the drive of some toward a "spiritual grouping" of Christians, so that "new convert" groups are isolated from the "mature" in order that they can be given the formal teaching they need. They may receive graded content. But the reality of what the Christian life is and how we respond to truth, which is communicated through modeling, will be unavailable to the new converts. And the mature will lose the joy of sharing the new believer's zeal and having their own commitment stimulated.

It can be the same with the "workers" groups in an institutional church. A group of sixty or so begin a new church. There is great enthusiasm and everyone is involved. Because churches must have them, a full church program is begun, with each of the sixty loaded with several tasks. Yet enthusiasm and communication in this relatively small group is high. And it continues as new people are added to the congregation. But a strange phenomenon takes place. Newcomers join but many do not become involved in the worker core. They accept the services provided but do not themselves serve. Over a period of time, as the church grows to several hundred, the original group is still the worker core. Newcomers, with a few notable exceptions, are somewhere on the fringe. As the size increases, the work load is increased and the early intimacy is lost. Staffing becomes a burden rather than a joy, and soon the burden of maintaining the institution for the uninvolved saps the strength and motivation of the original core. Distinct

341

groups have again developed within the body—one group has become a task group—and communication between the groups will seldom exist in a significant way.

One school of thought insists that for numerical growth homogeneous groups need to be encouraged. What we are saying is that for the church to be a body and to function as a body, communications need to be established *across* all such natural grouping lines. Our goal is a body that is segmented and exists as natural but isolated groups.

Norm Wakefield's church illustrates one of the many options available to us today for building communication in heterogeneous settings. On Sunday evenings his fellowship meets in homes. There for about forty-five minutes they have "intergenerational Sunday school." Norm uses a curriculum designed for interaction teaching (the program called Sunday School PLUS) to provide the theme and several learning activities. Adults and children meet together, and many of the activities are specifically designed to have children talk or do learning tasks with adults who are not their parents. This approach, not unique with Norm by any means, has led to the development of an "extended family" feeling for children and adults alike. Also single young adults, teens, and divorced or widowed believers discover the sense of family that they may have lost.

The main point of this section, then, is to suggest that spiritual leaders must be sensitive to the need to build an interpersonal communications network within the congregation. This network is formed not by formal structures but by the close and informal personal relationships we encourage. These relationships involve those who meet in face-to-face groups or with one or two other friends. The task of the leaders is to encourage the development of significant communication experiences in these settings both within and across natural groupings. Such communications networks are by nature nonformal; so leaders must utilize many nonformal means of helping them grow and remain aware of the need to consciously plan body activities to build and strengthen interpersonal communication.

WHAT IS COMMUNICATED?

Earlier in this chapter we suggested that what is communicated in the church's interpersonal networks is to be the reality of our lives. In several places Scripture makes it clear that in our new relationship with each other as brothers and sisters we are not to lie (e.g., Col. 3:9), but to speak "the truth in love" (Eph. 4:15). This biblical concept goes far beyond not telling falsehoods. It refers to an open and honest lifestyle in which the reality of our lives and our responses to others are expressed. We can express ourselves without love, in which case communication becomes gossip or backbiting or personal attack. We can love without speaking the truth, in which case we lose track of reality in our relationships. What is urged is a kind of communication that shares all significant data and is motivated by an honest love for others and a desire to know and minister to others as they really are.

There are many ways to look at what will be communicated in such a setting. Along the communication lines that we seek to build in the church, thoughts, ideas, expressions of feelings, and a revelation of attitudes and values will flow. People will share not only factual data but also "inner states" (what is happening inside).

A recent analysis of communications factors, developed primarily for use in marriage counseling, gives us helpful insights into the kinds of data that need to be shared if we are to know and understand—and love—one another. This analysis is found in Sherod Miller et al., *Alive and Aware: Improving Communications in Relationships* (Minneapolis: Interpersonal Communications Programs, Inc., 1975). The communications framework these authors suggest has five data levels. Each of these data levels is necessary for one person to truly understand another. Here are the levels:

Sense data

This involves telling what you saw or observed. For instance, "I saw you lean against the door as you came in, and I thought I saw a tear. Is something troubling you?" This communication includes the sensory data on which a conclusion was reached or a question raised.

Interpretation

This involves telling what you concluded or thought when you observed what you did. "I saw you lean against the door as you came in, and I thought I saw a tear. Jim, I think something is really troubling you. That isn't the way you usually act."

Feeling

Sharing sensory data and thoughts or interpretations is still only a part of complete communication. How we feel—our emotional response—also needs to be communicated. "Jim,

I've come to really appreciate you, and it hurts me to see your pain. I really feel concerned."

Intention

The communication is still not complete. Along with thoughts and feelings, we also need to share our "intention." This term is used by the authors in a specialized way. As they use it, it means verbally expressing what we hope for or want to occur. In this case we might add another statement to Jim. "Jim, I want to help if there's anything I can do. I hope you'll share your burden with me."

Action

Finally, there is another communication component: stating what action will be taken. "Jim, I'm coming over to your house right after church. Let's talk about it then." Or perhaps, "Jim, I'm going to be home all afternoon. Why not give me a call or drop in if you want to talk about it."

In this illustration Jim now has complete data from his friend and is able to understand his inner reactions, thoughts, and intentions.

This full communication is helpful in family relationships and in counseling settings. It is also something we want to develop within the body. All too often communication flows well only on the level of "interpretation." We tell someone our conclusions but not the observations we base them on nor the feelings they evoke in us. Or we say, "Carl, I want you to be more open with me," without letting Carl know our feelings, the reasons why we think he is not open, and anything we're willing to do to work toward openness.

It's true that not every aspect of communication is necessary in every situation. But it is also true that in many settings in which we are working toward a significant sharing of ourselves with others—as we are in the body of Christ—being aware of these levels of communication and using them will undoubtedly promote understanding.

Although communication skills can be taught, and possibly should be, it is still true that as a community the body of Christ usually develops and transmits its own patterns of life without formal training. As spiritual leaders develop communication skills and learn to share on each of the levels described above, others will learn from their example how to communicate well. As face-to-face groups become open and self-revealing, there will be greater freedom for freely sharing data on all levels. We need to have not only the ability to communicate but also, and more importantly, a community where loving acceptance gives each member the freedom to share his real self. Sharing our real selves will at times be threatening. But as we learn that in the body of Christ we are accepted *as we are* and that in that body our personalities can grow beyond their present level, we will find it easier to be open and honest.

In Christ's body this is the kind of communication we seek—and need.

PROBE

▶ *case histories*
▶ *discussion questions*
▶ *thought provokers*
▶ *resources*

1. Analyze along the following lines the networks that you as a leader have developed within the body:
   a. List times when your communication with others in the body is primarily task-oriented (i.e., involves "official business"). Prepare a chart of a "typical week" and mark all meetings, phone calls, or other get-togethers with body members that are task-oriented or formal in character.
   b. List times when your communication with others in the body is primarily personal. On the chart of your "typical week" jot down all meetings, phone calls, etc., with members of the body in which your personal lives and relationships with God are the topic of the sharing. Be especially alert for *informal* times of chatting or sharing. Don't fail to list a contact because it isn't "church business."
   c. Now take each item on the two contact lists on your chart and try to reconstruct the contact. Using a separate sheet of paper for each contact, list what you and others said, as nearly as you can remember. Divide each sheet of paper into the five categories, as in the example below, and jot down recollections under the appropriate categories.
   d. Now analyze your sheets carefully. What do you discover about the pattern of your sharing in the formal situations? What do you discover about the pattern of your sharing in the informal situations? How would you analyze the strengths and weaknesses of your own communication modeling?
   e. What goals can you as a body leader set for yourself that will help to build the interpersonal communications networks and skills recommended in this chapter? What areas of communication do you need to strengthen? How will you go about it?

FIGURE 47
COMMUNICATION ANALYSIS

Level of Communication	What was said	Who said it
Sense data		
Interpretations (thoughts, ideas)		
Feelings		
Intentions (hopes, desires)		
Actions promised		

NOTE: You may want to keep and use conversational analysis forms for several weeks as you train yourself to include communications data from all levels in your sharing with your Christian brothers and sisters.

2. The following chapter from *Building People*[2] tells of Don Bubna's relationship with Janet, a troubled young woman in the Salem, Oregon, congregation he serves. Underline the statements that say something important about communication. Then in about three pages describe Don's communications with Janet and their experiences in the local body.

LOVE ME AS I AM

"I want to withdraw my membership from the church!"
The slender woman spoke calmly into the microphone, and from the platform behind her I could see the shocked response of the people in the packed pews. Her parents' faces reflected quiet suffering as Janet's words rang through the sound system:
"I have been living a lie, and I can't continue to hide it."
Only a slight tremor in her voice betrayed emotion. "Please understand that I appreciate your friendship, and I want to continue as a visitor here. But I have discovered that I don't believe in Christianity as a valid philosophy of life. Therefore, I can't remain a member of this church."

[2]Don Bubna and Sarah Ricketts, *Building People* (Wheaton, Ill.: Tyndale, 1978), pp. 9-15. Used by permission.

Communication

Various people reflected their surprise, disbelief, and hurt, yet another response was becoming even more evident: a wave of compassion toward the lonely figure behind the microphone. Did Janet sense it too? I hoped so, and even as I thought it, I realized that what had happened was inevitable.

I had learned some things about Janet Landis over the last four years when she had made infrequent visits to my study to unburden her increasing pain and share her often unorthodox views. Janet had grown up in the church. Her father was an elder in the congregation when I first arrived as pastor ten years before. A determined and devout man of German-Russian descent, he had been pleased when Janet, the seventh of nine children, had gone to a Bible college. There she met and married her husband, Bob. When I came to Salem, Bob was still in college, working toward his Master's degree in education, while Janet was busy with three small children. After the birth of their fourth child, she too returned to college. I saw them only occasionally in church, until Janet began coming to my office for counseling.

Her immediate purpose was to share some personal difficulties, but I soon discovered that these only masked a deeper problem often experienced by young people who grow up in the church. Janet had sincere doubt that Christianity is anything other than a standard of behavior that makes us acceptable in the eyes of family and church. Janet had been a "good girl" all her life. A straight "A" student in Bible college, she was active in the missions program, was president of the honor society, and taught Sunday school in a black inner-city church. Yet since her early teen years she had lived with questions and doubts carefully hidden behind the "game of religion" she played so well.

Only after two years in graduate school, where atheistic and agnostic professors encouraged her doubts, did she feel free to tell me her honest opinion of Christianity.

"I have to answer for myself the questions of what is real, what is good and evil, and whether man is really free . . . ," she told me. Her voice was urgent. "Christianity is too narrow. I must find a philosophy of life by which I can live honestly with my imperfections and strive to be a better person on my own terms."

I felt the challenge in her dark eyes and was conscious of my own inadequacy. There was nothing I could tell her about the great truths of Christianity that she had not read or heard before. Instead I thanked her for her honesty and invited her to come by my office as often as she liked. "I will be interested to

347

hear where you are in your struggle toward a reality in your life," I said.

Janet looked as though she expected me to say something else, but after a brief silence she nodded with a quick smile. "Thanks, Pastor, for not telling me the obvious things."

Over the next two years she came often. Each time she voiced criticism of the church as a group of narrow-minded judges, and said she was continuing her search for a valid set of goals for her own life. She seemed progressively more depressed and frustrated. She told me she had chosen what she called an existentialist philosophy, attempting to decide her own standards of right and wrong, and it disturbed her that this did not result in the sense of peace and freedom she had hoped to find.

After two years, Janet received her Master's degree in education and moved with her husband and children to Alaska, where Bob became chairman of the English Department at Ketchikan High School. I only saw Janet when she returned occasionally to Salem for a visit, and I began to sense that she was moving dangerously close to despair.

"I have made some free choices," she told me, "but I can't rid myself of the idea that some of the things I've done are morally wrong." There were dark circles under her eyes, and new lines of pain etched around her sensitive mouth. She played nervously with the frayed seam of her jeans pocket. "It doesn't make sense to feel guilt when I don't believe there are any real objective standards of right and wrong . . . yet I am not finding freedom from guilt."

"I think I understand something of what you feel," I said slowly. "I can say that because guilt is a human condition, and I am very human. Men have tried to escape guilt simply by saying there is no right and wrong, and that our guilt feelings are the result of someone telling us we are bad. Yet I know of no philosopher or individual who has succeeded in convincing himself of that theory for very long."

Janet sighed and slumped in her chair. "I am beginning to see that. I may think there is no right and wrong, but I feel condemned. I am finding it more and more difficult to live with myself. I even feel alienated from my family." Her eyes were pits of despair as she lowered her voice. "No wonder existentialists dwell on death as the ultimate choice. Nothing else makes sense."

"I have found that some things make a great deal of sense," I said carefully. "If guilt is real—and we seem to agree it is—then it makes more sense to admit it than to deny it."

"So?" Janet's eyebrows were raised slightly.

"An admitted guilt isn't hard to define. It is concrete and real, like a debt you know you need to pay."

Janet looked apprehensive, and I smiled. "I know of only one effective way to resolve guilt . . . by forgiveness. I can live with my imperfections today because I know that my debt has been paid by Jesus Christ and I am forgiven."

My listener flinched. "You know I don't agree with that. It's too easy!"

"Not easy," I countered. "It involves the admission that I am not able to handle the guilt question myself, and that my ideas and philosophy are inadequate to explain what is real. It is never easy for me to agree with God that I am helpless and need his forgiveness."

"You seem so sure that God exists," said Janet. "He may be there as an impersonal power behind the universe, but many years ago when I thought of him as personal, I saw him as the judge who declared me guilty in the first place, and accepted me only when I was good. Today I consider a personal relationship with God impossible."

I ached for Janet in her dilemma—facing the reality of guilt, yet unable to accept the total forgiveness of God in Jesus Christ. I know the agony of guilt and few things overwhelm me with such gratitude as the awareness of forgiveness. My guilt is dissolved, and I know I am loved and accepted by God. This recognition always brings an intensified awareness that my relationship with God is intimate and personal. Only a God with personal attributes can forgive. No system of thought or philosophy can do that for us.

I wanted Janet to understand how the first man, Adam, broke his relationship with God through rebellion. Since then, down through history, God has taken the initiative to become reconciled with man by offering forgiveness, acceptance, and love. But there was nothing I could say to convince Janet that God already loved her. I could only attempt to accept her as I knew God had accepted me.

"I think I understand your position," I told her, "and I hope you can understand mine when I say I accept you as a person—not on the basis of your behavior, but because I choose to accept you as a friend. Can you buy that?"

"Perhaps," Janet shrugged. "But I would not be honest if I didn't tell you I find that hard to believe. . . ."

In Alaska Janet worked as a probation and parole officer, a year-round job that often took her away from home by floatplane to outlying Indian communities. In order to have more time with her family, she decided to return to college in Salem for one more term to earn her teacher's credentials. During those three months, she attended most of our church services, but managed to keep aloof from the people by slipping in late and leaving immediately after a service. In my office she continued to categorize the church as phony.

"They talk about love and acceptance, but I know it only applies to people who fit nicely into the right pattern." As if to prove her point, she deliberately did and said what she called "un-Christian" things. At times I smelled alcohol on her breath, and her attitude seemed to say, "Why don't you send me away so I can prove that you only accept me when I am good."

"Your idea of the church differs from mine," I told her. "I don't see us as a bunch of super-saints who've got it all together and are looking down our noses at those who don't. The Bible and my own experience tell me that the church is simply a group of imperfect people who know they are forgiven and accepted by God and are learning to forgive and accept one another."

"That sounds very nice, Pastor," Janet said softly. "But I know better. Remember, I grew up in the church. What do you think would happen if someone really different wanted to join your group—without conforming to your standards?"

"That would surely put to the test Paul's words to the early church, 'Welcome one another, therefore, as Christ has welcomed you, for the glory of God'" (Rom. 15:7 RSV). I smiled. "That means we ought to be learning to accept each other even in our sins, just as Jesus does."

An almost wistful look crossed Janet's face. "I've still got to be me." There was soberness in her voice. "Your cozy little in-group of a mutual admiration society just isn't my kind of thing."

"You've been open with me and I take that as an expression of trust." I looked directly at her. "Perhaps you ought to let the church know some of the struggles you're going through. They think of you as one of us, you know."

Janet looked startled. "You're right, I'm still on the membership roll. . . ." Gazing out the window where a soft drizzle darkened the day, she spoke slowly. "Perhaps I need to say something to the church. I may not know what I am or what I believe, but I know one thing for sure; I'm not a Christian. My life-style and my beliefs differ so drastically from what you people believe that the only decent thing to do is to tell the *church and withdraw as a member. . . . I'll feel better when I am not pretending to be something I'm not." Janet looked almost relieved. "Will you call me to the microphone at the end of the sharing service Sunday night? I won't have the courage to speak, otherwise."*

She had put me on the spot. The following Sunday evening was a special service. The church would be full, and there would be visitors.

I nodded. "I'll call on you . . . but think it over. Tell the people where you stand, and give them an opportunity to accept that."

The anguish was deep in Janet's eyes. "You are an optimist, Pastor. You believe in the church, but I don't expect to be accepted by them anymore than I expect to be accepted by God."

While the guest speaker delivered his message, I was acutely aware of Janet's pale face in the section of pews to my left. She was obviously determined to carry out her intentions. Her parents sat near the back of the crowded room. They would be deeply hurt by their daughter's action. I wondered what the response of the others would be.

Janet's eyes caught mine, as though she read my thoughts and was asking, "Are you going to let me down, or will you dare to have a lifelong member of the church stand up in front of all these people to say she does not believe in what you stand for?"

Her eyes followed me to the microphone. "Janet Landis has told me she has something to share with us. Will you come up here, Janet?"

There was an expectant silence as she came forward, long-legged in jeans and a loose sweater. Only someone who knew her well would be able to tell that she was under a heavy strain and that her words were carefully chosen.

". . . I can't pretend any longer. Please accept the withdrawal of my membership from this church."

Quickly she stepped from the platform and walked to the side entrance. As I took her place by the microphone, I was aware that one of our elders had followed her out the door. My heart ached as I spoke: "We have all sensed something of Janet's hurt. I have tried to help her in counseling, and I know something of the struggle she is going through. Now I believe that only as you people respond to her need can she come to understand that God loves her."

In those words, I expressed what I believe is the function of

351

the true church. I believe the church exists here on earth to demonstrate God's love in a way that can be understood and experienced by all who long to know him.

That was the challenge to our church that Sunday evening five years ago when Janet walked out of our building. Until then, most of the people had been unaware of her struggles. Now her pain was visible. Would we be able to respond in a way that would help Janet find the reality she sought so desperately?

Later that evening my wife echoed my thoughts. "I'm glad Janet felt free to share where she stands," Deloris smiled. "She said she wants to come as a visitor. . . . She must have felt reasonably sure we won't reject her. I think that is a good beginning."

Walking out of our auditorium was not the end of Janet's relationship with the church. Her public withdrawal had been a cry for help. Many of the people had understood and would respond, I was sure. In a sense, Janet's relationship with the true church, the family of God, had only begun.

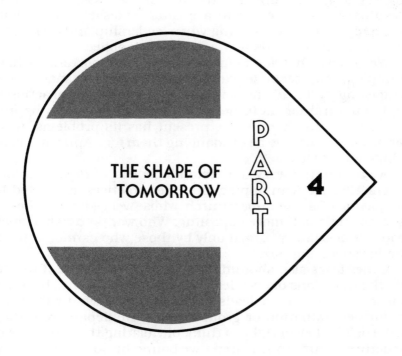

THE SHAPE OF
TOMORROW

PART

4

In 1970 Larry wrote a book called *A New Face for the Church.* It advanced some then-radical concepts about the nature of the church and spelled out some of the implications for the restructuring of our lives together as Christians. In the last section of that book there is a "science fiction" approach to describe an imaginary future church in Dunsea, Wisconsin, as an attempt to illustrate what a congregation structured on New Testament principles might be like in our culture.

We don't want to resort to fiction to conclude this book. Instead, we'd like to share some patterns of church life that are emerging and already exist in our own society. Each of these patterns expresses to a greater or lesser degree what may happen in a local setting when leadership and other concepts examined in this text are actually applied.

We believe that for many reasons it's important to have examples. One reason is fear of the unknown. No matter how compellingly biblical any of us may believe a course of action to be, it's natural for us to hesitate when action draws us into unknown paths. Even if the present has its problems, what new problems will we be exchanging them for? And what good things might we lose?

We also have a very understandable fear of *theory.* In our pragmatic American approach to life, practices suggested by the pastor of some superchurch whose very size testifies to "success" is much more appealing. Who wants to risk a lonely road to uncertainty, urged only by those who cannot point to similar success in size?

Other fears also abound. What will people think if we violate the traditions of decades? Won't some leave our church as this leadership course leads to change? And what will others in our denomination or group think if we depart from their patterns? Is it even right to think of violating the discipline or structure of our group? Aren't we bound by our constitutions to stay within established norms?

All these fears are valid. Most are realistic. It would be very wrong to suggest that adopting the leadership principles explored in this book will lead to anything but stress, trauma, and suffering for leaders. But it would be as wrong not to remind people that stress, trauma, and suffering was the price Jesus paid for commitment to God's way and will.

But enough. Let's move on and look at some of the fears and some of the possibilities. Let's see what *has happened* in congregations where the "renewal" approach to church life and leadership have been followed for at least a decade.

Let's explore the possible shape of *your* tomorrow.

PART 4

THE SHAPE OF TOMORROW

New Forms: The Flexibility of God
New Vitality: Tradition in Mission
Open-Ended Futures

*For several summers now, some of us have taught a School
of Ministry on the campus of Wheaton College. Last year the
theme was "Making Christ the Head of Your Church." Many
of the concepts in this book were taught.*

A number of men and women who took that course have

NEW FORMS: THE FLEXIBILITY OF GOD

*written reports on how they have begun to implement a
number of the leadership principles.*

*It's encouraging to see the enthusiasm and good begin-
nings made. But we wonder: What will such congregations
look like in a decade?*

One of the men taking the Wheaton course each year is the pastor of an Iowa United Presbyterian church of about three hundred members. He describes it as "steeped in the usual Presbyterian traditions." It is also a church rich in leadership and one experiencing God's special work of renewal.

In a report written some five months after the Wheaton experience, this pastor told of definite leadership steps he's taken based on principles explored in this text. Let's look at his report, part of which was quoted earlier.[1]

Our Sunday morning worship averages close to three hundred people. For the last several years we have replaced the traditional "pastoral prayer" with what we call a sharing time. It is a time when people can share prayer requests or things that have happened in their lives. Generally this has been a time of asking for prayer for the sick and others in need. After I came back from Wheaton, I suggested that during our sharing time people tell about something God had taught them from the Word or through experience during the past week. The next week a tenth grader stood up and said, "Last week pastor said we ought to share some things that God has taught us. I was reading in 1 Corinthians and God showed me. . . ." The look on the faces of the people said, "What was all that about?" This past Sunday a man in our congregation stood up and said that this week he had learned something new he wanted to share. He said that he had been studying the word "witness" in the Scriptures and found that most of the time it was a noun and not a verb. He had always thought of witnessing as something you do, rather than something you are. So maybe little by little the people are beginning to open up at the level of worship and learning that they are members of the body and can and should be able to share and teach what God has shown them rather than leaving the whole job to the pastor.

The main change, though, has occurred in our board of elders. Immediately on my return from Wheaton I began to ask the elders to lead in devotions at their meetings instead of doing it myself. I have asked them to try to share with us something out of their own experience rather than getting something out of a book somewhere. So far they have been able to do that. We have been spending more time during our meetings talking about our own needs as individual Christians and praying about them together and talking about the needs of our congregation. We do this in a collective way. We are asking, What are the needs of our congregation in general and how can we meet those needs? And we also talk about individuals. How are they coming along? What can we do to be of help? How can we serve them and encourage them in their Christian experience?

Since Wheaton we have had to wrestle with some special problems. What are we going to do about our church, since it is growing and there is no place to put all the people? As the elders began to work this through, they made every effort to include the entire body in their decision-making process by talking to individuals and calling for some congregational meetings in order to get the people's input. In these

_____
[1]See p. 290.

congregational meetings, the elders did a good job, I felt, pointing out that our growth was due to God's blessing on us and that we did not want to build a building or do anything that would not be in accordance with God's will. The elders prayed a lot collectively and individually. They encouraged the congregation to pray about the situation.

Since the church decided to build an addition to the church structure, there hasn't been a Sunday that has gone by that one of the elders hasn't spontaneously expressed during our sharing time what God has been doing—the miracle that He has done in our congregation—and thus endeavored to give God the praise and glory our head should have.

As the elders try to function as the spiritual leaders of the church, they are continually asking themselves, "What does Christ want us to do in this situation?" Recently the elders have stopped doing programs just because they have always been done or because the denomination wants them to be done. Rather they allow or carry out programs if they (1) honor the Lord, (2) meet needs in the members of the body.

The elders have become concerned that the entire congregation has an understanding of what is happening in the church. They are planning at our next congregational meeting to have a brainstorming session—a time when the people can share what they want and how they think it could happen.

As you can see, we are only getting started. I believe the elders are beginning to get a vision for what their jobs are as elders. They are trying to enter the role of servants. They want to be enablers. And for the most part they are trying to model the Christian faith as they understand it.

Our brother from Iowa *is* just getting started. The question we want to raise, however, is this: *Where is he going?* In this chapter we want to look at some of those possibilities, especially the possibility of an entirely "new" form.

A FIRST EXAMPLE: OUR HERITAGE CHURCH

For some twelve years now, Our Heritage Church of Scottsdale, Arizona, has been on the journey our Presbyterian brother has begun.

Our Heritage Church began as a mission of the Wesleyan Methodist Church in America. Its first and only pastor is Bob Girard, author of the book *Brethren, Hang Loose.*[2] For ten years or more the church has been organized into many small groups that meet during the week and an extended, two-to-two-and-one-half-hour service one Sunday morning a month. In the past year it has felt led to return its buildings to the denomination and move into a multiple house-church form.

Like other churches following the risky road of renewal, it has experienced many problems and tensions. Evangelism, a high priority and naturally functioning ministry of the members for a number of years, fell off for a considerable time.

---

[2]Robert C. Girard, *Brethren, Hang Loose* (Grand Rapids: Zondervan, 1972).

Elders committed to biblical principles of church life drew back from accepting New Testament responsibility for the life of the body. Bob Girard himself experienced guilt feelings as he was led with the congregation into patterns of ministry that did not fit the traditional role of the pastor. The congregation has struggled with Sunday school and how to minister to children in nontraditional formats. There have also been problems concerning how to minister to those who are offended by the freedom the church extends for sharing in its services.

Finally in a series of painful steps there came the unanimous conviction that God was leading the church to surrender its buildings to the denomination. At the same time the denomination chose to expel Our Heritage Church and its pastor.

Through several documents that were written at the end of the process, we can sense some of the agony the church experienced. The first is a newspaper article by Pat McElfresh that appeared in the *Scottsdale Press* in January 1979.

Church closes to meet in homes

A Scottsdale congregation is giving up its building and property to become "a church without walls," changing to what members believe is a New Testament–directed move to "house churches."

Instead of gathering on Sundays and midweek at the church, the 130 members of Our Heritage Church, formerly a Wesleyan Methodist congregation, will attend one of three "house church" locations in Valley homes, getting together for monthly "reunion" meetings elsewhere.

The concept, they believe, is set by example in the New Testament. "This was an 11-year pilgrimage into change," says Pastor Robert Girard. "We definitely feel this is the direction the church should go, based on a lot of biblical teachings, the example of Christ with his disciples and the early church.

"We know how they functioned, the kinds of things they taught. These were not institutional things but those based on the Beatitudes, about loving each other enough to die for each other, giving to each other when there is a need.

"The words of Christ say to me that his intention from the beginning was to create a family, not a company."

The new concept will have all ages meeting together under team leadership at each house church on Sunday afternoons or evenings. The focus will be on developing personal commitments to each other, to selves and to studying God's word, with goals of developing spiritual maturity, strengthening relationships and encouraging each person to become a minister in the church.

Girard said he almost left the ministry 11 years ago because of his frustrations. "We were trying everything we were supposed to do, yet the quality of life that the Bible talked about was nowhere in sight. So we decided to take these steps."

The steps, which paved the way for the big change, included meeting in small groups, simplifying programs, encouraging deeper relationships and participatory styles of meetings, dividing the pastoral leadership among a team of local elders and de-institutionalizing. "We were moving toward functioning not as a 'church' but as a family," Girard explains.

This meeting style brought sharing and participation, he says, of needs and hurts. "In the past, churches—and ours did it, too—have concentrated on the kinds of things that build an institution, an image, rather than real relationships between people, sharing of life and being each other's support. We're not against big churches but at the point where we are now, to become what we feel God wants us to become, we have to make this kind of move."

This past week that final move was made, out of the facility at 4640 N. Granite Reef Road. The first official services will be conducted Sunday evening in the Valley homes of three members. The congregation has become "denominationally independent," Girard said, using that term after the congregation was disassociated from the denomination, charged with being too far away from "the Wesleyan norm," according to a letter from the district superintendent.

The property the congregation is leaving is valued at approximately $230,000 and will be turned over to the Wesleyan denomination's area offices. The church office will stay there temporarily, and the Girards will occupy the parsonage for up to 90 days while finding a new residence.

The congregation will continue its commitments to individual missionaries, but Girard said most of the offerings will be taken for "people needs."

"Actually, we have been pretty free about our budget for some time. We have had no pledges for 10 years and haven't taken offerings for five or six years. We just have a receptacle or let people mail in offerings. We want people to give whatever they do out of response to what God is saying to them, and out of love. We feel the pledge drive or passing the plate are artificial pressures."

This de-emphasis on a fixed budget led to Girard serving since the first of July without salary, relying on income from speaking engagements and the books he has written. The four "elders" on the pastoral team selected by members also serve without pay.

"They were chosen over the last five years as men who had the kinds of gifts that lent toward a pastoral ministry. One of our strong emphases in the past 10 years has been to get away from the whole idea that only professionals can do something. Every believer is a priest; it is a matter of personal talents and gifts and sensitivity; it has nothing to do with training. In counseling, many are more adept than I am by their spiritual gifting and the experience they have had in the past."

Girard said in small group experiences during recent years, people have found out they can help just by caring and loving. "From the human standpoint of tradition, there is risk in this but we are excited by the possibilities of acting like a family. This is happening all over the country, all around the world."

Girard foresees hundreds of people in house churches, predicting "aggressive growth." He said there already are many house churches but he does not know of any congregations which have left a building.

Our Heritage's house churches are in north-central Scottsdale (5135 N. 86th St.), south Scottsdale–east Phoenix (2502 N. 53rd St., Phoenix) and north-central Phoenix (14411 N. Sixth St., Phoenix). Each of Sunday's 5 p.m. meetings will be followed by a potluck supper.

New Forms: The Flexibility of God

The elders are Howard Graham, a sign maker; Pat Porter, an electronics engineer; Larry Richards, an ordained minister, writer and conference speaker; and Rod Wilke, with an air conditioning firm.

The newspaper article gives an overview. But what were the reasons for the new forms and what is the new life pattern? That is explained in a newsletter prepared by the elders for all the members of the church.

The next step: A church without walls

On an eleven-year pilgrimage into change, the congregation of Our Heritage Church has been led into (1) small groups, (2) simplification of programs and ministry, (3) relational style of church life, (4) participatory style of meeting, (5) shared pastoral leadership by a team of local elders, (6) refocusing of giving priorities to comply with New Testament teachings that say Christian giving is basically for people needs, and (7) de-institutionalization—moving toward functioning not as a "church" but as a family. All these have involved considerable change in church structure.

"The next step" grows naturally out of this long process of refocusing and renaissance. The most intense period of concentration has been the five-year struggle of the church's leadership team to ascertain the mind of the Holy Spirit for their own ministry and for this particular congregation.

In order to provide a more flexible "wineskin" (Mark 2:22) that will more effectively stimulate real growth into Christ and responsiveness to His headship, we are committed to the following actions:

1. *On Sunday, January 7, 1979, we shall begin meeting weekly in several "house churches."*

From that date on, by deliberate choice, we shall no longer meet at 4640 N. Granite Reef Road. (These buildings are being voluntarily turned over to The Wesleyan Church.)

Characteristics of the house churches:

    a. *Geographical location.* Body members will be urged to join the nearest house church, but there will be freedom for each person or family to choose (Acts 2:44-47; 5:42; 12:12; 16:40; 28:23, 30-31; Rom. 16:5, 23; 1 Cor. 16:19; Col. 4:15; and Philemon 2).

    b. *Team leadership.* Each house church will be shepherded by a carefully selected team of pastors and teachers (elders and others who are gifted by the Spirit for teaching and pastoral care). Team members of all the house churches will meet weekly for mutual discipling and for sharing and praying concerning the needs of each house church and the larger body (Acts 13:1-3; 14:22; 1 Tim. 3:1-6; 1 Peter 5:1-4; Heb. 13:17).

    c. *Sunday afternoon and/or evening meeting time.* A time frame allowing development of greater freedom of thinking, attitudes, and meeting style.

    d. *Participative meeting style.* Similar to our present Sunday meetings. Planned to include singing, worship, sharing, and teaching of the Word (1 Cor. 14:26; Acts 4:23-35; Eph. 5:18-21).

    e. *The shape of a family.* The body will be encouraged by its setting to *see* itself as a family and will be stimulated by its structure to *live* as a family (Mark 10:29-30).

    f. *Closer personal relationships.* Both localness and size will contribute to greater concentration on developing significant relationships with

361

people. The church, unencumbered by the murkiness of institutional expectations, has a chance to *be* what it is by nature, a network of relationships (John 13:34-35; 15:12-13; 1 Cor. 12:12-27).

g. *Completely duplicatable structure.* This simple, dynamic church form can be developed in any neighborhood without financial or professional limitation. Body members will be built up and sent out as the Spirit leads and supplies pastoral leaders to form new house churches (Matt. 28:19-20; Acts 1:8; 13:1-3).

2. *There will be monthly gatherings of the larger body in which all the house churches will come back together.* The general pattern is expected to be: (1) meeting in the house churches for three Sundays, and (2) on the fourth Sunday, all house churches cancel their meetings in order to gather for the larger celebration and "family reunion." (Occasionally these larger meetings will take the form of a retreat.)

Purposes: (1) to maintain identification with the larger body, to guard against becoming ingrown or cultic; (2) to share spiritual gifts (such as teaching) with the other house churches; and (3) to stimulate a common sense of mission.

Content of these meetings: worship and celebration, concentrated biblical teaching, fellowship and relationship-building.

Place of meeting: rented or borrowed places such as retreat centers, hotel meeting rooms, schools, public recreational facilities, and restaurants. There are many such places available in the Valley.

Added opportunity: other house churches, such as the Shared Life Fellowship (at Wakefield's) and Grace (at Klagge's), will join us for these gatherings.

3. *A stronger discipling ministry will begin when the house churches are launched.* It will be titled, "Discipleship: Training for the Kingdom" or, "Do You Want to Get Over Being a Baby?"

For the "disciplers" and the "discipled," the program consists of

a. Personal commitment to each other
   (1) to spend time together—regularly, casually, and as needed (in an emergency)
   (2) to feel with each other, to develop empathy
b. Personal commitment to yourself
   (1) to face honestly what God reveals
   (2) to seek changes in life-patterns, from those of the culture to those of the kingdom, and from the lower to the higher nature
c. Personal commitment to study (seeking information on which changes—personal and relational—may take place)
   (1) to honor God's Word, no matter what it says
   (2) to honor the "voice" of the Spirit through meditation and sharing with others

(The specifics of the program and how the discipling process will function will constitute an additional paper.)

4. *Small groups will continue.* The weekday small groups that have been part of the life of Our Heritage Church for more than a decade and that have carried on its indispensable ministry of "spontaneous discipleship" will continue as is. New groups will be formed as needed. Yokefellow groups will carry on their special ministry.

5. *The goals of these actions include:*
   a. *Spiritual maturity:* (1) that all may have the mind of Christ, (2) that all may bear the family likeness of God's Son, and (3) that all may

know what is spiritual and what is not (Rom. 12:1-2; Eph. 4:11-16).

b. *Priesthood development:* that each believer may become an able minister with his gifts (Rom. 12; 1 Peter 2:5, 9).

c. *Practical ministry:* that the network of relationships that the church is by nature may be strengthened and freed to become more real (1 Cor. 12:12-27; 13:1-13; 1 Peter 1:22).

d. *Growth:* that the church may grow with the growth that is from God—in numbers of people and in love (Eph. 4:16; Col. 2:18-19)—in a manner and context that is a biblical response to the Lord's Commission to "Go . . . make disciples . . . baptizing . . . teaching them to observe all that I have commanded . . ." (Matt. 28:19-20).

e. *Body Life:* that the church may cease to be in any important sense an institution and may be what it is—a body, a family, a shared life (John 18:36; Acts 2:42-47).

Come On Along! Let's Take the Next Step . . . Together.

For many years Our Heritage Church had followed a path that led to increasing conflict with *The Discipline* [constitution] of the denomination of which it was a part. When the buildings were turned over to the denomination, a request was made that the congregation be retained in fellowship, or at least Bob Girard's Wesleyan credentials be continued. Two letters exchanged between Girard and the General Superintendent of the Wesleyan Church give a hint of the gracious— and yet painful—manner in which the request was heard and at first rejected. For Our Heritage Church to follow what it believed to be the leading of God did mean official separation from the organization. It is possible that following the practices suggested in this book will lead others to such a painful separation as well!

Here are the two final letters, which make clear the points of view, both of the denomination and of the local congregation:

December 20, 1978

The Reverend Robert C. Girard
4640 North Granite Reef Road
Scottsdale, Arizona 85251

Dear Brother Girard:

It was with regret that I received the announcement of the plan for voluntary withdrawal from The Wesleyan Church of the pastor and members of Our Heritage Church for the purpose of establishing another type of organization which "sets aside *The Discipline* of The Wesleyan Church." I recognize, as you pointed out in your correspondence, that this step grows naturally out of the process you have been pursuing for the last several years. However, I had hoped after our conversation at last Conference time that you and the people there would move to "the Wesleyan norm" of church operations and practices.

Please, Brother Girard, accept my deep gratitude for the ethical and forthright manner in which you and your people have acted in this matter. We appreciate you letting the district officials know in advance of your organizational plans and of your intention of vacating the property the first of January. This will enable the officials to plan for the utilization of all the properties in a continuing ministry of The Wesleyan Church there.

The kind of relationship you requested for the group does not appear to be proper. "The Wesleyan Church is a denomination consisting of those Christian believers, who as members of the Body of Christ, hold the faith set forth in the Articles of Religion of The Wesleyan Church, who have been duly received as members of The Wesleyan Church and formally organized according to its *Discipline*, who acknowledge the ecclesiastical authority of The Wesleyan Church, who support its worldwide mission, and who meet together regularly for worship, edification, instruction, and evangelism." The concept set forth in the new plan of organization is not compatible organizationally or philosophically with that of a denominational organization or plan of operation. This does not question the Christian testimony or the Christian integrity of the withdrawing group. Neither should it prevent a harmonious working relationship between The Wesleyan Church in that community and those who plan to be a part of the new organization. The greatest possible spiritual impact is needed in that city. May God be pleased to use each group to accomplish His will.

A continuing ministerial relation for you also appears to be impractical and improper. Membership in a local Wesleyan Church with all of its attendant privileges, responsibilities, and requirements is necessary for one to remain an elder in The Wesleyan Church. It would be difficult if not impossible for you to meet these expectations while ministering in and promoting the new work as outlined in the plans for "A church without walls."

It would be to your advantage, it seems to me, for you to request a ministerial letter of standing when or just before the new work is launched. This letter of standing is in effect for one year and may be used to unite with any group with which there is a framework for such a relationship. It carries a recommendation to the Christian confidence of those to whom the letter may be presented.

Much latitude, as you indicated, has been granted you in the work there. It was hoped that this would permit you to develop a church that would fit "the Wesleyan norm." Evidently you have decided to pursue another course. Knowing you as I do, I am sure you are taking the step you now feel you should. I sincerely wish the very best for you and for your people in your new venture. My past association with you and your family has been enriching. I look forward to continued fellowship as opportunity may afford. I feel a sense of personal loss in this decision.

I am sure the members of the Arizona District Board of Administration as well as the members of the District are disappointed in the developments. They are a great group and they will be fair and Christian in their future relationship with you.

Sincerely in Christ,

(*signed*) Virgil A. Mitchell
General Superintendent
Western Administrative Area

New Forms: The Flexibility of God

January 8, 1979

Dr. Virgil A. Mitchell, General Superintendent
The Wesleyan Church
Box 2000
Marion, Ind. 46952

Dear Dr. Mitchell:

We had hoped and prayed that your decision concerning our relationship with the Wesleyan Church would be different.

We have considered the possibility of appeal (because of the biblical instruction to "make every effort to keep the unity of the Spirit," Eph. 4:3), but the tone of your letter made it clear that, for the church here, such an appeal would be fruitless, since we are as a congregation clearly not in step with *The Discipline.*

The grounds stated for concluding that "a continuing ministerial relation" for me "also appears to be impractical and improper" seemed less substantial and inconsistent with the practice of many Wesleyan districts of continuing relation for elders who serve in non-Wesleyan churches and organizations. I myself, in earlier years, served Free Methodist and Evangelical United Brethren Churches, under license from the Iowa Wesleyan District, and later served in the Billy Graham Evangelistic Association, as an elder in the Wisconsin District. And there are many others, who maintain local Wesleyan Church membership, while serving elsewhere. On this basis, founded both on *The Discipline* (paragraph 1174) and on precedent, I briefly considered the possibility of appeal. But, again, the tone of your letter is quite final, and I definitely see my life deeply entwined with the people of Our Heritage Church (if they are guilty, then I am guilty with them of departure from "the Wesleyan norm"), so neither will I appeal your decision.

I will, as you suggest, request a letter of standing.

I want to correct an apparent misconception in your understanding of what we are doing.

You referred to our "plan for voluntary withdrawal from the Wesleyan church" and later spoke of "the withdrawing group." It is true that in our plans and in many of the changes that have taken place over the last few years we have "set aside *The Discipline*" in favor of a direct response to Scripture. But it is not true that we have been planning to *withdraw* from The Wesleyan Church. If you will reread my letter of Nov. 30 you will discover that nearly half of it is an appeal to allow Our Heritage Church and me "to remain spiritually connected to The Wesleyan Church."

I stated in that letter that our chief reason for not wanting to withdraw or to be put out of the denomination was solidly based on clear biblical teaching—i.e., 1 Cor. 3:1-3, 12:12-25, and Eph. 4:1-3—that the body of Christ is one and that as disciples of the Lord we are commanded to live out unity of Spirit with each other in practical terms. We cherished the hope that this Word of God would speak more loudly than the voice of *The Discipline* to spiritual men such as yourself. We hoped that together we might be able to risk the beneficial struggle that would be involved in seeking to be one on the basis of mutual allegiance to Christ and love for each other, even though it might stretch "the Wesleyan norm."

While it may be argued that our local choices have led to your decision on this matter, the truth still remains that it has remained our sincere desire to *continue* in relationship, and if possible that the relationship might actually be deepened. I sincerely hope that if this matter is discussed or reported in official Wesleyan circles and elsewhere it will not be reported that Our Heritage Church and I have "withdrawn," but that it will be told that our relationship with The Wesleyan Church has been officially terminated by action of the General Superintendent.

I realize that I am in no position to demand such a thing. But I appeal to the truth.

Even as I write this, I am keenly aware that the failure at unity is a two-sided affair. While Audrey and I have been personally, deeply involved in district life, and have given rather persistent effort to trying to keep the lines of communication open, neither district leaders nor the local congregation have really pursued the matter of interaction that might have led to understanding and trust.

Both our local congregation and district people seem to have been waiting for each other to do something. We needed "the district" to come in and get involved with us and investigate us and listen to us and to see if God was in fact at work among us, and to explain itself to us. When it did not happen we should have gone as a local leadership group to the district leaders and demanded such intercourse. But we waited too long. I can only guess that the district, on the other hand, was waiting for us to conform without such interaction before they could enter into open discussion. Perhaps both mistakenly thought that *my* involvement at the district level was all the communication needed. It was not. And we all waited ourselves into a colossal, fear-filled communication-and-understanding gap that has us speaking different languages and in desperate need for someone to interpret.

Having said that, I must admit to the fear that, even if the languages had been clearly understood, denominationalism's insistence on conformity and ours on freedom would have eventually led to our expulsion anyway. But then again . . . maybe not.

Be assured that I will seek to maintain good relationships with my brothers and sisters in the Wesleyan Church (which certainly will include whoever the district sends in to pioneer the new Wesleyan work here in Scottsdale). The most painful aspect of this time of transition in our lives is that it will unmask those friendships that have been purely institutional—only the *real* relationships will remain. It always *seems* more desirable to live in the *illusion* that you are loved than to know the truth. The good thing that rises up through the grief involved is the freedom to concentrate on the real friendships and stop wasting emotional energy on relationships that are only part of the institutional facade.

My hope is that the respect you and I have seemed to hold for each other will prove true and lasting.

Sincerely,

(signed) Robert C. Girard

Copies to: General Superintendents, District Board of Administration members, and others concerned about what is happening at Our Heritage Church

---

Epilogue: In July, 1979, the California District of the Wesleyan Methodist Church received Bob into its fellowship

New Forms: The Flexibility of God

with the full approval of the general superintendent, Dr. Mitchell. This gracious action was deeply appreciated by Bob as a reaffirmation of the fellowship in Christ that has meant so much to him and his family for over three decades.

A SECOND EXAMPLE: CHRISTIAN LIFE CENTER

Our Heritage was a "traditional" church of some two hundred people a dozen years ago when the transition began. In spite of active evangelism through small groups and personal witnessing, in which many times that number have been won to Christ, the congregation itself did not grow. In fact by the time of the division into house churches only some 130 were full participants.

In contrast, Christian Life Center in Spokane, Washington, which built on exactly the same principles of church life and leadership, shows a very different pattern. C.L.C. began with ten persons in the home of Jack and Mary Lou Woods. In some six years that congregation has grown to around nine hundred. The congregation's life takes a variety of forms—many small groups, open congregational meetings on Sunday—and it meets in neither a home nor a church building but in a former YMCA facility.

Like Bob Girard, Jack Woods has gone through many personal struggles, including depression related to redefinition of his own role from that of the kind of "pastor" he was taught to be to that of the kind of spiritual leader he became convinced God wanted him to be. Recently Larry had the opportunity to interview Jack and Mary Lou, who share the story of the congregation of which they are a part:

LARRY: Jack, tell us about Christian Life Center.

JACK: The Christian Life Center is basically a church that we founded. I say "we," but the Lord really founded it. That was the unique part about this work—we felt that the Lord *was* responsible for it. I have been responsible for starting and pastoring other works, but we decided that we wouldn't make a mess out of *this* one, and we would try to let the Lord do it.

LARRY: What was your earlier experience like?

JACK: I started pastoring when I was very young down in the Southern California area and was there for fifteen years. So I became swept into the church world in Southern California, which was then very oriented to spectacularism and colossalism. I even brought an elephant to church one day. I was an

367

THE SHAPE OF TOMORROW

associate pastor at this time and of course the big appeal was numbers. It was very simple—the goals were simply to grow, to get bigger at any cost. So we pulled rabbits out of the hat and had Sunday school contests coming out of our ears and gave away Volkswagens to teenagers and did a whole lot of things. But through it all I became very empty inside and began to "work like the devil" for the Lord—so active in this colossal program—that I really lost the reason for the whole plan; I lost touch with my family and I really felt I had lost touch with biblical truth.

LARRY: That's when you moved to Spokane.

JACK: That was six years ago. We began our first meeting with ten people—five of them were my family—and it was in a building we leased for ten dollars. It was the north branch of the YMCA. But we always felt that it would be the Lord's one day, and we actually walked around it a few times, just as Joshua did around Jericho, and in about three years' time we actually were able to purchase the twenty acres with all of the facilities of the YMCA, including a lodge-type building and two office buildings. One building is now used for the Children's Center. We have a swimming pool, and the grounds are just lovely.

LARRY: What's Christian Life Center like?

JACK: We have two meetings every Sunday morning because our building holds only about three hundred people and there are about one hundred children in the Children's Center. But we are a very nonstructured church. Practically every denomination is represented; we do not emphasize dogma or doctrine at all—just the basic belief that Jesus is Lord. Charismatics and Catholics also attend.

MARY LOU: One day before the church began to grow, I remember, I expressed concern over growth because that was what we gaged our success on in the past—miracle growth. And I remember Jack saying, "Whether this church survives or not is entirely up to the Lord; it is His church, His problem. So I just gave it to Him." I don't know what that would mean to others, but as a pastor's wife, it was like a huge burden off my shoulders because I felt responsible for the church. Then I knew that it wasn't my responsibility after all; it was the Lord's.

JACK: So we tried to follow all the principles that you believe in and teach, Larry, including the priesthood of all believers. That was one of our foundational principles. We refused to call people laymen and clergy. In fact, we tried to do away with all distinctions between laymen and clergy. We have never taken up an offering in six years—we have a little box in the back and we are amazed at the way the people give so willingly. They are so ready for concepts; it seems that they have all been through the same things we have been through and are just ready for something like this. And we have been practicing plurality of leadership—or plurality of ministry, as we call it. There are about seven men now who function as elders and we all share together. We have a policy among our elders that we all agree before we move on anything. We feel that the Lord is very capable through His Spirit to give us unity and harmony as we prayerfully seek Him in decision making.

We now have three full-time ministers, including myself, on the staff. Dave joined us about four years ago and Bill about two years ago. They were members of the body and were worshiping with us. We have felt that our position as leaders is not to appoint leadership at all; we don't feel that is our responsibility. Our responsibility is to confirm the divinely appointed leaders and to make room within the nonstructured structure for them to function. So those elders have come right out of the body. Some of them have then become paid staff or salaried ministers.

LARRY: How do you help your people really *be* ministers? You said you stressed the priesthood of all believers.

JACK: Our way is to provide freedom for people to discover their own giftedness or their own ministries. Rather than forcing them to conform to a hierarchy or deciding where they are to function, we just give them the freedom and support they need. It may be conducting a ladies' fellowship group, visiting the sick, caring for the needy, or presiding as an elder or what we call an undershepherd. We want people to discover their giftedness and have room to function without feeling they are interfering with some superstructure we've set up.

LARRY: Are the majority of the people in your fellowship new Christians or have they been in churches before?

JACK: I would say about half and half.

MARY LOU: At the beginning of the development of the Center, we acted on the conviction that the foundation was really the family. In most of the churches we had participated in, time with the family was squeezed out by the church's demands on the family. We worked with families, the news traveled, and a lot of counseling resulted. Many people were brought to Christ through the counseling ministry. Jack and Dave both counsel. We also have another counselor who comes in on Tuesdays and we have other trained counselors in the congregation. In fact, the offices are in use all day long.

LARRY: So counseling is one of your ministries to the community as well as to your own body?

JACK: Yes. We have several volunteers we call "maintenance counselors." They are in the office just to listen. If people aren't able to meet with one of the staff members or if they just need to pray with someone over the telephone or find a shoulder to cry on, these maintenance counselors are available. One woman is working on a degree in counseling while she is counseling at the Center on a volunteer basis. Then we have a very experienced older gentleman who is both minister and counselor. He has volunteered to oversee the counseling staff. We meet once a week at breakfast to exchange our caseloads and talk about problems we feel need more help than we can offer. Also, I work with a board of professional people, including a medical doctor, a couple of clinical psychologists, and some legal personnel. I find a lot of security in bouncing my problems off them!

LARRY: So how would you summarize the key biblical principles expressed in the body's lifestyle?

JACK: I see it as the priesthood of all believers. It's the ability of the people to welcome into the fellowship as the Scripture says, the person who has just received Jesus as Savior. They put the splitting of doctrinal hairs aside, declare the lordship of Christ, and "embrace" him into the fellowship! We actually don't have a membership of any kind. We don't have

370

            people sign pieces of paper or agree to doctrinal codes or standards or dogma, although we try our best to funnel them immediately into support groups. A great deal of growth takes place as they rub shoulders with the rest of the Christians.

MARY LOU: Worship is a basic principle, too. Bill came into the fellowship about two years ago and began to conduct our worship and lead the people toward the exaltation of the Lord. We aren't a perfect congregation in worship, but worship is a key to our life as a church.

JACK: It hasn't been easy to get people to focus upward rather than inward. No two of our services are alike, though; we let the Holy Spirit guide us. The people feel free to ask a question or to interrupt at any time. We don't get uptight about that, but with three hundred people at each service, it is difficult sometimes, so we don't encourage interruption! The service is pretty free-flowing, with a lot of warmth. We are very affectionate people. We encourage people to reach out to one another and we often group up and are close in this way. Sometimes we have so little contact with the work of the Lord among the people that we don't hear until the following week that someone became a Christian in one of the groups. But what a miracle it is when the Lord becomes real to someone. The fruit remains to this day. And what a thrill it is to know that God doesn't need us professional clergy to bring souls to the kingdom and to touch hearts. It's exciting!

A THIRD EXAMPLE: WORD OF GOD COMMUNITY

It may be helpful to look at one other new form of church life. Like the other two, the Word of God Community stresses the need for intimacy, the role of elders in spiritual leadership, and the importance of evangelism. It comes from yet another Christian tradition—the Catholic.

Recently Larry interviewed one of the founders of this Ann Arbor, Michigan, community. Here's their story, as told by Kevin Perrotta:

LARRY: Kevin, give me a little of the history of the Word of God Community—how it came about, and what God has been doing.

371

KEVIN: Our particular community began in the mid-1960s with a number of Catholic lay people who were involved in the Cursillo movement. The Cursillo movement began not only as a movement to bring individuals to experience a personal relationship with Jesus as Lord but also as a pastoral approach to bring renewal to the Catholic Church. Some of the leaders of the movement in the United States, such as Steve Clark and Ralph Martin, had a vision for renewal in the church. Their vision drew on some Cursillo insights. They developed a plan for renewing the church as a Christian community—not simply renewing organizations within the church or adding programs to the church but renewing it as a Christian environment that would support people in everyday faith. From this there developed a new vision for leadership in the church: leaders who had a gift for creating a Christian environment would arise.

Some of these people—four single men—came to Ann Arbor in the fall of 1967. They had become involved in the beginnings of the charismatic renewal in the Catholic Church. This renewal gave them a much deeper awareness of the working of the Holy Spirit in pastoral and evangelistic work. When they first came to Ann Arbor, they worked as lay assistants to the Catholic chaplain on the campus of the University of Michigan and did some person-to-person evangelism on campus. They also spent a fair amount of time praying. They had a very clear sense when they came that God was leading them, but they didn't have a specific plan or program.

Partly as a result of their evangelism on campus and partly through word of mouth, people started attending the weekly evenings of prayer that they held in their apartment. A number of people—both Catholics and Protestants who had been living the Christian life for quite a while, people who had been only nominal Christians, and people who had not been Christians at all—experienced a personal conversion to Christ. Also the four wanted to introduce people who were Christians to a deeper experience of the Holy Spirit's activity in their lives.

What resulted was an awareness that people

need more than an initial conversion or openness to the Holy Spirit. People who were coming needed a lot of teaching about living the Christian life and developing closer relationships with one another as Christian brothers and sisters. From the beginning there were Protestants and Catholics. We agreed that our people should continue to attend their own churches as well as the weekday services on campus. They still do.

LARRY: Why do you think the community grew so quickly?

KEVIN: I think one of the important things about the growth of the community here was simply that the men who were here in the beginning had many pastoral gifts and a deep commitment to serving God's people. Under their leadership we recognized we were being called by God to commitment to one another as Christian brothers and sisters, even though some retained membership in other churches. We talked as a community about what that commitment would involve. We talked about supporting and caring for one another not only in spiritual matters but also in a whole variety of practical and material ways. We talked about contributing our time and money to support the missions the Lord was giving us. We realized that because we were joining our lives—not just forming an organization—our leaders would affect our lives directly. They would be concerned about every aspect of our life. That was why we wanted to be a community in the first place—to grow in the Christian life together.

What has developed is a leadership of fifteen or eighteen elders. Annually we invite our members to recommend those in the community they feel have the character and gifts to coordinate. The present coordinators look at all the recommendations. There are usually two or three who are recommended by a large number of people, since they are recognized as those who are already functioning with some degree of leadership in the community.

LARRY: It is simply a recognition of gifts that God has already given them?

KEVIN: Yes, it's a process of recognizing both gifts and character. The coordinators are responsible for the whole life of the community. We agree to follow their pattern of life and teaching and receive the personal pastoral care they provide. I don't mean strict imitation of their personal lives. I mean a spirit of "teachableness," a willingness to accept their pastoral care.

LARRY: There is a very interesting passage in the New Testament that has been translated "Obey your leaders" (Heb. 13:17). Literally it means, "Be responsive to those who are your guides and don't shut yourself off from their ministry." It sounds very much like what you are saying.

You mentioned a commitment that community members make. Is this a formal kind of commitment—a covenant?

KEVIN: Yes. Several years ago when we began to commit ourselves to one another, we drew up a statement about the nature of that commitment. Then we invited one another to make the commitment. Since then, we simply have a reading of that statement at one of our community meetings. Those who enter into it stand up and say, "I, _____, want to give my life to God and live as a member of the Word of God." That is understood as an explicit agreement with the statement of commitment to one another.

New people who join our community are required to wait at least two years before they make that commitment.

LARRY: Approximately how many people are influenced by the community?

KEVIN: There are about eighteen hundred adults and children who are now members of the Word of God Community. About fifteen hundred are adults, and somewhat more than half have publicly committed themselves to community membership. The rest are what we call "under way" members.

We also have an evangelistic program called "Life in the Spirit Seminars" to help people commit themselves to the Lord and to the Holy Spirit. A lot of people who go through this seven-week program do not become members of the community.

LARRY: You said something earlier about the mission God was giving you as a group of Christians. What is that mission?

KEVIN: To bear witness to the kind of community life that God initially intended the church to have.

LARRY: Being the body is one of the key focuses?

KEVIN: Yes. Another important aspect of our mission is its ecumenical or interdenominational character. We are able to have a rich life together and yet be members of different churches. Also we are not, as Catholics would say, "indifferent" members of our churches. Differences in our different traditions are important to us, but by and large they are not obstacles to sharing our lives. That is an important lesson the Lord has for the church in our day. It is possible for His people to share their lives and to work together for Him, even without all the differences between them being resolved.

LARRY: Describe the life of the community.

KEVIN: We have about a dozen divisions we call districts. Most are simply the geographical areas in which the members of the community live. Each district has about one hundred adults. Three are in the campus areas of the University of Michigan and Eastern Michigan University in Ypsilanti.

Each district has a weekly gathering on Sunday afternoon. On alternate weeks we also gather either as a whole community or as a group of districts. Districts share life in a number of ways. Men and women are in small men's and women's groups that meet weekly for a couple of hours. They share, study the Bible, work, and play together. This produces close fellowship and friendship. In addition we invite each other over for dinner, go out for an evening together, or garden in the summer. When one of the women has a baby, the women in her group often help by cooking meals for her family, cleaning the house, or taking care of her other children. When a family moves, men and women often get together and help. We frequently work together on each other's houses. We do a lot of informal evangelism—simply sharing with friends, relatives, and neighbors. But some of our evangelization is more carefully planned. For instance, the university dormitory district witnesses by making friends rather than simply knocking on doors. But the members really work together to bring people to the Lord. Some of the older men have a weekly prayer breakfast. A number of us are involved in other types of outreach.

About twenty members of the community moved to Brussels, where they have been working with the Catholic cardinal Leon Joseph Suenens, the highest official in the hierarchy involved in charismatic renewal in the Catholic church.

LARRY: So the idea was to go over to Belgium and be a Christian community and in the process bring in the Belgians and teach them how to be a community too? It's a different approach to missions.

KEVIN: Right. A few of the people who have been in Belgium are now going to be moving to London to begin a similar work there. We also have a number of people in a community in Aguas Buenas, Puerto Rico, and others in Managua, Nicaragua, and elsewhere.

LARRY: Do you see a number of people from the community beginning to develop a sensitivity to the church's world mission?

KEVIN: Yes, some people are directly involved in it and have felt God sent them out to these various places. They continue to be supported financially and spiritually by the rest of the community. And we know them as friends. They are not simply people we support but members of the body. That has done a lot to develop our consciousness of the worldwide church.

We also produce magazines, books, and tapes that involve maybe forty or fifty people. This helps us become conscious of our relationship to the church at large. Some members of the community, of course, have a much clearer sense of that mission.

LARRY: One of the questions that I am constantly asked is, "If you begin to move in the direction of renewal, aren't you self-centered? Don't you lose a sense of mission to the world?" Do you feel that renewal fosters a sense of mission?

KEVIN: We did turn inward at one point, Larry, for about three years. We didn't consider it retreating into a shell. But, just as Steve Clark and Ralph Martin and some of the other leaders in the Catholic charismatic movement who had very heavy commitments to the Cursillo movement, we cut back when we realized that we needed to establish a pattern of life together if we were going to become a community. We needed to ask a lot of questions about basic Christian teaching, family life, and pastoral duties.

Moving toward a community takes a lot of time and effort. But out of the move comes the strength to serve others outside the fellowship.

LARRY: In what new directions do you see yourself moving, Kevin?

KEVIN: What we are trying to do at the moment is form fellowships within the community. We want Lutherans, Catholics, and the people in the Reformed tradition to be able to express some of their distinctive traditions within our community. We have so far established a Free Church Fellowship and a Catholic Fellowship that has been recognized by the authorities of the Catholic Church. Under the leadership of Catholic coordinators it will provide a sacramental and teaching life for the Catholics in our community. We are working to establish something similar for Lutherans and people in the Reformed tradition.

LARRY: Do you see these fellowships developing into the churches of the people from those traditions?

KEVIN: That is what is in fact happening. The Catholic Fellowship isn't operating as such yet because it wants to wait until the Lutheran and Reformed fellowships become established. These fellowships will eventually provide a full church life for their members. We are not, of course, going to be able to do it for all traditions. For instance, we have only a handful of Anabaptists.

LARRY: Why did you decide to form these fellowships?

KEVIN: We wanted to continue the different traditions our members cherished. Also, some of the members found it hard to be active in both our community and their own churches. To resolve that tension we felt we needed to help them in such a way that they could continue their traditions and yet experience the benefits of our community.

SUMMING UP

In the churches described in this chapter we see new, nontraditional forms a local congregation may take. These forms are both exciting and threatening. They are exciting because they offer an intimacy and commitment to serving that is often lost in the impersonal "programing" of the traditional church. The small group meetings build close, face-to-face re-

377

lationships and permit its leaders to function "among" the members in significant ways.

Yet these forms are threatening because as they emerge they produce unanticipated problems that need to be worked through and place real strains on the leaders as they struggle with issues of personal identity and calling.

It should also be noted that each congregational form we have described is essentially a "believers' church." That is, unlike the "state church" in which most denominations have roots and which accept the growth of wheat and tares side by side, these congregational forms assume that all who participate are or will soon become true believers.

Each congregation has a lot of freedom. None stresses doctrinal conformity as a test of fellowship. None demands strict behavioral conformity. Yet without any doubt these forms call for a level of commitment to the community that is likely to come only after a conversion experience. The congregation makes no attempt to develop structures that will attract and hold the "social" Christian.

This issue of commitment and active faith is an important one. When a congregation takes such a nontraditional form, it comes into conflict with cultural ideas of what a church should be. As a result, it will lose members or potential members. Yet its firm choice is to move toward a congregation that is a company of the committed, not an association of the interested.

To many, this "believers' church" pattern is in fact *the* pattern: it reflects the biblical nature of the church that, it is felt, should be expressed in the local congregation. The kind of leadership stressed in this study is most likely to lead to some form of congregational life that is, in significant ways, like one of the models we have presented.

To answer the question implicit in our Iowa friend's exciting beginning of a new leadership style—"Where will it lead?"—his course *may* lead to a new form of congregational life. It may also lead to increasing conflict with existing Presbyterian structures, causing increasing tension within the congregation as some respond and others react.

Over the next decade, new and surprising facets of God's infinite greatness may be revealed in the emergence of yet another unexpected form of congregational life and worship.

New Forms: The Flexibility of God

PROBE

▶ case histories
▶ discussion questions
▶ thought provokers
▶ resources

1. What problems do people experience when they think of an "open ended" future—one in which they have no assurance of what will happen, or when, or how?

   Imagine yourself as a board member of the Iowa Presbyterian Church whose pastor was quoted at the beginning of this chapter. List as many reasons as you can why you might *not* want to follow the direction indicated in this text.

2. Reread the descriptions of the three churches or communities described in this chapter. Which one most appeals to you? List some of the reasons why it attracts you.

3. Under the leading of God for over a decade at Our Heritage Church, the congregation decided to depart from the denominational "norm." This decision led to expulsion from the denomination. What moral issues are raised by this decision? What are some practical issues that might emerge? For example, at Our Heritage Church the pastor and his family lost the home in which they had lived for twelve years. Would you be willing to follow the leadership principles outlined in this text if you knew ahead of time they would bring you and your congregation into a similar conflict with your denomination or association? Why or why not?

4. Some denominations or associations find it impossible to accept diversity in form, although they accept great diversity in doctrine. What does this imply? Is there room within your own group for the kinds of differences affirmed in this text? What churches in your group are actually implementing "renewal" principles? How do denominational offices and others perceive them?

Many people assume that the spiritual leadership patterns examined in this text will lead to one of the unusual forms of church life described in the preceding chapter.

That is not necessarily so. In fact it is more likely that churches setting out on the journey of commitment to biblical

NEW VITALITY: TRADITION IN MISSION

leadership principles will retain their traditional form. New life may well be expressed within the tradition rather than burst the tradition's "bonds."

Let's examine three congregations that have experienced new vitality within traditional frameworks.

CASE HISTORY ONE: MIDWESTERN METHODIST

Midwestern Methodist is not the actual name of this church. It does, however, indicate its location. And it is a real congregation with a history of well over a hundred years. It is a small-town church. Yet it is influential because of its historic support of denominational programs and missions.

Midwestern Methodist has its roots in the evangelistic efforts of an earlier day. It was not unusual in the thirties or forties for traveling evangelists to stop at the church for a week of meetings and not at all unusual for dedicated members of that congregation to come down the aisles for a fresh commitment to Christ. In the framework of the fundamentalist-liberal controversy of the twenties, this congregation was solidly in the fundamentalist camp.

In the past three or four decades Midwestern Methodist has had many different pastors, following the rotating concept of the denomination. Some have been liberal, some neoorthodox. One was an older man whose preaching left much to be desired but who was a very effective personal evangelist. Yet, no matter who the pastor was, the church's vitality remained.

CHAPTER 25

Denominational programs, curriculums, and missions came and went, but the stability and vitality of the congregation seemed unaffected. The church has participated in lay witness missions and undertaken its own mission to a prison in the area. There have also been other ministries: to those in a nearby mental hospital, to the needy, etc.

Midwestern Methodist with its councils and commissions and boards seems to function just like other Methodist congregations. When one examines the church more closely, however, he discovers a fascinating phenomenon. Alongside the formal structure there is an informal structure—among the women.

Over the years the women of the congregation have continued to meet in small groups for Bible study and prayer. Over the years there have been quiet women whose spiritual leadership through these groups and within the formal structures has been very much of the "example" and "servant" pattern described in this text. Official decisions may have been made by the boards, but spiritual life has been nurtured and shared through the women's groups.

When one looks at the history of the congregation, he finds that the interest in missions, the raising of funds, and the support of most of the other activities that have kept the congregation the "highest per-capita givers" in the district are all the result of the activities of the women. Vacation church schools and many other local ministries, including a very active youth ministry that has seen young people called to go into the ministry, have also been spearheaded by the women.

All these years the congregation has accepted and affirmed good ministers and bad, those in theological harmony with the congregation and those whose theology has been repugnant to them. In a quiet and loving way the differences have been accepted and handled, and the heart life of the congregation continued unaffected by either.

What has in fact developed in this congregation is a believers' church functioning within a denominational framework. This pattern has been duplicated—sometimes with the understanding and encouragement of the pastor and staff and sometimes without—in multiplied congregations across our country.

The formal structure and the informal structure, the official leadership and the spiritual movers, the association of the interested and the company of the committed have existed side by side in many churches for decades.

And who is to say that this is not a valid expression of what God seeks to do through Christ's body in the world? Who is to say that what is institutionally known as the church must in fact be the whole identity of the church? And who is to say that a "pure" form of the believers-only body must be reflected in an organization as well as in an organism?

CASE HISTORY TWO: FAR WEST ADVENTIST

Once again we identify this congregation only by its geographical area and tradition. It is a real congregation with its own history and an alternative lifestyle within a traditional framework.

Like many other churches in the Adventist camp, Far West tended to be legalistic. Most of the children were sent to Adventist boarding schools for education. Most of the members tended to hold tightly to the traditions of the group but lacked personal experience of a vital relationship with Jesus Christ.

This began to change some ten years ago when one of the members and his family felt a new touch of life at a Campus Crusade training session in Arrowhead Springs. There the message of freedom in Christ brought to many hearts by the Holy Spirit caused an exciting awakening. Through this influence, the church began to encourage family Bible studies and other small-group activities. A number of other members also experienced a spiritual awakening.

Over the next few years there was some tension between the "traditionalists" and the "renewalists" in this congregation, but in general the traditional format was retained. Most of the members of the congregation found more meaning in the formal services than in the Bible studies and sharing. Most also maintained a rather narrow interpretation of their church's teachings with little stress on any personal relationship to Christ. Yet there was a strong "new life" core in the church. Within the organizational church an organism lived.

Then a new young pastor came. He was theologically in harmony with the renewal group. At the same time he was sensitive to the concerns of the others and aware that he was called to minister to them as well. Members of both persuasions learned how to accept each other. The pastor's commitment to both groups and their concerns gave both confidence in him.

As he continued to minister, the church began to grow. Everyone was enthusiastic about the number of young adults who were joining the fellowship. At this point the pastor went to the board and pointed out that their various classes and organizations had the capacity to absorb only so many people. If the church were to continue to grow, it would be necessary to set up structures that would absorb the new people.

The board was enthusiastic. None of the established patterns or programs of the church would be threatened. The congregation would still have the same ministries for the original group that had always been there. The new structures would make room for more and more members to be added to the congregation. Official sanction for a believers' church within the traditional church was enthusiastically given.

This too is a not-uncommon pattern. It can be found in congregations ranging from Lutheran to Baptist, from Presbyterian to Church of God. Double structures to meet the perceived needs of very different persons within congregations can be established and maintained without any serious strain.

This is possible, however, only within congregations where there is an acceptance of a kind of diversity not possible in the "believers' church." Only where the official leadership is aware of the issues and willing to serve all members of a divided church is it practicable.

CASE HISTORY THREE:
SALEM CHRISTIAN AND MISSIONARY ALLIANCE

The Salem Alliance Church also has a long history. It's a church that has not violated "denominational norms" but has been recognized as a model congregation within its fellowship. I explored its history with Don Bubna, whose book *Building People,*[1] coauthored with Sarah Ricketts, tells more fully of the exciting developments in this model congregation.

The following interview focuses on the vitality of the church and its leadership:

LARRY: I'd like to chat with you about your congregation. I see Salem Christian and Missionary Alliance Church as an example of a congregation that is traditional in its format but not traditional in the reality of its life.

DON: We are in a capital city where things tend to be perhaps even more conservative than in the rest of the state. So I came into a church in a part of the country that I knew would be different from San Diego, which I left fifteen years ago when I was thirty-four.

I came with the conviction that I needed to change things very slowly. I followed a man who was considerably older and very settled; so I knew I should be cautious in making changes and needed to establish my credibility. The differences in my personality alone were all the church could handle!

A Christian brother took me to lunch and said, "These are very conservative people. I married a girl from this church and I know. I have been in it for ten years. These people think you're really 'far out.' But they will follow you because they believe you love them." That gave me an awesome responsibility, but the message was one I needed to hear.

I began to work with the leaders in an effort to become part of their lives. Hospitality was an important part of this: lunches together, coffees, getting inside their places of business. I remember going to eat in a school cafeteria with one of our members, a janitor in a local school. These contacts were all important.

After that we began to change the services. Even having a communion service at night was difficult. I tended to be uncomfortable with traditional altar calls. Tension resulted, and we had to work that through. I also had to convince the members that it was not necessary for me to be doing all of the pastoral care in terms of visiting and praying for the sick. Next I began a more open, sharing kind of service. Our transformation had begun.

---

[1] Don Bubna and Sarah Ricketts, *Building People* (Wheaton: Tyndale, 1978).

In recent years we have also been doing interesting things with multimedia. The last couple of summers we have dismissed the choir and had a very creative kind of worship experience where different people, usually staff members, would take the responsibility for the first fifteen minutes of the service. They sometimes presented a multimedia program or a drama and sometimes they followed a very traditional format.

Two years ago we moved into twenty subparishes, as we call them; they're really mini-congregations. We moved from a church board, which was called an executive committee, to a genuine board of elders. Each of the men who serve on the elders' board also oversee a subparish of from twenty to twenty-five people. Some of the businessmen who had been leaders no longer felt comfortable with the board. We both accepted the fact of their discomfort. But we felt that it was the right move to make, and there was a lot of enthusiasm. The new leaders began to say, "Hey, we are really fulfilling pastoral functions!" and I said, "That's right!"

LARRY: It's taken many years in our congregation for the elders to be able to accept that responsibility and feel comfortable with it.

DON: Recently our elders have even been baptizing people. Most of the subparish meetings take place in addition to our regular Sunday or Wednesday evening service. However, a number of them meet on Wednesday night. A couple of times a year we cancel the Sunday evening services, and each subparish has an *agapé* feast or other form of celebration.

LARRY: In many churches in which there is new life, a divided congregation results. But apparently you are maintaining the believers' church, and gradually incorporating the whole congregation into it.

DON: This is one of the unique features of this group. The people we began with are still with us.

LARRY: What would you say is the key to maintaining cohesiveness in the entire congregation in this process?

DON: One key is a relationship based on love and commitment. Our members learned it first about me, and then it became increasingly true about the rest of the staff. I still make house calls. All of us do. And all of us are involved in the pastoral ministry. We are not all administrators or preachers. Another key is retreat if there is too much concern or opposition. Come at it again later when people are more ready. A third key is to make the people a part of the process. I am not an autocratic person. I think I could be. Because I am a strong leader, I have learned to have a holy fear of things happening just the way I think they should! Therefore I depend in a special way on the other elders. We try to make people a part of the team.

I still think preaching is the cutting edge of change. I favor a strongly expository biblical preaching that is also life related. I frequently give messages on the church whether I am doing a special series on the church or not. When I was preaching through the Book of Acts, the nature of the church's ministry constantly cropped up in my preaching.

LARRY: So the people really understand the new trends they are seeing modeled.

DON: Right. And they understand that it is biblical. Then, too, there are people in our church who were leaders in the past who are not now and who have basically said, "It's right, but I can't handle that much change." Or "That's not where I'm at, be patient with me."

LARRY: Earlier you said when you came to Salem fifteen years ago you recognized the need to change very slowly. That tells me that when you came you already knew in general where you wanted to go. How clear was your thinking at that time?

DON: Not nearly as sophisticated as it is now. But I had a vision of a caring, loving church. I remember when I candidated that I preached about eating with sinners. It was a message about what we would call friendship evangelism, building relationships, building bridges.

LARRY: Did it take long to implement?

DON: Patience is important. Scripture says so much about it. The fruit of the Spirit includes patience. The word refers to trying people rather than trying circumstances.

In our culture there is a change from the functional to the relational. Pastors need to stay so they can develop relationships and grow themselves. Frequent moves make this impossible.

LARRY: True. Don, I know the church in Salem has grown numerically. Didn't I hear that you have started another congregation?

DON: We were averaging about two hundred when I came. We are now running about a thousand. After careful study, we decided we should start a second congregation within the community but couldn't find the one hundred people we felt were minimally necessary to do so. Not enough people were willing to be part of the new, smaller group. We then sponsored fifty-five Cambodians, most of whom were new Christians. Subsequent to that, we sponsored sixty-five Hmung refugees. The Hmung have their own pastor. We are also helping a Vietnamese group; so we have Cambodian, Hmung, and Vietnamese congregations meeting in our facilities. Some of them are also becoming part of our own body.

LARRY: Could you tell me about your in-service training ministry? You must have been doing this for about ten years.

DON: We have been doing it for twelve years. The impetus came from Henry Tournidge, who is a member of our congregation and a farmer and school teacher. In his younger days he was a pastor. He is greatly concerned about young pastors. He came to me one day and said, "Don, whatever it is that these young pastors are supposed to be doing, they're not doing it. We need to help them." To use his words, "They don't have a program. [He really meant that they don't have a sense of direction.] You have a program."

So we first brought in groups of ten men at a time for a three-day session. Rather than lecturing, we used writing exercises to find out where they were and to see if they could put together a strategy for their own situation. We later saw that they needed a support system. So we started a group with ten men who came in once a month for half a day. Then we expanded until we have had five groups now for about five years throughout our district. We all meet about once a month for support and prayer and for a time to define what we are trying to do. We have a waiting list of young pastors who want to get into the program.

LARRY: I've talked to more than one pastor who's said that being in your in-service program really saved him in terms of his ministry.

DON: That is a very gratifying part of our church's commitment.

In the past five years we have also trained about

thirty interns. A couple of them were mavericks from my own congregation who did not fit the guidelines. But they were thinkers who were committed to new forms and loved the church but were frustrated by it. I had difficulty getting them accepted by some of our leaders because the leaders were afraid of them. The interns started a group they called "Community," which soon became part of the total church. That group has now gone on for about four years, and its leadership comes from our congregation. It is made up largely of disenchanted people, people frustrated by the institutional church. They are often our critics and yet they know we love them, understand them and are open to them when nobody else is. They are the fellows who have pressed me the most, and I owe them the most. They are the ones who say, "If you really believe this—and I know you really believe it—why aren't you out here like we are? Why aren't you changing the church more quickly?" They're saying there is a place for the institutional church, but they're trying to model for us a different form, an alternative form. And they do not understand why it takes us so long to adopt these biblical changes.

I think they would say they owe a lot to us, too. That's a very healthy tension. And one of these leaders is an adjunct staff man here, a counselor in our church. I think that we almost have both worlds.

LARRY: In your book you said that only about 10 percent of the people had captured the concept of hospitality and are doing it effectively. Is that still about right?

DON: Yes, it is my conviction that one can move only a significant minority. Of the remaining 90 percent, probably only half have some commitment to hospitality, and the other half would agree with the idea but find it a bit too threatening.

LARRY: Some people would say that only the 10 percent were followers of Christ in the congregation, so that the 10 percent were the real functioning church inside the larger church organization. Do you think that is accurate?

DON: No. I think we have 10 percent who are enthusiastic types, 45 percent who are cooperative and definitely moving in the right direction, and another 45 percent who are a little scared. The last group gives mental assent to the idea of hospitality and like what is hap-

390

pening, but they are only occasionally involved or not involved at all.

LARRY: But they are still receiving the benefit of being part of a body and belonging to a family.

DON: Larry, your book *A New Face for the Church* was the basis for a discussion on vulnerability we had at one of our officers' retreats about twelve years ago. That book did a lot to help change attitudes.

LARRY: How many people do you have on your staff now?

DON: There are five of us on what we call the pastoral staff. In addition, there is an educational assistant and a counselor who is an adjunct staff member. Being a staff member is like being married. Becoming a staff member should not be a stepping stone to something better. It's got to involve commitment. That's why we tend to have few staff changes and long-term service.

SUMMING UP

Our survey of the three churches in this chapter suggests several important conclusions. The first is that it may not be necessary to attempt to identify the organism and the organization. In the "believers only" church tradition there is a strong drive toward purity. It is assumed that every member of the local congregation must be a true believer. Even when time is provided for those coming into the fellowship to move to a personal relationship with Christ, the assumption remains that in time there will be a conversion experience for everyone in the local body.

In two of the churches sketched in this chapter that assumption has not been made. Pluralism of belief is acceptable, and while there is usually a desire for conversion to take place there is a tolerance and even willingness to accept into active leadership those who would not, in the believers' church, be considered Christians.

The second conclusion is that we must not be too quick to attempt to separate the sheep from the goats, or the wheat from the tares. Even in this chapter the reader may have made the unfortunate inference that we can accept as "true Christians" only those who are in the "renewal," as opposed to the "traditional," camp. That is an inference that must not be made. There are individuals in all three churches who have a real faith, yet are distinctly of the traditional mold. These brothers and sisters are committed to traditional patterns and ways and work to the glory of God within the institutional frameworks criticized in this book.

So it is important *not* to assume from the "church within the church" pattern that all true believers will be found in the one camp and none in the other.

A third conclusion relates to the commitment of the pastor and the other spiritual leaders. In the churches described in this chapter, the leadership was committed to a concept of the church that demanded expression in new forms. This was not only a biblical vision. For many it may also have been a personal reaciton to the institutional church. Personal tensions may make it impossible for some people to accept life in churches so far from their ideals.

But for others life within the institution may be a calling. It should be accepted as a valid calling, an expression of servanthood that has its burdens but also its rewards. Certainly those who minister in Christ's way within the traditional framework and exercise a spiritual leadership should not be criticized or rejected by those whose commitment is to the believers' church.

A fourth conclusion has to do with an important distinction between official leadership and spiritual leadership in a congregation. Often those who make organizational decisions have little or no impact on the organism. It's important to realize that spiritual leadership need not have formal sanction to exert its influence!

Each of these conclusions helps us to realize that vitality can and does exist within the traditional church and that the kind of spiritual leadership explored in this text can be exercised in the traditional setting.

However, to exercise such leadership in such a setting effectively, the ideal of a "believers' church" must be rejected, and the leader must be satisfied to minister within a system in which organizational structure and the true church need not coincide.

Not everyone can accept this condition but must drive toward his ideal. But to those to whom it is acceptable, the traditional church is an exciting place of ministry, and within the organization can be found vital expressions of the church over which Christ is head.

PROBE

▶ *case histories*
▶ *discussion questions*
▶ *thought provokers*
▶ *resources*

1. It is often assumed that biblical *forms* protect us against errors or problems. The following article is on the subject of consensus,

something the authors believe is a biblical approach to decision making in the church. Yet, as the article suggests, this approach can be just as fallible as any other for discerning the will of God. Read the article thoughtfully and try to answer the questions at the end.

CONSENSUS: THE ANSWER?

The Bible seems to teach that working toward unanimity is God's way of guiding decisions in the body of Christ. The Acts Council spoke with confident authority when it wrote, "It seemed good to the Holy Spirit and to us" (Acts 15:28). The peace God brought served as an umpire in the hearts of the members of the body at Colossae, and as one body they taught and admonished one another (Col. 3:15-16).

Yet we must guard against the assumption that if we make our church decisions by consensus rather than by the "unspiritual" method of voting, we are protected against error. The former approach to decision making may be theologically correct—but carnally applied. Or some of the limitations on decision making may be ignored. So let's look at several ways in which the consensus method can go wrong.

1. False Consensus. The key concept in the consensus approach is that the decision-making team unanimously agrees that the decision made is God's will—for now. This requires a high level of integrity on the part of each team member. I must be willing to say no if I am against a decision, even if I am the only one. I must be willing to share my doubts and fears and uncertainties even when all the rest may be enthusiastic. In time, as God continues to lead, a decision may be reversed or an approach changed (but I must not then say, "I was against it all the time").

Any loss of integrity or withholding of opinion for any reason will distort the process.

2. Unresponsible Decision. No, not irresponsible, unresponsible. The key to the consensus processes is that those who are responsible for an area of ministry or activity are the ones who must make the decisions affecting that ministry.

This is a problem in any church where the elders in the congregation perceive themselves to be "board members." In our culture, board members set policy and make decisions for, and control, those "under" them. Decisions are made for those responsible to God for a ministry (for example, Sunday school or home Bible studies).

But biblical elders serve among the body, and their function is to disciple, mature, teach, encourage, and guide members of the body to freedom and responsibility to Christ.

Thus, the decisions made by a consensus of the elders will relate to their ministry in and to the body. But their decisions should not be made for groups, teams, or agencies in the body. To begin to make decisions (even by consensus) for others is to violate Peter's warning against "lording it over those entrusted to you" (1 Peter 5:5).

For this process to function effectively in any local body, it must be carried out by those responsible to God for the ministry or activity in question. God never gave us the unanimity principle as a method of making decisions to bind others. They too must be given the freedom to respond to Christ, the true head of the church.

3. Constitutional Freezing. Another common misuse of the unanimity principle is to apply it to make binding decisions. Constitutions and by-laws that are later referred to with such statements as "the Constitution says we must do it this way" or "the By-laws say we can't do that" can unfortunately be substituted for the living Word of the Holy Spirit.

We always need to remember two truths: we are fallible, and we are in process. Our fallibility means we must always hold open the possibility that even our most confidently made decisions may be wrong. Our awareness of process requires us to look at every decision as a for-now solution.

God does not reveal His complete will for an individual or a local body at one time. We understand His plan for us in an unfolding way. As we walk step by step with Him, He shows us our next step—not the whole road.

This means that our current understanding should not limit or bind us in the future. We always need to be open to that next step. When our consensus decisions are frozen into constitutional or by-law form, we run the risk of letting our past, rather than our God, be Lord of the future.

4. Loss of History. Although we must not let past decisions control us, we must not lose our sense of history and God's working. We should keep a record of how God has led, what decisions were made as a result of seeking His leading, and why those particular choices were the outcome of our search for unanimity.

Such a history of God's leading can be both confirming (reminding us of God's past work among us) and helpful (reminding us of the factors we considered and helping us to evaluate different factors that may exist in a new situation). If we fail to recognize the Lord's guidance in the past, we will less readily and confidently seek His guidance for every new decision.

5. Prayerless Process. *Strangely, another danger is that we might turn consensus seeking into a mechanical process rather than a spiritual exercise. Coming to search out the mind of Christ, we enter into a deep, significant, and mystical relationship with the Lord Himself.*

Yet decision making in the body can also be a carnal, almost flippant exercise. "Anybody against? Great: consensus! Now what's next?" Such an attitude or approach misses both the significance and the seriousness of fulfilling an area of our responsibility under Jesus' personal leadership.

The appropriate attitude is one of prayer and searching. Searching involves a careful examination of every factor we can consider that relates to the issue. It also involves a careful probing of each other so that we may in honesty and openness scrutinize our thoughts and feelings. This entire process is a distinct spiritual service to God. Thus we must seek His guidance and His Spirit's ministry to help us discover His will.

What do these five problem areas in consensus decision making tell us? Not that the approach is wrong. Instead, they do tell us that the method is not infallible, that our confidence must always be in God Himself rather than in ourselves, even when we follow His principles. We are fallible human beings whose only hope is in a total dependence on the sovereign grace of God. So let's guard against any carnal use of God's methods and seek His Spirit's intervention to guard us as we search out and do the Father's will.

Questions to think about:
a. If it is possible for a biblical approach to decision making to go wrong, is it equally possible that Christ's headship might be effectively exercised in voting or other methods of making decisions?
b. What is the advantage of one approach over another, if we admit that the "biblical" approach is not infallible and the "cultural" approach can be a vehicle for the expression of God's will?
c. What other principles or practices suggested in this book must be regarded as "fallible"? Develop a list and try to suggest how each might break down.
d. If we are convinced that one particular approach to church life and leadership is more fully in harmony with biblical principles than others, are we obligated to implement that approach or not? Why?

2. Would you personally be able to work in "church within a church" system? Why, or why not?

3. Look again at the letter of the Iowa Presbyterian minister on pages 357–58. Which outcome do you feel is most likely to move toward a "new forms" church? Toward a "church within a church" pattern? Why?

PART 4

THE SHAPE OF TOMORROW

New Forms: The Flexibility of God
New Vitality: Tradition in Mission
Open-Ended Futures

There is one basic, underlying conviction expressed in this text: that Jesus Christ is the living head of the church. Our whole task as leaders in the body of Christ is to bring ourselves and members of the body into a responsive relationship to Him. Our burden has been to explore the New Testament principles that guide spiritual leaders in the church in their allegiance-building task.

In our exploration of biblical principles and practices,

OPEN-ENDED FUTURES

we've tried to avoid suggesting any "plan" or translating principles into programs. There is no formula that can be applied to a given situation, no five-step program for churches with over two hundred members or six-step program for churches over one thousand.

In the place of programs and plans, there is the promise of a daily relationship with Jesus Christ, who Himself must and will guide the process.

As biblical principles of leadership are practiced, Christ will guide His body into the future that He has designed for it in all its local manifestations. Because of the complexity of the wisdom of God, we cannot know in advance the pattern of life He intends for our local body.

This means that if we are going to follow the course recommended here, we need the courage to open ourselves up to an uncertain future. It means that we need patience to work through a process that will certainly take years as God's shape for our congregation is revealed.

But *process* and *years* are words that apply to any living, growing organism. A child is not born to reach the full strength of adulthood in a few days or weeks or months. A child grows over the course of many years, and what the child will be as an adult cannot be fully known in advance. We should not be surprised, then, if congregations grow and find their identity over a span of years and if in the process they pass through different stages. To live with process and to live with it for years is part of the commitment anyone who chooses to lead a church as we have suggested must make. One must also accept the fact that during the years of process and development very little evidence of "success" may exist.

CHAPTER 26

Why then would anyone choose the type of leadership suggested here rather than one of the "success" models taken from secular management systems or recommended by "superchurch" promoters? We can think of only one compelling reason: *It is biblical.* It honors Jesus as the living, capable head of His own body, and we must honor His instructions.

As to whether this book does in fact accurately describe a biblical approach to spiritual leadership, each must decide for himself. But to the extent that it *is* determined to be scriptural and theologically sound, to that extent the principles are compelling. For in the last analysis, it is not whether principles or practices "work" or have the sanction of tradition or even are accepted by others in our group that should motivate us to personal commitment. The only consideration that can persuade us is this: Have we heard the voice of Jesus speak?

Will we obey?

INDEXES

Indexes of Persons

Aaron, 47
Aberbach, Moses, 133
Adam, 18
Apollos, 209
Appley, Lawrence A., 181-82
Argyris, Chris, 162-64
Arn, Wynn, 81, 283
Atkinson, David S., 177

Bauer, Walter, 19
Bennis, Warren, 168, 171
Bradspies, Robert W., 184
Bromiley, G.W., 239
Brown, J.A.C., 163-64
Bruce, F.F., 18
Bryant, Jack, 263-64
Bubna, Don, 70, 230, 345, 386ff.

Carlisle, Howard M., 167-68
Clark, Steven B., 284, 372, 376
Coleman, Robert, 116
Crenshaw, Donna, 262

David, 237
Dayton, Edward R., 191
Diaz, Isidro, 81
Dick, Henry, 228
Draper, James, 89-90

Engstrom, Ted W., 27, 89-90, 137,
    191, 337-38

Fayol, Henri, 161, 167, 177
Fiedler, Fred, 171
Follett, Mary Packer, 162
Fortes, Meyer, 127-28
Franklin, Richard, 314

Getz, Gene, 232
Gilbreth, Frank, 161
Girard, Robert C., 358ff.
Graham, Howard, 361
Gulick, Luther C., 167

Herod, 237
Herzberg, Frederick, 165-66
Hoeldtke, Clyde, 77ff., 88, 150, 157,
    193, 245, 294, 296, 310-11

Isaiah, 306

James, 106, 307
Jaquith, D.A., 182-83

Jenkins, Gary, 263-64, 303
Jephthah, 16
Jethro, 16
John (apostle), 61, 63, 91, 93, 106,
    237
Joshua, 368

Kahn, Robert L., 155
Kast, Fremont E., 153-54
Katz, Daniel, 155
Kilinski, Kenneth, 32, 54-55, 143,
    285-87
Koontz, Harold, 184

LeBar, Lois, 33
Levi, 47
Likert, Rensis, 40
Louden, J. Keith, 182, 186
Luthans, Fred, 170-73

Martin, Gib, 258, 261, 265, 277
Martin, Ralph D., 248, 372, 376
Maslow, Abraham, 165
Mayo, Elton, 163
McElfresh, Pat, 359
McGavran, Donald, 81, 283, 285
McGregor, Douglas, 164-66
Miller, Sherod, 343
Mitchell, Virgil A., 364-65, 367
Moore, Charles, 182
Moses, 16, 38-39, 119-20

Oncken, William, Jr., 137

Pastore, Joseph M., 179
Paul (apostle), 15, 18-20, 22, 30-31,
    37, 45, 49, 52, 63-64, 67-68, 75,
    90, 93-94, 102, 109, 114-15,
    119-21, 126-27, 129, 134, 138,
    141-42, 152, 154, 206, 209-12,
    218, 220, 236, 283, 295-96, 308,
    320ff., 350
Perrotta, Kevin, 371-77
Peter (apostle), 80-81, 90-93, 134,
    142, 206, 209, 213, 218, 220, 237,
    296, 394
Philip, 134
Phillips, J.B., 206
Pollard, Harold R., 161, 163
Pontius Pilate, 237
Porter, Pat, 361

INDEX OF PERSONS

Index of Subjects

INDEX OF SUBJECTS

INDEX OF SUBJECTS

INDEX OF SUBJECTS

INDEX OF SUBJECTS

INDEX OF SUBJECTS

INDEX OF SUBJECTS

INDEX OF SUBJECTS

Index of Scripture References

INDEX OF SCRIPTURE REFERENCES

INDEX OF SCRIPTURE REFERENCES